THE POLITICS OF THE AYODHYA DISPUTE

(Rise of Communalism and Future Voting Behaviour)

THE POLITICS OF THE AYODHYA DISPUTE

(Rise of Communalism and Future Voting Behaviour)

PRADEEP NAYAK

Commonwealth Publishers

NEW DELHI-110002

(INDIA)

THE POLITICS OF THE AYODHYA DISPUTE

Edition : 2026

ISBN : 81-7169-252-4

Published by :

Ajay Verma

COMMONWEALTH PUBLISHERS

4378/4-B, Gali Murari Lal, Ansari Road, Darya Ganj

New Delhi-110002 (INDIA)

Phone : 3272541

Printed at :

Stylish Composing Agency

Bhajanpura, Delhi-110053

Dedicated to the sacred memory of those innocents who fell victims to the communal orgy spawned by the brutal politics of Mandir-Masjid.

ACKNOWLEDGEMENTS

As an avid observer of the Indian political scene, the Ramjanmabhoomi-Babri Masjid dispute interested me much as I found it is not only worthwhile to do research on such a challenging and multi-dimensional problem but it would also enrich the existing level of our understanding of the Ayodhya dispute. The Ayodhya dispute no longer remains confined within the exclusive academic domain of the historians and anthropologists because the Mandir-Masjid issue is sine-qua-non a political question. That is why the students of Indian politics must address themselves to this problem.

The idea of doing research on such a volatile topic developed during my M.A. days but it finally took shape during my discussions with Dr. Zoya Hasan. She not only suggested that I do research on this topic but extended all sorts of help in preparing my synopsis. I am very grateful to her for providing valuable guidance and help especially at the initial stage of my research.

My frequent discussion with Prof. Romila Thapar, Prof. K.N. Panikkar of the Centre for Historical Studies, JNU, Dr. Asghar Ali Engineer, Director, Institute of Islamic Studies, Bombay, Prof. S.N. Jha, Dr. Imtiaz Ahmad and Dr. Kiran Sexena and Prof. Kuldeep Mathur proved very useful in clarifying ambiguities and other difficulties while writing my dissertation. I take this opportunity to record my sincere gratitudes to these renowned scholars for sparing their valuable time and the kind interest they took in my topic.

I am also indebted to my teacher Prof. Balveer Arora, Dr. Manzur Alam, Chairperson and Dr. A.R. Agwan, Director of the Institute of Objective Studies (IOS) for offering much help and guidance in undertaking my field studies in Ayodhya and Faizabad.

My field trip to Ayodhya-Faizabad and its remote villages would not have been quite fruitful and pleasurable had it not been the warm hospitality extended to me by Ms. Suman Gupta, Mr. Mitrasen Yadav, Mr. Yunus Siddique and Mr. Majeed Ansari and their invaluable help in collecting the data and the relevant information pertaining to my research. I am also grateful to my friend Yoginder Sikand who proved a useful companion in my field study. Braving the scorching sun and sweltering heat of May, Yoginder accompanied me to remote villages, smoothly interpreted local Hindu language and helped me to carefully collect the relevant data from interviews and public meetings.

I owe a great deal to Mr. Jaideep Nair, Centre for Political Studies, who right from the preparation of my synopsis to the writing of my conclusion, has been instrumental in my developing academic curiosity in the subject. I am thankful to my friends especially P. Sahdevan, Subhra Mohanty and Paul Rozario who went through several portions of my dissertation and offered their useful comments.

I want to thank the staff of JNU book shop, processing sections and press clippings sections of the JNU Library for taking enough care in collecting the latest books and useful material for my research and providing it at the earliest. I am very thankful to Mr. B.R. Verma of Commonwealth Publishers for showing his keen interest in bringing out the volume in the shortest possible period.

Last but not the least. I wish to thank my father to whom this work owes much.

Pradeep Nayak

CONTENTS

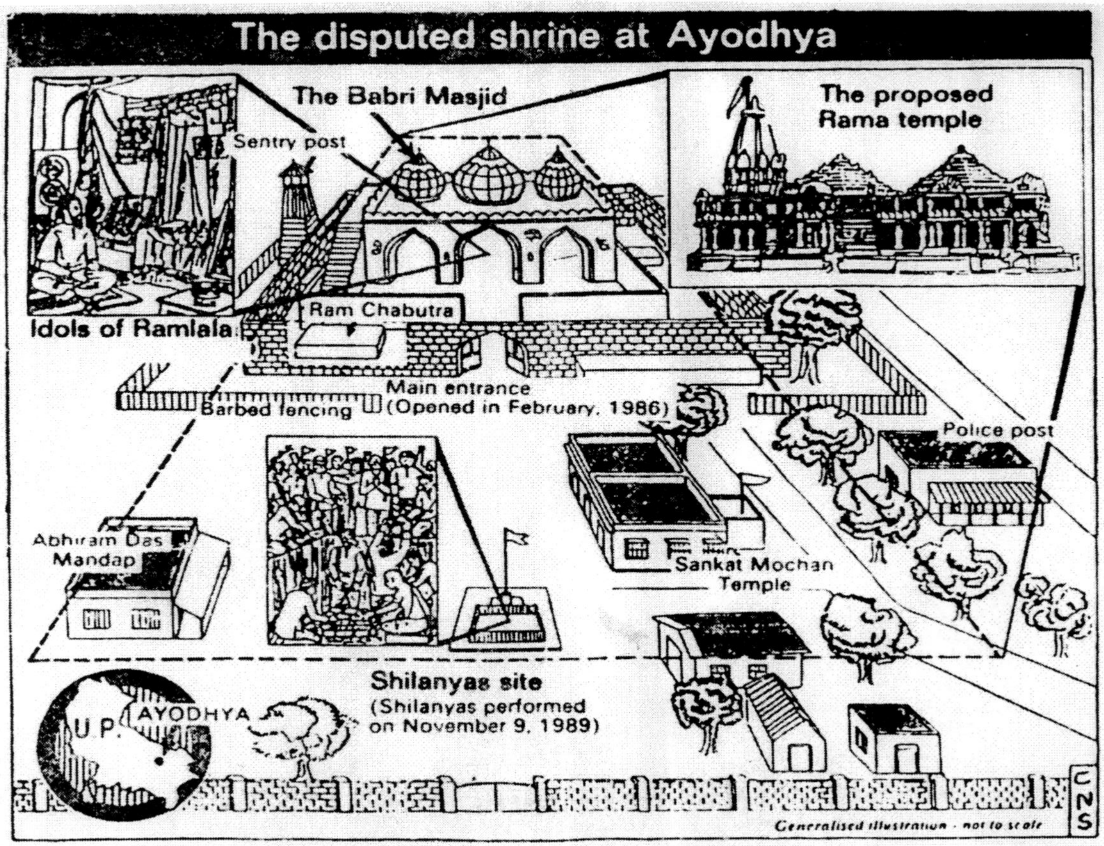
The disputed shrine at Ayodhya
The Babri Masjid
The proposed Rama temple
Sentry post
Idols of Ramlala
Ram Chabutra
Main entrance
(Opened in February, 1986)
Barbed fencing
Police post
Abhiram Das Mandap
Sankat Mochan Temple
Shilanyas site
(Shilanyas performed on November 9, 1989)
U.P.
AYODHYA
CNS
Generalised illustration - not to scale

1

Introduction

The Ram ki Nagari (the city of Ram), Ayodhya, literally means a place where there can be no battle, a place of peace, seems to have lit communal fires across the country between Hindus and Muslims. Ayodhya is now in every one's mind not because of its association with Ram legend but because communal forces and some political parties have blown over a local legal dispute over the title of a dilapidated mosque into a major national issue and pushing back the burning socio-economic problems to the background. The dispute over a crumbling and ugly structure named variously as Ramjanmabhoomi-Babri Masjid by the communal groups belonging to two communities in recent years, has become the most important reason for a sharp deterioration of inter-communal relationship and communalisation of political process. The Ramjanmabhoomi-Babri Masjid dispute at Ayodhya undeniably, has dramatised the political process as never before. It has been instrumental in the downfall of the two ruling parties at the Centre and has virtually opened the door of a real definition of secularism in India. The backlash from the raging controversy at Ayodhya has spread the fumes of religious hate to the hitherto unaffected countryside while triggering a series of communal conflagrations in the cities. Hundreds of people have lost their lives and incalculable amount of property has been reduced to flames in the wake of the Vishwa Hindu Parishad's nationwide Ramshila campaign and Advani's long Rathyatra from Somnath to Ayodhya.

The vary name of Babri Masjid on Ramjanmabhoomi (birth place of Lord Ram), if uttered by an outsider in Ayodhya-Faizabad, create a kind of peculiar and sharp response from the people in these two cities who had prided themselves for maintaining a harmonious inter-communal relations for decades. Undoubtedly, the dispute at Ayodhya, originally related to the claim over the ownership of the property has been the focal point in dividing the hearts and minds of Hindu and Muslims throughout the country. The controversy over the Babri-Masjid is smouldering like an erupted volcano, and has become a symbolic issue of redefining the nature of Hindu-Muslim relations for both the self-appointed spokesmen of the two communities and it also raised some fundamental issues governing the nature of our polity. While the BJP/RSS/VHP combine claim over the Babri Masjid is not supported by any sort of historical evidences but only based on mythic history and popular beliefs, what indeed strange is that the people have not only chosen to believe mythical history but also 'shown their willingness to face death, rather than to search for truth. Moreover, the Mandir-Masjid feud in Ayodhya has very little to do with 'restoration' of Babri Masjid or 'reconstruction' of Ramjanmabhoomi temple on a piece of disputed land. But it symbolises the assertion of the majority community against a perceived injustice perpetrated culturally centuries back by the alien invaders.

What is indeed tragic is that the self-styled 'secular' parties, who tactically mechanised the controversy over the so called Ramjanmabhoomi, are busy in pitting both the communities against each other. The dispute is not a religious issue concerning merely the sentiments and emotions of the two communities, the dispute is political which has been motivatedly turned into an acrimonious controversy with deep political ramifications and no sign of its solution seems in the near future.

I

The origin of the communal controversy over the Babri-Masjid goes back to the British period and after the partition the dispute surfaced ominously in 1949 but since then it confined with endlessly fruitless legal battle between the two communities in the subordinate courts of Faizabad district, hardly evoked any attention of the so-called champions of Hindus' and custodians of Muslims' interests.

In the beginning basic questions arise, as how this dispute attracted the national attention only in the 80's ? Can its origin be attributed to the mere opening of the gates of Babri Masjid or the political realities and developments influenced in opening the gates ? The political process in India passed through a major shift in the beginning of 1980's, after the ascendancy of the Congress Party led by Mrs. Indira Gandhi in the political scene. Her unabashed courting of Hindu communal sentiments and softening of her attitude to the Hindu communalists and aggressive posture towards minorities had indicated a perceptible shift in the style of her politics. The Babri Masjid-Ramjanmabhoomi controversy turned into an electorally useful issue only in the mid 80's when communal politics received their legitimacy in the changed style of ruling Congress Party led by Mrs. Indira Gandhi and her son Rajiv Gandhi. Prior to the communal conflagration over the Ayodhya tangle, other political developments like communal situation in Assam, Punjab, J & K and Meenakshipuram conversion had made fertile ground for the upsurge of communal and fundamentalist forces.

The Babri Masjid-Ramjanmabhoomi controversy is very complex issue and challenging one for an objective study. While the emotions, faith and identity vitiated the controversy, the space for a reasoned and impartial inquiry at the intellectual level is shrunkened. Free intellectual approach to the controversy by the scholars was denounced by the campaigners for Ramjanmabhoomi temple, terming them as "traitors of Hindus" for not respecting the 'sentiments' of Hindus. The dispute being the product of a specific stage in the development of party politics, is also a multi-actor phenomenon. The controversy unfolds a complex interaction between various parties to the dispute like the communal organisations, religious leaders, political parties, non-political organisations, the state, the intelligentia and progressive sections and the media. Each of the actor's perception to the dispute varies and articulation of their role also is determined by other parties. The interaction of the multiplicity of actors with the Ayodhya dispute reveals the political nature of the dispute.

The vigorous nationwide campaign by the protagonists of Ram temple has made large sections of Hindus fall into the communal trap laid by the Hindu fundamentalist forces and these Hindus now believe that, a place which is now called 'Ramjanmabhoomi' is the real birth place of Lord Ram which had been desecrated like many other Hindu temples in the medieval period by the Muslim invaders, and after centuries of domination by the Muslim rulers, now, they feel, the time has come in their favour, to take revenge on the history. The present communal mobilization for the Ram temple at the supposed birth place of Lord Ram, we are told, has "brought to the fore a suppressed chapter of India's history, namely the large scale destruction of the Hindu temples by the Islamised invaders."[1] Further, for the campaigners of the 'liberation' of Ramjanmabhoomi, the faith is the only legitimate basis of their action which transcends the evidences on judicial process and even openly transgresses the right of others. But when the faith is challenged by historical facts, then attempts are made to set aside or disprove the historical facts by presenting alternative set of 'authentic history', but still their hopes are not belied on their faith. The unflinching determination to demolish the Babri Masjid and erect a magnificient temple dedicated to the memory of Lord Ram in its place through resort to sheer force and violence, (symbolised with the catchword, Saugandh Ram ke Khate hein hum Mandir wohin Banayenge) by the Hindu communalists, reveal that it is not merely to rewrite symbolically the so-called unhappy chapter between Hindu-Muslim relations but to assert, in a crude way, the hegemony of Hindus as a majority community and politically subdue the Muslims. The main stimulus for such a bizzare and frightful move among the sections of Hindus is due to the fact that they have been made to convince through false campaign that the state has denied them of their right to construct a temple by putting the fetters of legality in their move, while the state has appeased the Muslims in removing the judicial verdict when it

1. Arun Shourie *et. al. Hindu Temples : What Happened to Them.* (New Delhi : Voice of India, 1990), Preface.

came the questions of supremacy between peroneal law of a community and the law of the land.

The language of 'faith' and vindication of national honour through removing the Babri Masjid do not help us to comprehend the real meaning of Ayodhya controversy. The movement for 'retrieval' of Ramjanmabhoomi from the "control of descendants of Babur", the proponents of Hindutva believe, would be a catalytic for the construction of an "imagined Hindu community", which would in the long run pave the way for establishing Hindu cultural hegemony over society and to redress the "historical humiliation of Hindus". The Ram symbol has been catapulted into the centre of the stage of Indian politics by the Hindu communalists who found a historic opportunity to consolidate and unify the heterogeneous Hindu society by a popular and powerful unifying symbol. Hence, Ram has been projected before us as the Maryada Prushottam and 'National Hero' where Babur has been branded as a foreign invader—a Muslim. This sort of thinking helps to portray the Babri Masjid as a Muslim movement which has displaced Hindu cultural honour and prestige.

For the lovers of Babri Masjid, a semi-abondoned and obscure mosque believed to have been constructed by Babur, is symbolised as a matter of protecting their Muslim honour and dignity in a predominantly non-Muslim society. And now the secular state, judiciary, rule of law become the sacrosanct institutions for the Muslim fundamentalists who paid their scant regard when the Supreme Court gave its verdict on the Shah Bano case in 1983. The aggressiveness and confrontationist attitude taken by these self-proclaimed Muslim leaders help the Hindu communalists to make campaign for demolishing the Babri Masjid with an overzealous and strident overtones. The controversy over the Babri Masjid also provide the golden opportunity for the Muslim communalists to strengthen their weakening hold over the Muslim masses and to wean them away from the influences of the secular political parties and ghettoise them to a point of no return. Like the Shah Bano case, the movement for the restoration of the Babri Masjid has provided the political legitimacy to the Muslim fundamentalists and emerged as spokesmen of their community at the cost of secular and progressive Muslim leaders.

II

Several aspects of the perplexing Ayodhya imbroglio indeed calls for the inter-disciplinary approach as well as independent study. The judicial, historical and political aspects to the controversy have inter-relationship with each other and can be fruitfully be studied to arrive at a meaningful understanding of the nature of dispute. The present work makes an attempt to study the various aspects of Ramjanmabhoomi-Babri Masjid controversy from the political perspective.

Contrary to the dominant historical and anthropological approaches to study Ramjanmabhoomi-Babri Masjid controversy and Ayodhya's development as a sacred religious centre, the present work seeks to study the dispute from a political perspective on the assumption that the dispute no longer confined within the exclusive domain of historians rather it is decidedly a political issue.

Unlike the historians, I saw the dispute not emanating from the past rather, it emerge from the changes in the political processes. Even though it is argued that the present politics of Ramjanmabhoomi received its 'sanctity' from mythic history as well as distortion of historical evidences and facts, for the supporters of the movement for Ram temple, still the dispute is political in realm than historical. It is now widely accepted that the divergent claims and counter-claims, interpretations and inquiries of historians and archaeologists have further obfuscated the Ramjanmabhoomi-Babri Masjid controversy and eluded the hope for a solution of the present impasse. Worse, while the Vishwa Hindu Parishad's claims of the Babri Masjid based on myth and faith and contorted historical evidences, the AIBMAC's claims to the disputed mosque is based on the appropriation of secular historiography. In the so-called debate on the historicity of Ram's Ayodhya, the logic and rationality and objectivity is lost because of the involvement of communal forces and their ideologues. The secular historians' attempt to challenge the historical veracity of Ramjanmabhoomi temple, have in the process, made them to surrender the space of history to the unhistorians and untrained persons who have received credence to their views while dismissing the factual history with spurious reasonings.

The historians' claim to assert their role in the dispute is however not free from ambiguities. While a historian has questioned the involvement of historians in the dispute as "academically a non issue", another historian exhorted his colleagues with a view that, "It is not for historians to 'prove' or 'disprove' as right or wrong every instance of an assertion made by a political or cultural group as social winds blow this way or that."[2]

Apart from the multidimensional nature of the problem, its repurcussions on the political process and inter-community relations in India and her neighbouring countries prove that the issue is political in its essence. In the political level, the Ayodhya dispute raise one of the most vital questions which would shape the nature of Indian polity. The dispute has forced open the controversy over the definition of secularism in India. The aggressive Hindutva campaign by the RSS/BJP/VHP for Ram temple and directing their communal mobilization against the Muslims and the 'pseudo-secular' policy of the political parties and intelligentia, has drawn up the most serious controversy over the prevalent concept of secularism.

What has made an explosive dimension to an apparently local religious issue about the ownership of a piece of land, is that political parties with different hues and ideological predilections have, converted the Babri Masjid-Ramjanmabhoomi wrangle into a haunting ground for vote banks. The political antagonisms nurtured by the dispute centring on Ayodhya

---

2. Majid H. Siddique, "Ramjanmabhoomi—Babri Masjid Dispute : The Question of History", *EPW*, 13 January 1990, p. 98.

inevitably are dressed up as a confrontation between communalists and those who unwaveringly adhere to the secular creed. Whether or not the VHP and the Babri Masjid Action Committee would give up their confrontationist postures and resolve the dispute in a manner which would save the nation from further communal carnage seems to depend very much on whether political parties and their leaders choose to subordinate their short term objective of vote catching strategems to the larger need for promoting secular values and harmonious inter communal relations.

III

In our study, we have identified major political parties like the BJP, Congress (I) and the Janata Dal as mainly responsible for politicising the sensitive dispute and manipulating the religious sentiments for their political objectives. The role the communal forces play are also important for the purpose of our study but we have ascribed them a secondary role because it is the attitudes of political parties to the communal forces that determine the latter's role. It is also fruitless to study two communal outfits, the Vishwa Hindu Parishad and the Bharatiya Janata Party separately when the dividing line between these organisations has been blurred with regard to their involvement in the Ramjanmabhoomi-Babri Masjid controversy.

In the first chapter, an indepth analysis has been made to study the development of political and social processes and the changing interactions between the state and society. The keystone of our argument is that communalism of today and the controversy over the Babri Masjid at Ayodhya can be best understood if we look into the specific political developments emerged since the 1980's. In the second chapter, various aspects to the Ayodhya dispute-legal, mythical historical and political—have been studied and interlinks between them have been established. In the third chapter, we have examined the politics of communal mobilisation over the Ayodhya dispute and attitude of political parties to the dispute with special reference to the study of Ayodhya dispute in the Ninth General Elections campaign. In the fourth chapter, the political nature of the Ayodhya dispute is further buttressed by our study of Tenth General Elections and Ramjanmabhoomi-Babri Masjid issue which played a crucial role. In the final chapter, our study concludes with reference to the issue of secularism, challenges posed to it by the Mandir-Masjid feud and the involvement of the political parties with secular credentials in the communal issue for their electoral advantage.

2

Shifts in Indian Politics : The Emergence of Communal Politics since the 1980s

Since the beginning of the eighties, we are witness to the menacing rise of ethnic and religious upsurge in our body politic. The wave of terrorist violence, widespread communal riots and tension, vicious communal campaign and mobilization and the surging tide of fundamentalism, have seized large sections of people belonging to different region and communities of India. The aggressive assertion of religious identities can be seen in the mushrooming of Shakhas, Parishads, Senas, Dals, Jamats and leagues throughout the country. Taking into consideration the fact that communalism and politics were both interlinked even in the past, it must be underscored that never before in the history of Indian politics has the communal virus attempted to swamp the Indian polity as we now witness in recent years. These events and developments undeniably prove, the retreat of the Nehruvian secular consensus, which had long been perceived as one of the vital ingredients to India's modernisation and nation building process.

The assertion of religious identities in the political process has led India to the stage where the political process itself has already undergone a considerable change. Despite the remarkable flexibility and resilience shown by the centrist politics and ideology since independence, in recent years we notice its decline. In the present social and political scenario, religion is being viewed as the sole criterion of community formation. The conscious attempt to construct a community on the religious identity tends to polarise the Indian society on religious lines.

A new arena of competitive politics emerges, which moves from centrism to extremes which are becoming the basis of political mobilization. The search for political parties now moves from a common ideological background to mutually exclusive issues that set one apart from the other. The polarisation in the politics is taking place not on the basis of socio-economic issues, but rather, on the precapitalist identities like religion and ethnicity. The centrist space of India's politics mainly represented by the Congress (I) is declining progressively due to this polarisation.

Two important shifts have taken place in the Indian political processes. Firstly, there have been major changes in the people's participation from the radical socio-economic issues to their steady involvement in their communal and sectarian conflicts. Secondly, since the beginning of 1980s, communal mobilization is becoming a dominant mode of political activity in a long term trend of politics. Essentially democratic, secular and anti-authoritarian, the political mobilization in the 1970's which was based on serious socio-economic problems has changed altogether. By contrast, the mass discontent and dissatisfaction in the 1980's were not frequently articulated in the democratic movements.[1]

I

Our attempt here has been to study the present communalisation of Indian politics, with reference to the political changes that have taken place in the larger arena of party politics. The main emphasis here has been to study the dynamics of communalism. Changing interactions between the political and social processes and to underline its political realities.

In the noisy discourse of communalism, one would find bewildering definitions and interpretations of communalism. Communalism has been described as an "ideology", "a false

1. See Zaved Alam, "Political Articulation and Mass Consciousness in Present Day India in Zoya Hasan *et. al.*, eds., *State Political Processes and Identity*, New Delhi : Sage 1989, pp. 237 ff.

consciousness", "a struggle for scarce resources", "competition for jobs", "an urban phenomenon", "an instrument of ruling class politics", and the basic causes of communalism are said to be "cultural and psychological" and so on. The unending search for a definition of communalism by the social scientists, social activists and journalists have tended to homogenise the complex socio-political and economic factors and experiences and have thereby, overlooked their variety and dynamism. Communalism no longer derives its sustenance from the middle class or the petty bourgeoisie from the urban centres.[2] The communal ideology has today spread much beyond its urban middle class base and receive its widespread support base among upper castes, backward castes, feudal classes and lower classes. The British used the policy of "divide and rule" to further their control. On the other hand, caste and religious arithmetic has always been exploited by the ruling class politicians in their electoral game of numbers. But what we have seen since the eighties is that conscious attempt to unite and consolidate the majority community under a common ideological banner has gained momentum.[3] The sole motive of the RSS and its affiliates behind the Ayodhya dispute is to strive for achieving a pan-Indian, undifferentiated and monolithic Hindu society and to redefine the national identity in terms of Hindutva (Hinduness). To achieve this purpose, distortion, misappropriation and mythification of history is made not only for "correcting the mistake committed in the past" but also to de nounce the composite cultural traditions of India.[4]

In the present study, our analytical framework rests on the assumption that, the present communalisation of Indian politics is essentially a political phenomenon. Communalisation of politics in India is, apart from other things, a political mobilization

---

2. Bipan Chandra, *Communalism in Modern India* (Delhi : Vikas, 1984), pp. 46-51.

3. K.N. Panikkar, "Communalism in India—A Perspective for Intervention", *People's Democracy*, 17 March 1991.

4. R.S. Sharma, *Communal History and Ram's Ayodhya* (New Delhi: PPH, 1990), pp. 8-18.

on the basis of a religious identity of a community by the political elites to serve their interests of achieving or maintaining political power. By "political" here we mean those activities and events, which can only be understood in terms of their relationships with public postures or wider goals and the decision making structures. In the present day communalism, the phenomenon must not be understood in the givenness of the categories like Hindu, Muslim and Sikh communalism. It should be perceived as a state of consciousness and a strategy of mobilization of a community for political purposes. Further, the communalism of today must not be identified with issues of faith and beliefs, rather, it is a conscious attempt to form a political community out of religious issues. The communalists present before us the Ayodhya dispute as a religious one, when we study the actors in the dispute and their motives, we get a political picture of the dispute.[5] It is being believed that people belonging to a common faith must have some common identity, perception and social-political outlook. The contemporary communal mobilization derives much of its sustenance from the construction of a community on the basis of religion. Religious issues and identity are instrumental in the mobilization for Ram temple at Ayodhya and the same case can be attributed

5. For example, some scholars have perceived differently the present communalisation of Indian politics mainly from the political context. Prof. Romila Thapar says, "Communalism has to be seen for what it is ; an intermeshing of ideology and power, where groups aspiring for power use a particular religious ideology to subvert a social order and replace it with an order that is based on sharp differentiations between those who accept the ideology and those who do not. It also places power in the hands of the authors of that ideology. *See*, "Politics of Religious Communities", (*Seminar* No. 365, January, 1990, pp. 28-29.) Asghar Ali Engineer argues that, "The communal phenomenon is political in genesis and can be defined as the skilfully manipulating the religious sentiments and the cultural ethos of the people by its elite to realise its (elites) political, economic and cultural aspirations by identifying those aspirations as those of the entire community". (*See*, *Communalism and Communal Violence in India : An Analytical Approach to Hindu—Muslim Relations* (Delhi : Ajanta, 1989), p. 225.

to the growth of fundamentalist leadership in the Muslim community.

Communalism in Indian society, operates at multiplicity of levels starting from the individual and local levels to regional and national levels. The communal riots and communal mobilization play a crucial role in maintaining a linkage between different Social levels and political arena.[6] The present communal mobilization can be properly understood from the context of inter-relationship between politics and society ship. From this perspective, communal politics of recent times, can be viewed in two inter-related ways. Firstly, it is an attempt to create a state of community consciousness on the basis of religion, and secondly, to use that community consciousness not merely to capture the state power but also operate in various social, economic and political domains and levels. Communalisation of Indian politics has been reflected in the heightened community consciousness and prejudices, recurrent communal riots and mobilization of a community by manipulation of its religio-cultural symbols in the political arena. It is also to be seen on attempt to divert the peoples' attention from the glaring failure of the ruling as well as opposition parties, to solve the serious socio-economic crises.

Crucial to the understanding of the contemporary communalism and the shift in the political discourse, are of two main aspects. First, communalism and politics have become complementary to each other. Communalism receives its wider acceptance and legitimacy in the political process. Second, the role of the state has been seen as being one of communalising the political process which can be proved in the case of the Punjab problem, the Shah Bano case, and the Ayodhya dispute.[7]

---

6. Panikkar, n. 3, p. 5.

7. I have developed these two points after an extensive reading of the following articles :

   (*a*) C.P. Bhambri, "State and Communalism in India", *Social Scientist*, Vol. 18, Nos. 8-9, August-September, 1990, pp. 25-26.

(*Contd. to next page*)

II

What role do political parties play in the development of the group consciousness in the political sphere? Political parties have been perceived by a number of contemporary scholars as the product of the societal cleavages. A number of research works point out the dependent role of the parties but they explicitly concede the fact that parties also play causative and dependent roles and influence the dynamics of societal cleavages.[8] Paul R. Brass's study shows, the North Indian party politics provides three broad patterns of relationship between the political parties and social and ethnic cleavages, but, in all these three factors the leadership in political parties plays a crucial role in determining the outcome of such events. Hindus and Muslims in UP are divided on the basis of mutually reinforcing ethnic cleavages but, the political parties and voluntary associations have worked towards the reinforcement of the cleavages.[9]

(Contd. from previous page)

(*b*) Randhir Singh, "Communalism and Struggle against Communalism", *Social Scientist*, Vol. 18, Nos 8-9, August-September, 1990, pp. 5-26.

(*c*) Anil Nauriya, "Relationship between the State and Religion", *EPW*, 25 February, 1989, pp. 405-6.

(*d*) T.N. Madan, "Secularism in Its Place", *Journal of Asian Studies*, Vol. 46 (4). November 1987, pp. 747-59.

(*e*) Dipankar Gupta, "Communalising of Punjab (1980-85)", *EPW*, Vol. X, No. 28, 13 July 1985, pp. 1185-90.

(*f*) Achin Vanaik, *The Painful Transition : Bourgiois Democracy in India* (London : Verso, 1990), pp. 147-49.

(*g*) Gyanendra Pandey, "Ayodhya and the State", *Seminar* (*365*) December 1989, pp. 39-43.

(*h*) Ashis Banerjee "Comparative Curfew: Changing Dimensions of Communal Politics in India" in Veena Das ed., *Mirrors of Violence : Communities, Riots and Survivors in South Asia* (*ND-OUP*) 1990, pp. 44 ff.

8. See Paul R. Brass, *Language, Religion and Politics in North India* (Delhi : Vikas, 1974), pp. 36 ff.
9. *Ibid.*, p. 41.

There are broadly two categories of parties in relation to their linkage with communalism as such. There are parties which are organised around the communal ideology and goals, like the Akali Dal, Muslim League and Hindu Mahasabha during the pre-Independence period, and in the post-Independence period—there are parties like the IUML, the BJP, and Shiva Seha, which are examples of "confessional parties". The latter kind of parties are the best examples of present day communal parties. The BJP and Shiva Sena are exclusivist parties and base their ideology on the Hindutva or Hindu nationalism. These parties believe that a creation of homogeneous Hindu consciousness is essential precondition for making a "Hindu Rashtra". The sustained effort to create an emotionally charged community consciousness by manipulating the religious symbols like the "Trishuls" and "Rathyatra", "Ram" are meant to attain their goal of bringing about a qualitative transformations in the social configurations and ideological structure of Hindu society.

Another type of political party which is not based on religious idiom but which covertly uses communalism for its political mobilization is the Congress (I). This party reversed its earlier electoral "strategy of mobilization with the steady erosion of its support base. The Congress party during Nehru's period relied on the left-of-centre values of socialism and secularism to secure political mobilization and legitimacy. Indira Gandhi resorted to populist socialism in the late sixties and seventies as her main electoral strategy. Since the beginning of eighties, the Congress moved to the right and appealed to Hindu chauvinism which we will discuss subsequently.

The developments in India's political process can be studied through continuities and changes in the party system and the forces within the system, because the parties provide the main channel of communication between the state and society in an open democratic system. To emphasise changes in party politics, we can categorise the changes in the political process into some phases. The first phase of India's party politics is known as "one party dominant system" covers the period from 1947 to 1967. The second phase of party-politics starts from the Congress party's decline of its dominance in 1967 election to its defeat in the elections in 1977.

III

From the early eithties, Indira Gandhi's political and policy orientation in the post-Janata period were different from her earlier regime. This period is the most important phase in India's party-politics and during this period, a set of new and quite different trends in Indian politics began to emerge.[10]

Indira Gandhi slowly adopted a political strategy which had hitherto been the exclusive strategy of the right-wing Hindu communal parties. It was noticed in her policy pronouncement that Indira Gandhi was less ideological and more pragmatic. Despite her frequent rhetoric on socialism and economic independence and self-reliance, her shift of emphasis from anti-poverty programmes and move to the IMF to accept loan with stiff conditionalities signalled the changes in the policy persuasion of the Congress Party.[11]

Behind her changing orientation of politics from the left of centre path of development, deeper social and economic factors were at work.[12] As we have mentioned earlier, Indira

10. James Manor, "Parties and Party System" in Atul Kohli, ed., *India's Democracy* (Princeton University Press, 1988), pp. 80-91.

11. For this aspect see, Atul Kohli, "Politics of Economic Liberalization", *World Development*, Vol. 17, No. 3, 1989, pp. 308-09.

12. But scholars belong to liberal democratic persuasion view this shift from different perspective which is based moreover on appearance than the underlying political realities. They view that, the political awakening of the masses heralded with the political decay of the parties. The deinstitutionalization of the Congress party and the centralization of party structure and the political institution resulted in the growing failure of the system to respond 'creatively' to the pressures from society. This also contributed to another change, which was the failure of the state to act as an agency of social and economic change. So, the decline in the infrastructure of democracy account for the shifts in the political discourse and idioms of the Congress Party. See for example, James Manor, n. 10, pp. 77-91.

Gandhi's populist and rhetorical socialism failed to effect comprehensive economic and social changes, because of the class composition of the state and its inherent structural constraints. There is a growing frustration and disillusionment due to the failure of the system to deliver goods and to remove economic hardships. The development path that has been pursued since independence had led to further immerserisation and alienation of vast segments of the people, and the consequent their cynical attitude to the state's ability to solve their problems. The state has tackled the popular unrest by resorting to undemocratic and authoritarian tactics. The political are not in a position to present radical socio-economic programmes to the people.[13] In a desperate bid to hold on or capture political power, it is not the socio-economic issues but the appeal to the caste and community sentiments of the people that has become an effective strategy of these parties. All these developments in the sphere of political economy can be linked to the rapid decline of the congress party's support base and collapse of its earlier social coalition. In the 1980 elections, the Lok Dal secured its victories in the Muslim dominated areas. The voting analysis also revealed that the backward and the middle peasantry had overwhelmingly tilted towards the Lok Dal and Janata Party. This was also further realised when the party suffered humiliating defeat in Andhra Pradesh and Karnataka assembly elections which had been its stronghold in the South India. All these trends led to a sense of insecurity and desperation in the Congress leadership and the search for a new electoral strategy.

The rightward shift alongside communal appeal, couched in the language of threats to India's unity was accepted as the "creative strategy" to win back the Congress Party's traditional support base comprising of rural poor, backward castes and minorities as well as to gain support from the petty bourgeoisie

---

13. See for example, Randhir Singh, "Communalism and Struggle Against Communalism", *Social Scientist* (New Delhi), Vol. 18, Nos. 8-7, August-September, 1990, pp. 7-21. See also, C.P. Bhambri' "State and Communalism", *Social Scientist* (New Delhi), Vol. 18, Nos 8-7, August-September 1990, pp. 24-26.

who had provided a strong support base to the BJP which posed a threat for the BJP in North India.[14]

The logic of the move to the left, after the 1969 split of the Congress and her move to the right since the early 80's was similar in objective. Her populist radical posture during the beginning of the 70's was meant to undermine to the potents of the left force, while her later move to the right was guided by her political compulsion.

Indira Gandhi's move from the left-of-centre values of secularism and socialism, to appealing to Hindu chauvinism and the pro-business stance, must be viewed from the context of a overall shift in the political orientation. Because, in India's political culture, there are two alternative paths of developments, which will ensure the ruling party the political legitimacy and popular support. The shift from the Nehruvian path of socialism and its acceptance of secular mobilization as its inherent political logic was abandoned by Mrs. Gandhi after her "soft victory" in 1980.[15]

Mrs. Indira Gandhi sought to capitalize the growing communal sentiments of Hindus in North-Western India, over the killings of Hindus in Punjab by Sikh terrorists. By taking a confrontationist posture towards the Akalis, Assam agitation and J&K Chief Minister Farooq Abdullah, she successfully projected herself as the protector of the national interest. She also, frequently visited Hindu temples, hobnobbed with the Acharyas, Yogis and Tantriks. It it most surprising to note that inspite of Mrs. Gandhi's change of attitude there to was a frequent occurrence of communal riots. By contrast to the sixties and seventies, whereas the ruling Congress party identified the Muslims as the victims of communal riots and denounced the communalism of Hindu community. But from the early eighties Mrs. Gandhi's main attack was on communal "violence"

---

14. James Manor, n. 10, p. 10.
15. Zoya Hasan, "Changing Orientation of the State and Emergence of Majoritarianism in the 1980s". *Social Scientist*, Vol. 18, Nos. 8-9, August-September 1990, pp. 29-30.

and not its source.[16] A number of communal riots which took place in the beginning of eighties like in Moradabad and Allahabad in 1990 where the Provincial Armed constabulary (PAC) played most blatant role in the riots. But Mrs. Gandhi never condemned the PAC for its partisan role.[17] In one of her public meetings, she openly attacked the minorities for creating problems in Punjab and Assam and said in a meeting at Kurukshetra, that a Dharmyudh (hold-war) was underway to resist the challenge posed, by the minorities.[18] Soon after "Operation Bluestar", Mrs. Gandhi, in her public meeting at Gharwal, said openly that, Hindu religion was under attack from the minorities.[19] By evoking Hindu sentiments she had begun to inject a sense of insecurity and anxiety in the minds of the majority community about internal threats to the national unity posed by the aggressive minorities.

The careful strategy of counting the Hindu majority paid dividends in the Assembly elections in Jammu and Kashmir, the Municipal Corporation elections in Delhi, wherein the Congress (I) defeated its main rival the BJP by driving a wedge between the former and the RSS. Further, numerous RSS activists deserted their political organ, the BJP, and campaigned in favour of the Congress (I) in the elections. In Maharashtra, the Congress (I) formed an election alliance with the Shiva Sena to fight the Municipal and Panchayat elections. This new

---

16. D.D. Sheth, "Sympathy Vote on Communal Wave ? The electoral Scene in 1984" (mimeographed). (Centre for Study of Developing Societies : Delhi), pp. 10 ff.

17. See Mohammad Aslam, "State Communalism and the Reassertion of Muslim Identity" in Hasan *et. al.*, ed., n. 1, p. 274.

18. For this aspect see, A.G. Noorani, "Indira Gandhi and Indian Muslims", *Economic and Political Weekly*, 3 November, 1990, pp. 2417-2418 ; Rajni Kothari, "Communalism : The New Face of Indian Democracy" in his book *State Against Democracy* (Delhi : Ajanta, 1989), pp. 246-247 ; Rober L. Hardgrave Jr., "India on the Eve of Elections : Congress and Opposition", *Pacific Affairs*, Vol. 57 (3), 1984, pp. 424-25.

19. Rajni Kothari, "*Political* and *the Peoples : In Search of Human Agenda*" (Delhi : Ajanta, 1989), Vol. 2, pp. 437-60.

strategy appeared to the ruling Congress (I) as the only viable electoral option, to ensure the party's victory in the next parliamentary elections. What prompted the party to adopt the new electoral strategy is the humiliating defeat of the Congress (I) in the Andhra Pradesh and Karnataka Assembly elections, which made Mrs. Gandhi to believe that the South might not support them in the next Parliamentary elections, and North Western and Central India would be crucial for her survival in the office. With the menacing rise of contrifugal forces in the Punjab, Jammu and Kashmir and Assam, Mrs. Gandhi succeeded in cultivating an evocative theme like threats to India's unity from anti-national minorities in the border states and the opposition parties collusion with the anti-national forces abroad, and maintaining that strong centre would be the only antedote against such divisive forces.

Till 1980, "Hindu confessional politics" had been confined among the upper strata of the Hindu society in the Northern India. With the rapid development of communication and social mobility and economic transformation, Hindu religious festivals gradually transcended to the local horizons and indicated the growing community consciousness among these sections of Hindus. Communally sensitive issues like the Meenakshipuram conversion in 1983, adulteration of vanaspati ghee made the hitherto dormant communal organisations like the RSS, VHP and Jamait-e-Islami to rise. These events created a favourable condition for the Hindu communalists to launch nationwide mobilization to save Hinduism from India's proseletyzing minorities.[20] The supporters of backlash alleged that the majority community is being beseiged by the minorities as the latter are being pampered by the Indian state.[21]

Much of the social support for the resurgence of religiousity comes from the newly "nouveau riche" in rural areas and

---

20. L.I. Rudolph and S.H. Rudolph, *In Pursuit of Lakshmi : The Political Economy of the Indian State* (Bombay: Orient Longman, 1987), pp. 41-42.

21. M.J. Akbar, *India ; The Siege Within* (England ; Penguin, 1988), pp. 196-98.

entrepreneurs and professionals in the urban centres. These middle class found that patronising Hinduism and practising it in new ways not only earned them respect but also provided them a type of satisfying world view and social identity. The proliferation of religiousity can be traced when these classes are eager to channel a part of their newly acquired wealth to religious activities like the building or reclamation of the temple, festivals and gospels. But this quest for a positive social identity by a section of Hindu society also proved to be a source of tension and controversial identity in inter-communal relations in India.[22]

By the mid eighties India's centrist secular image received no longer a commitment from its post-independence political elites. In the closing years of Indira Gandhi, the Congress party moved slowly from a Nehruvian secular image to a "Hindu Confessional Party."[23]

After the assassination of Mrs. Indira Gandhi, the generational change that was heralded by the rise of Rajiv Gandhi at the helm of affairs of the nation, failed to augur a new era in Indian politics. Rather, it strengthened the new trends of politics set by his mother. To say that Rajiv Gandhi's politics marked a "deviation" or a "new phase", is based on the mistaken notion of understanding Indian politics. Rajiv's regime was part and parcel of the politics and economics of Indian political process and it would be futile to expect any perceptible change in his style of politics.[24] Rajiv Gandhi inherited the legacy of his mother and mistook her political opportunism as political sagacity.

Many observers on Indian politics had likened the last years of Indira Gandhi regime to the 1977 political situation. There were speculations about the possibility of a coalitional politics in the face of Congress Party's steady erosion of its support

22. Panikkar, n. 3, 13 March 1991.

23. Rudolph and Rudolph, n. 20, p. 46.

24. See for example Moin Shakir, "Political Economy of Rajiv Regime", *Link* (New Delhi), 25 February 1987, pp. 12-15.

base and hold over different regions. Even average Congressmen were sceptical about the victory of the party. But, after Indira Gandhi's assassination, the political scenario had changed dramatically. Sensing the favourable moods of the electorate towards the party, Rajiv Gandhi announced the holding of Eighth General Elections.[25]

The 1984 verdict, was catastrophic in nature. The Congress party secured unprecedented victory, and for the first time, negative votes were turned not against the Congress (I) but against the Opposition. It has been widely accepted by the noted scholars on Indian politics that the 1984 landslide victory of the Congress Party was more to do with other factors than due to 'sympathy vote' for the 'personality' of Rajiv Gandhi. Rather completely different issues and new electoral strategies of the Congress party gave it a massive mandate in the Lok Sabha elections. The pre-assassination political situation was gradually being built up with the slow communalisation of Indian politics.[26] The sudden death of Mrs. Gandhi only consolidated the winning strategy which was accomplished by Rajiv Gandhi.

In the 1984 elections, the Congress (I)'s slogan was to preserve national unity and integrity and political stability.[27] Rajiv Gandhi inherited his mother's style of politics and a similar kind of attitude to opposition parties. In his election meetings, Rajiv Gandhi warned the people about the "grave" internal threats posed by the terrorist and secessionist forces in the Punjab, Jammu & Kashmir and Assam and threats from across the border. Like his mother, Rajiv Gandhi branded the Opposition as anti-national and attacked the opposition parties.

---

25. Sheth, n. 16, pp. 1-8.

26. Kothari, "Behind the ballot", *Seminar*, No. 306, February 1986, pp. 12-14.

27. The Congress (I) hijacked the age old slcgans of the Hindu chauvinist forces like *Desh Akhand—Desh Bachao* (Unite India—Save India) and made as its main poll plank. See for example, Myron Weiner, "*Indian Paradox* : *Essays in Indian Politics*" (New Delhi : Sage, 1989), p. 297.

for supporting the Anandpur Saheb resolution. Despite the prompt denial by the opposition, Rajiv Gandhi continued to level that allegation against the Opposition. The RSS leaders like Nanaji Deshmukh and Bala Saheb Deoras openly supported the Congress Party in the elections but Rajiv Gandhi refused to disavow the RSS support.[28]

In his election Campaign, Rajiv Gandhi projected Mrs. Gandhi as not only his mother, but the mother of all the patriotic Indians, who sacrificed her life for the cause of India's unity and integrity. By campaigning in such a style, Rajiv created an impression in the voters mind that only the Congress (I) can protect and safeguard the unity and integrity of the country. For the first time in the Congress party's election history, the party was less concerned about securing the Muslim votes. Even the local Congress' leaders of U.P., in the public meetings expressed open antagonism to Muslims and lumped them together with the Sikhs, as internal threats backed by the external enemies.[29]

The Congress party's failure to check the virulence of the communal riots such as in Bombay-Bhiwandi (1984), Moradabad (1980), Ahmedabad (1982), Allahabad (1980, and Hyderabad (1983), the "Operation Blue Star" (1984) and anti-Sikh carnage after Indira Gandhi's assassination in which the local level Congressmen were involved, had alienated the minorities from the Congress party. Despite Shahi Imam's appeal to Muslims to reject the Congress (I) in the elections, the SGPC and Akali Dal's support to the Janata Pary and Jammu & Kashmir's then Chief Minister Mr. Farooq Abdullah's campaign for opposition parties, Congress returned to power with overwhelming majority.[30] Further given the lacklusture performance of Indira Gandhi's regime, the party

28. See for example, Manor, n. 10, p. 82. Also, H.K. Paranjape, "The Wave", *Seminar*, No. 306, September 1985, p. 16.

29. For details, see Paul R. Brass, "1984 Parliamentary Elections in U.P.", *Asian Survey*, June 1986, Vol. 26, June 1986, p. 663-64.

30. Pranjape, n. 28, p. 16 ; James Manor, n. 10, pp. 85-86.

was left with no option but to mobilize the voters on a completely different set of issues. Economic hardships faced by the people and growing corruption at high places hardly played any role.

The complete reversal of the poll strategy paid unexpected dividends to the Congress party. It not only saved the Congress Party from the fast erosion of its social support base but won back a huge mass of Hindu votes, so much so that, the BJP failed to bag a single seat from its Hindu heartland. The Congress Party also made a significant dent in the Lok Dal's and Janata Party's backward-caste support base and deprived them of their chance of winning majority of Lok Sabha seats.

The foregoing facts and events bring home the point that the pre-conditions had been created already before the assassination of Mrs. Gandhi for a 'wave' by politicizing the communal issues. Indira Gandhi's death which though it generated "sympathy vote" served as an "icing on the communal electoral cake" already prepared by the Congress (I).[31] The party's victory was not due to the "sympathy wave" (contrary to the widespread superficial view) rather sympathy for a bereaved son whose mother had laid down her life for a "Hindu cause" (or for national unity ?).[32] The 1984 election results proved that, there is presumed to exist a "Hindu vote" which can be mobilized for the sake of national unity and threats from Sikh extremism and Muslim separatism and can bring a landslide victory to a party.[33]

The dramatic reversal of the poll strategy and political shift on the part of the Congress Party, only helped the marginal and dormant political parties, like the BJP and Shiva Sena to rise. Indeed, the humiliating defeat of the BJP in the 1984 elections forced it to abandon its liberal and moderate posture and move to an aggressive and uncompromising stand

31. Seth, n. 16, p. 12.

32. Rudolph and Rudolph, n. 20, pp. 46, 149.

33. Paul R. Brass, *The New Cambridge History of India : Politics of India Since Independence* (Hyderabad : Cambridge, 1990), p. 14.

on the issues of secularism and nationalism. The BJP leadership convinced that, evoking the theme of majoritarianism and a confrontationist attitude towards the minorities would enable it to garner Hindu votes. Further, the Congress party's role in the Shah Bano Case and Ayodhya controversy determined the BJP to thwart the possibility of Rajiv Gandhi playing the "Hindu card" in the Ninth General Elections. "We must not lose Hindu votes by letting him do that" quipped Mr. Vajpayee.[34]

For the students of Indian politics, Rajiv Gandhi's regime would be long remembered in the history of Indian politics, not because of his effort to move India towards the twenty first century, but, because of the unprecedented growth of the fundamentalist and communal forces during his regime. The young technocrat-turned-politician's assumption as the Prime Minister of India promised a new beginning and style of Indian politics. But within a brief period of his rule, it was undeniably proved that his regime was the logical extension of the regime headed by his mother. Rajiv Gandhi's five years of tenure as the Prime Minister witnessed an ominous growth of communal and fundamentalist forces, centering around the two most contentious issues of the secular polity—the Shan Bano controversy and the Babri Masjid Ramjanmabhoomi dispute. It is our assumption that Rajiv Gandhi government's dubious role in the Shah Bano case and the Ayodhya controversy, has brought the issue of secularism and communalism to the centre stage of Indian politics, and pushed Indian politics and society towards communal polarisation. The assertion of ethnic and religious identities in the political process had become the most distinctive feature of Indian politics in the Rajiv era.

The Shan Bano case represented one of the most important political crises for Rajiv Gandhi, in which he had demonstrated his utter indecisiveness to handle the controversy. The controversy generated around the Shah Bano case highlighted the role of ruling Congress party in permitting the upsurge of fundamentalists, and its questionable move to nullify the Supreme

34. See his interview with the *Times of India*, 2 October 1989.

Court judgement, which in turn aroused sentiments among, the Hindu middle class against the so-called "minority appeasement" policy of the government.

On 23rd April 1985, when the Supreme Court of India delivered a sensitive judgement on a divorced Muslim Woman's plea (Shah Bano) for maintenance which was perceived by the Muslim fundamentalist as the attack on their 'shariat' (Islamic Law) and it led to the massive agitation and turmoil among the Muslims.[35] The Supreme Court addressed itself primarily to the issue of applicability of Section 125 of the CRPC to a divorced Muslim woman's plea for maintenance allowances, unable to support herself. The Court ruled that section 125 of the CRPC is applicable to all citizens irrespective of their different personal laws. In case of conflict between the Muslim Personal Law (MPL) and Criminal Procedure Code (CRPC), the latter would prevail upon the former. Aware of its strong repurcussions on the Muslim psyche, the judges of the Supreme Court delivered their judgement after having gone through number of authoritative interpetations and translations of the 'Shariat' and the holy book. But apart from the women and theologians belonging to All-India Muslim Personal Law Board (AIMPLB), Jamait-ul-Ulema, Jamait-e-Islami and leaders of the Indian Union of Muslim League (IUML), Muslim Majlis-e-Mushawarut, and the Janata Party leader Shahabuddin strongly denounced the judgement as the perceived it as the Court's interference on their Personal Laws.[36] The Muslim Personal Law according to the theologians and Ulemas based on the Shariat which is divine and immutable and its adherence is an indispensable act of each Muslim.

Interestingly, the Shah Bano case was not the finest of its kind in granting maintenance allowance to muslim woman. Earlier in the case of Tahira Bai vs. Ali Husai Fiduli Chothia

---

35. Zoya Hasan, "Minority Identity, Muslim Women Bill Campaign and the Political Process", *Economic Political Weekly*, 7 January 1989, p. 44.

36. See for details, Asghar Ali Engineer, ed., *The Shah Bano Cont oversy* (Hyderabad : Orient Longman 1987). pp. 35-36.

and Fazumbi vs. Khader Ali cases in the 1970's, the then Supreme Court Judge Mr. V.R. Krishna Iyer had granted maintenance to Muslim women under Section 125 of the Criminal Procedure Code. While none of these judgements generated any protest among the Muslim leaders, the Shah Bano judgement unleashed a great turmoil among the Muslims.[37]

The reason for such a strong protest of the Muslims must be under in the context of the larger changes that had taken place in the Indian political process since eighties. As has been mentioned earlier it would suffice to say here that, the last phase of Indira Gandhi witnessed marked polarisation of Indian society on communal lines. Nearly, 4,000 people and been killed in the communal riots that broke out in the early eighties. The Congress party had taken over the role of the protector of majority, interest and the procurement of the ideology of Hindu nationalism. The deteriorating economic conditions and discrimination against the Muslims in employment opportunities and the steady erosion of Congress party's support base among the Muslims had made large sections of Muslims receptive of fundamental ideas. The Vishwa Hindu Parishad (VHP) launched series of agitations like the Ekatamata yanja (sacrifice for unanimity), the Ramjanmabhoomi Mukti Yanja (A sacrifice to liberate the spot on which Ram was born), Ram Janaki Rath and the "Tala Kholo agitation (open the locks) and the partisan role of the State Police forces during the communal riots had created a deep sense of insecurity and anxiety in the minds of Muslims.[38] These developments made it possible for communally oriented Muslim groups to occupy the political vacuum created by weekening of the Congress base.

The Supreme Court judgement in the Shah Bano case, provided the fundamentalists and the so-called custodians of Muslim identity a much needed opportunity to retain their

37. Zoya Hasan, n. 35, p. 45.
38. Mushirul Hasan, "Indian Muslims : In Search of Integration and Identity", *Third World Quarterly*. 10(2), April 1988, pp, 830-38.

fading leadership and social status and to emphasize the distinctive identity of the Muslim community. Intense agitations were organised by these leaders throughout the country. The spontaneous response by the Muslims gave a lease of life to the Muslim non-political organisations which were starved of action literally.[39]

The Shah Bano judgement was symbolised as a matter of protecting the Muslim political identity. The Muslim leaders perceived the judgement as an unique opportunity to homogenise the Muslims around a common symbol, transcending their socio-economic barriers. As Shahabuddin wrote, "Ours is not a communal fight. It only amounts to resisting the inexorable process of assimilation. We want to keep our identity at all costs."[40] The campaign against the Supreme Court judgement by the fundamentalists received further momentum due to vociferous campaign by the Hindu communalists in favour of the Supreme Court judgement and their demand for enacting a Uniform Civil Code for all Indians.[41] The clergy saw the Supreme Court judgement on Shah Bano's appeal as a grave threat to their power and authority over the Muslims.

Despite their divergent socio-economic, regional and linguistic backgrounds the Muslim fundamentalists unanimously denounced the Supreme Courts judgement. The controversy over the Shah Bano judgement took a new twist by the intervention of specific political processes and developments on the political arena. The initial reaction of the Congress to the Supreme Court judgement was positive, when one of Rajiv Gandhi's Council of Ministers, Mr. Arif Mohd. Khan strongly supported the Supreme Court judgement on the floor of Parliament with a tacit consent from Rajiv Gandhi. But on 20 December 1985 another Union Minister, Mr. Z.R. Ansari virulently criticised the Supreme Court's authority (of the Supreme Court) to interpret the Shariat.[42] Later when the

39. Engineer ed., n. 36, pp. 13-14.
40. *Mainstream*, 10 May 1986, p. 33.
41. Engineer ed., n. 40, pp. 14-17.
42. Hasan, n. 38, p. 840.

Congress Party suffered reverses in the Lok Sabha by-elections held on 25 December in several constituencies with sizeable Muslim population, and the massive victory of Sayed Shahabuddin—a fundamentalist Muslim leader who was leading the movement against the Supreme Court judgement, finally convinced the Congress leaders about a steady alienation of the Muslims from party. Fearful of further electoral reverses, Rajiv Gandhi's government bowed to the fundamentalist pressure of annuling the Supreme Court judgement. After consultation with the members of AIMPLB (All India Muslim Personal Law Board) and the IUML, the government adopted the Muslim Women (Protection of Rights on Divorce) Bill, 1985 on 5 May 1986 in Parliament and used the party's brute majority to pass the bill, despite strong protests from the opposition parties and several non-political and progressive organisations. The most anti-secular and regressive provision of the Bill was that, it overruled the Article-14 which guarantees the equality before law by the Article-15 which safeguards the freedom of religion.[43]

The Law Minister strongly defended the government's stand and contended that "the consistent policy of the government that in the matters pertaining to a community, priority would be given to the leader of that community."[44] The Prime Minister argued that, the government had to enact the Bill, to allay the fears of the Muslim leaders (theologians and a section of M.Ps.) who perceived it as a threat to their identity.[45] The government by according the status of leaders to the fundamentalists and theologians, thus, overlooked the views of other secular, democratic and progressive Muslims leaders. The reversal of the Supreme Court judgement solely due to electoral compulsion, darkened the progressive and secular

43. Engineer ed., 36, 15-17; Hasan (Z), n. 35, pp. 44-48.

44. *The Telegraph* (Calcutta), 4 December 1985.

45. *The Telegraph*, 12 March 1986. See M.J. Akbar's interview with Mr. Rajiv Gandhi. See Kewal Varma, "Rajiv Gandhi and Secularism: Lessons from Muslim Women Bill Debate". *Mainstream*, 24 May 1986, p. 51.

image of Mr. Rajiv Gandhi. By enacting the Bill, Rajiv Gandhi's regime exposed a serious weaknesses in India's secular polity. In the name of secular polity, a multi theocratic secularism was promoted and the religious sentiments were given protection over all other considerations. The aggressive opposition of the Muslims to the Supreme Court judgement had a very adverse impact on the Hindu minds.[46] The Hindu communal forces saw the government move to nullify the Supreme Court judgement as capitualation to the Muslim fundamentalist and obscurantist forces. This, also strengthened their view that while the Hindus are secular in their outlook, the Indian Muslims are fundamentalist and communal. The government, the politically conscious Hindus felt, has clearly gone back from its duty to uphold the judiciary and the Constitution and subverted these institution for its electoral compulsion.

The sustained mobilization by the RSS and VHP for the liberation of Ramjanmabhoomi undeniably had given a new dimension to the Muslims' protest of the Supreme Court's judgement. In fact, the decision to enact the Muslim Women's Bill was a sequel to the communal pressures mounted by Hindu communal organisations for reopening the Babri Masjid-Ramjanmabhoomi complex. The Talakholo agitation which started during Mrs. Gandhi's regime was suspended due to her assassination and it was revived again on 23 October, 1985 in 25 places of the country.[47] Arun Nehru, once a close confident of Rajiv Gandhi and Minister of State for Home said, "In early 1986, the Muslim Women's Bill was passed to play the Muslim card and then came the decision on Ayodhya to play

---

46. See for details, A.A. Engineer, "Hindu-Muslim Relations Before and After 1947", in S. Gopal ed., *Anatomy of a Confrontation : The Babri Masjid Ramjanmbhoomi Issue* (New Delhi : Penguin 1991), p. 191.

47. A.G. Noorani. "The Babri Masjid-Ramjanambhoomi Question" in Asghar Ali Engineer ed., *The Babri Masjid-Ramjanmabhoomi Controversy* (Delhi : Ajanta, 1990), p. 62.

the Hindu card. It was supposed to be a package deal. I know it was a dangerous thing to do. I did not agree.[48]

The locks of the Babri Masjid were thrown open on the 1st February 1986, on the order of the Faizabad District Court and the Muslim Women's Bill was introduced on 25th February 1986, in Parliament. The Central Government felt compelled to open the gates of Babri Masjid only to distract the attention of the Hindus from its next move of introducing the Muslim Women's Bill to nullify the Supreme Court judgement on the Shah Bano Case. Further, by introducing the Muslim Women's Bill after a few weeks, the government hoped to divert the attention of Muslims from the opening of the Babri Masjid for the Hindus to offer worship.

Though the origin of the dispute dates back to 22nd December 1949 when the idol of Lord Ram was sureptitiously kept in the Babri mosque, the dispute attracted public attention only when the Faizabad District Magistrate opened the locked gates of the Babri Masjid on the order of Faizabad District Court judge and it received wide publicity by the public as well as private media. The judgement, was, by all accounts controversial and politically calculated. The procedure adopted in passing the order is unprecedented in so far as the whole affair was conducted with undue secrecy and haste, as the verdict was given within two days and executed within half an hour.[49]

The judge in his verdict said, "If the Hindus are offering prayers and worshipping the idols, though in a restricted way, for the last 35 years, the Heavens are not going to fall, if the locks of the gates O and P are removed". But unfortunately, within 24 hours of the opening of the gates, all hell was let loose and 30 people were killed in the communal riots by the 6th April 1986.[50] The 1986 verdict brought the sterile dispute

---

48. See the English version of Arun Nehru's interview with Akhbar-e-nau (Delhi based Urdu Weekly) in *The Statesman*, New Delhi edition, 17 August 1989.
49. See, M. Mahmud, *Facts, vs. Fiction* (Faizabad : *n. d.*), pp. 36 ff.
50. See, Aswini Bhatnagar, "Opening the Flood Gates"', *Illustrated Weekly of India* (Bombay). 6 April 1986, p. 32.

on to the streets and subsequently to the political arena. Uttar Pradesh became communally the most sensitive state and between the January and June, 238 communal riots occurred over the Ramjanmabhoomi-Babri Masjid controversy.[51]

The introduction of Muslim Women's Bill failed to distract the attention of the Muslims from the Ayodhya dispute. The Babri Masjid haunted the minds of various cross sections of Muslims more than the Shah Bano case because they perceived it as another attempt to deprive them of their distinct socio-cultural and push them back to the dark days of medieval politics. The Muslim fundamentalists and certain communally minded leaders also treated it as one more issue before them, which would help them to strengthen their weakening hold over the Muslims, through whipping up the religious fervour of the Muslims against the illegal control of the Babri Masjid by the Hindus.

The so-called victory over the Shah Bano case, encouraged the Muslim reaction in several different ways, over the Babri-Masjid dispute. In March 1986, the Babri Masjid Action Committee was formed which was followed by a nation wide mobilization of the Muslims over the reopening of the Babri Mosque for the Hindus. Such a militant and aggressive stand by the Muslim leaders generated strong passions among the Hindus and protest by major national political parties.[52] This, was followed up by the biggest ever public protest by the Muslims since independence, held in New Delhi, to demand the full possession of the Babri Masjid. Muslim leaders like Syed Shahabuddin, Shahi Imam of the Jamma Masjid, Sayed Abdullah Bukhari made objectionable and provocative speeches.

The Babri Masjid has become a symbolic issue for the Muslims in their struggle for protecting their threatened identity.

---

51. See the *Illustrated Weekly's Review*, "Who will get the Muslim Vote", 9 July 1989, pp. 14-15. Also, Mohd. Aslam, *State Communalism*, n. 17, p. 276.

52. *Sunday* (Calcutta), 25-31 January 1987, p. 45 ; Engineer, n. 47, p. 12.

As one leader of the AIBMAC (All India Babri Masjid Action Committee) viewed, "The Babri Masjid is surely not our Mecca but if we lose the mosque to Hindus, the already oppressed minority will lose whatever little reason they have to be citizens of the country."[53] The politics of Babri Masjid raises the question of identity, faith of the Muslims, but in reality, the lovers of the Babri Masjid are neither the champions of restoring their Babri Masjid, nor genuinely concerned about safeguarding the interests of Muslims. The Babri Masjid movement leaders are well aware that the chances of restoring the Babri Masjid, surreptitiously captured by the Hindu chauvinists in 1949, is bleak and the Court verdict in directing the Hindu communalists to hand over the Babri Masjid to Muslims is well nigh impossible. But dispite the fact that these self proclaimed leaders have adopted an irreconciliable stand and are itching for a confrontation with the Hindus, and have identified the unimpressive and Crumbling Babri Mosque as a matter of their faith and identity. In more than six years of communal mobilization over the Babri Masjid, the Muslim community has suffered the worst. Though the campaign for Babri Masjid, can never take its campaigners to the seat of power, it certainly has provided an all-India platform to the Muslim fundamentalists and some communalists leaders, and has assigned them the legitimate and representative voice of the Muslim community. The sustained and counter communal mobilizations by the leaders of Babri Masjid movement have made cross sections of Muslims of realize the symbolic importance of the Babri Masjid for the Muslim community as a whole.[54] The handing over the disused Babri Masjid to Hindus, the Muslims have been told, would end their distinct cultural and social identity and inaugurate "a fascist rule based on Hinduisation". Muslims are being incited by the firebrands and hot headed leaders, to

53. Quoted in Koenraad Elst, *Ramjanmabhoomi vs. Babri Masjid : A Case Study of Hindu-Muslim Conflict* (New Delhi : Voice of India, 1990), p. 97.

54. Imtiaz Ahmad, "Muslims and Boycott Call : Political Realities Ignored", *Times of India*, 14 January 1987.

be ready to shed their blood for the protection of the mosque. Since the issue of restoration of Babri Masjid has been symbolised as a critical determinant' of the Muslims' social life in India, many Muslims are prone to feel that they are unequal and inferior to Hindus, by virtue of being Muslims. This kind of insecure feeling is further reinforced by the steady decline of the secular forces in the body politic, especially, the changed style or posture of the Congress party during Mrs. Gandhi's and Rajiv Gandhi's period.

IV

The Shah Bano case and the Ayodhya controversy must be understood in the context of larger changes and developments in the political process. Even though religious sentiments and feelings are attached to the Ram temple agitation, this can not be understood in isolation from the political process in which they have occurred and are managed.[55] The Babri Masjid-Ramjanmabhoomi dispute which had been a non-issue in the fifties, sixties and seventies, has attracted the attention of the political parties since the beginning of eighties, with the shift in the political discourse.

The Ayodhya dispute has become one of the most important tools for communal mobilization by the BJP and the Congress and the Janata Dal. The dispute also revived a debate about the nature of the Indian secularism as formulated and practised by Jawaharlal Nehru.

For the campaigners of Ramjanmabhoomi the existence of Ram's birth place is a matter of faith and that the very place is the birth place of Lord Ram and which can neither be ascertained by the Government nor by the facts of history. "In religion, it is a matter of faith and not of proof......So, by faith and faith alone, Christians accept Jesus Christ to be the son of God, and by faith and faith alone, Muslims believe Muhammad to

---

55. Peter Vander Veer, "God must be Liberated : A Hindu Liberation Movement in Ayodhya", *Modern Asian Studies*, 21 (2), 1987, pp. 285 ff.

be the Prophet of Allah and by faith and faith alone, Hindus believe Ramjanmabhoomi at Ayodhya to be the birth place of Rama" (emphasis added).[56] The question of faith also takes the form of asserting the identity of a community and seeks to redefine it. "The present agitation to liberate the Ramjanmabhoomi "we are told", is no less than a battle for national self-assertion. It is, in fact, nothing short of a phase for the liberation of the national soul."[57]

56. See K.S. Lal, "Ramjanambhoomi-Some Issues" in Engineer ed., n. 51, p. 87. Also see the pamphlet *Political Abuse of History* published by the Centre for Historical Studies, JNU, New Delhi-67.

57. H.V. Seshadri, "Wiping out the Blot of Foreign Slavery", *Organiser* (New Delhi), 4 January 1985.

3

Myth, History and Politics of Ramjanmabhoomi

I

The Ayodhya dispute is undoubtedly one of the most sensitive communal issues after the partition of India. Since Independence no other issue has generated such heightened communal passions, widespread communal riots and tends to polarise India's two major religious communities. The dispute is very complicated and multi-dimensional because of the involvement of the multiplicity of actors like the state, political parties, communal forces, religious leaders, the media and the intelligentia. It is difficult to understand the dispute purely a from historical point of view although this aspect appears to be central to the understanding of the Ayodhya tangle.

The present controversy can be traced back to more than 100 years of litigation over the Babri Masjid. The roots of the controversy has more of its legal aspects than the historical. It is assumed here that the failure on the part of the judiciary to solve the legal nature of the controversy has turned it into a political issue with some historical facet.

A perusal of the legal aspect of the controversy is essential as it would enable us to understand the other dimensions of the controversy. Because the present turmoil over the Babri Masjid basically originates from the upshot of a judicial decision in February 1986. As it is being viewed from many quarters, it would be no exaggeration to say that the Ayodhya dispute has posed the gravest challenge to India's democratic institutions and mechanisms like the constitution, the judiciary and the rule of law. Further, the study of the legal nature of the controversy would enable us to comprehend attitudes of the main parties to the dispute, the Vishwa Hindu Parishad (VHP) and the All India Babri Masjid Movement Coordination Committee (AIBMMCC) on the All India Babir Masjid Action Committee (AIBMAC)[1].

While the VHP has expressed its unwillingness to accept the judiciary's role in solving the controversy, the AIBMAC on the other hand has placed all its hope of recovering the Babri Masjid on the outcome of the judicial verdict. Interestingly enough, though the Ayodhya dispute has gone beyond the ambit of legal wrangles over the ownership and possession of the particular site where the Babri Masjid stands today, it is being sought by the most political parties and non-political organisations to find a solution to the problem through the judiciary, if the out-of court settlement fails to achieve any tangible result.

The legal history of the Babri Masjid shows that in the beginning, the "chhabutra" (platform) constituted on 23 February 1857, inside the boundary wall of the Babri Masjid was known as the janamsthan (birthplace). Raghubar Das claiming to be the Mahant of chhabutra janamsthan, filed a civil suit on 27 January 1985, against the Secretary of the State for India in Council, in the office cf the Sub-Judge Faizabad for a decree awarding permission to construct a temple over the chhabutra janamsthan" situated outside the mosque, measuring 17×21 feet in area, "restraining the defendant from prohibiting and obstructing the plaintiff in the construction of the temple". In that case, the Sub-Judge of Faizabad, Pt. Harikishan Singh, having heard from the plaintiff, the Government of Uttar Pradesh and the defendant and undertaking an inquiry on the spot in the presence of the parties to the dispute, rejected the plea of the Mahant Raghubar Das on the ground of the threat to the public law and order situation. The judge observed that, if a temple is constructed on the

1. The Babri Masjid Movement Coordination Committee formally split on 26 November 1988 when some leading members left the committee and formed the AIBMAC later on.

chhabutra which is so close to the Masjid, then it would "lay the foundation of death and murder."[2]

The plaintiff, Mahant Raghubar Das on 18th March' 1886, moved to Faizabad District Court with an appeal to dismiss the judgement of the lower court and allow him to construct a temple on the Ram Chhabutra. The District Judge in his judgement on 26 March 1886, dismissed the appeal and recorded his judgement, "I found the Masjid, built by Emperor Babur, stands on the border of the town of Ayodhya, that is to say to the West and South it is clear of habitation. It is most unfortunate that a Masjid should have been built on the land especially held sacred by the Hindus. But as that occurred 356 years ago, it is too late now to remedy the grievance. All that can be done is to maintain the parties in *status quo*. In such a case, as the present one, any innovation would cause more harm and derangement of order than benefit."[3] (emphasis added). The judge further observed that, "the entrance to the enclosure is under a gateway which bears "Allah"-immediately on the left is the platform or chhabutra of masonry occupied by the Hindus......This chhabutra is said to be the birth place of Ram Chander". He also struck down the words from the judgement of the sub-judge, which conceded that the property is owned by the Mahant.

The Mahant on 25 May 1886, moved the highest Court in the province seeking to quash the orders of the District Judge, but it was dismissed by the Judicial commissioner of Oudh, in his judgement dated 1 November 1886, and upheld the judgement of the District Judge.[4]

---

2. See the Records of the Suit Relating to *Janamsthan Chhabutra*, 1885 in *Muslim India*, March 1986, pp. 105-7.

3. See S.K. Tripathi, "One Hundred Years of Litigation" in Asghar Ali Engineer, ed., *Babri Masjid-Ramjanambhoomi Controversy* (New Delhi : Ajanta, 1990), p. 18.

4. See A.G. Noorani, "Legal Aspects to the Issue", in Sarvepalli S. Gopal ed., *Anatomy of a Confrontation : The Babri Masjid-Ramjanmabhoomi Issue* (New Delhi : Penguin, 1991), pp. 66-67.

With the dismissal of the Mahant's appeal, the first legal battle by the Hindus to claim the right to build a temple on the Chhabutra inside the mosque compound ended in a fiasco. Except serious communal riot that took place in 1855, the legal battle from 1883 to 1886 hardly evoked the public attention until 17th April 1934, when communal tension was created over the slaughter of a cow by the local Muslims of Ayodhya. The Bairagi Sadhus (an ascetic Hindu sect) captured the Babri Masjid and badly damaged it but was saved from further destruction due to the intervention by the local administration. Later, the mosque was repaired with the fines collected from the Hindus but the intervention of the administration in no way helped to subside the tension.[5]

The Civil Judge S.A. Hasan's judgement on the Mutwallaship of the Babri Masjid dated 23 March 1946, shows that Muslims, both Shiahas and Sunnis, prayed in the mosque till that time, though both Shiha and Sunni Wakf Boards litigated over its possession, and no challenge to Muslims' right to offer namaz (prayer) had been thrown by the Hindus.[6]

In the twentieth century, the nature of Babri Masjid-Ramjanmabhoomi controversy was shaped by the socio-political changes and configurations in North India. "The Suddhi movement", the cow protection movement". Hindi-Urdu language controversy had their impact on the political development of Faizabad also.[7] Since 1920s, two distinct kind of political idioms that found their prominence in the party-politics of United Provinces were the "secular modernist idiom" of Motilal Nehru and "indigenous communal idiom" of Pandit Madan Mohan Malviya. Hindu-Muslim communal politics was legitimised by the Muslim League in the 1926 General Elections and 1937 provincial elections.[8]

5. See for example Sushil Srivastava. *The Disputed Mosque* (New Delhi : Sage 1991), pp. 48-49.
6. See S.K. Tripathi, "One Hundred Years of Litigation", n. 3, p. 20.
7. See for example Srivastava, n. 5, pp. 46-47.
8. See for details in Gyanendra Pandey, *Construction of Colonialism in Colonial North India* (New Delhi : Oxford, 1990), pp. 207 ff.

In the late 1930s, the inter-communal harmony had been disturbed in U.P. due to the recurrent communal riots, the insensitivities of the administration to check the spread of riots, the involvement of the local Congress workers in the riots and the Congress party's political and ideological failure to challenge the vicious communal mobilization and sectarian politics of the Muslim League in the province.[9]

In 1937 provincial elections, the Indian National Congress literally surrendered Faizabad-Sitarpur-Bahraich urban constituency to the Muslim League and the result was the League's electoral success. In the 1946 General Elections, Faizabad electoral politics had been polarized communally and the success of the Muslim League candidates in the Muslim dominated constituencies were a foregone conclusion.[10] In the 1948 by-elections, the Indian National Congress leadership in U.P. exploited the religious sensibilities of Hindus in Faizabad to secure electoral gains and to ward off their principal political rival, Acharya Narendra Dev in the region. The Congress strategist filed a "saintly" politician Baba Raghab Das against the socialist leader Acharya Narendra Dev and in their election campaign they had succeeded in turning "the sacred city" of Ayodhya against him by claiming that as a Marxist, Narendra Dev was an atheist Launching the Congress party's campaign. Chief Minister Govind Ballav Pant declared at Ayodhya that, Acharya Narendra Dev was not a devout Hindu and as Marxist, he did not believe the divinity of Ram in Ayodhya.[11] The "Ayodhya Strategy" had paid off for the Congress as the popular socialist leader of Faizabad, Acharya Narendra Dev, lost to the Congress candidate in the elections.[12]

9. For a discussion on this aspect see Mukul Keshvan, "Communal Violence and its Impact on the Politics of North India", *Occasional Papers*, NMML, New Delhi, pp. 36 ff.

10. See Harold A. Gould, "The Emergence of Modern Indian Politice : Political Development in Faizabad-II : 1935 to Independence", *Jr. of Comparative and Commonwealth Studies* (1974), Vol. 20, No. 42, pp. 165-73.

11. *Ibid.*, p. 178.

12. Harold A. Gould, *Caste and Politics*" (Delhi : Chanakya, 1990), pp. 76-77.

The communal political climate in Faizabad after the defeat of Acharya Narendra Dev found its appearance in the capture of Babri Masjid on 22nd-23rd December 1949, night.

The events on the last week of December 1949, had given a decisive twist to the Ramjanmabhoomi-Babri Masjid controversy in Ayodhya. In this regard Akshaya Brahmacthari's (then President of the Faizabad Congress Committee) memorandum to Home Minister Lal Bahadur Shastri is really historic in importance.[13] According to Mr. Brahmahari's account, based on an information, he personally went to the Babri Masjid and observed that graves hear Babri Masjid were being dug-out. In front of the Babri Masjid, there was a nine-day long non-stop recitation of Ramayana being held. Public meetings and fastings were being organised near the mosque and Hindus were being exhorted through the loud speakers to through near the mosque and participate in the ceremony. It was also being announced that, the Babri Masjid was going to be converted into Ramjanmabhoomi temple soon. The apathy of the district administration to these happenings near the Babri Masjid impressed the people of Faizabad-Ayodhya that the show had been organised by 'the Akhil Bharatiya Ramayan Mahasabha, in connivance with the government and local administration.

On 23 December 1949, he was informed by the Faizabad District magistrate that the idol of Ram had been implanted in the precincts of the Babri Masjid on the preceding night. Accompanying the District Magistrate, he visited the Babri Masjid on that day itself and saw the idol of Ram in the mosque and gatherings of large number of Hindus. The loud speakers near the Babri Masjid were announcing the appearance of Lord Ram in the mosque and urging the Hindus in nearby areas to assemble there for a darshan. Handbills were being distributed about the miraculous appearance of Lord Ram inside the Babri Masjid. At that moment the image could have been removed and the Masjid could have been saved from forceful conversion, had the district administration wished. While

13. *Muslim India*, June 1988, p. 252.

the Government took possession of the mosque, under section 145 of Indian Penal Code, but Hindus were allowed to worship in the mosque and the Muslims were prevented from offering the namaz. These events had terrified Muslims in Ayodhya and many of them had fled away for good. The Muslims were also threatened of dire consequences if they do not cease their claims over the Babri Masjid ...

Despite his effort to draw the attention of the local administration about these serious events, he failed to achieve his objective. He stated, "I do not view this question as one of saving the mosque or Muslims. I view it as saving the great ideals of the Congress and Mahatma for which we all have been struggling in all these days. If we do not resist these reactionary ideas with all the forces at our command, the ideals of the Congress will become extinct and reactionary forces will sweep the country".[14]

These events are also corroborated by uncontroverted and incontrovertible official records. The incident on 22nd December 1949, night, which converted the Babri Masjid into Ramjanambhoomi temple and subsequently resulted in its padlocking, was reported by the Police station at 9 a.m. The FIR lodged by Sub-Inspector Ram Dube, Police Station, Ayodhya, on 23 December 1949, was certified by the Office of the City Magistrate on 11 February 1986. The English translation of message as follows :

"According to Mata Prasad (paper no. 7) when I reached to (sic) Janambhoomi around 8 O'clock in the morning, I came to know that a group of 50-60 persons had entered Babri Mosque after breaking the compound gate lock of the mosque or through jumping across the walls (of the compound) with a stair and established therein an idol of Shri Bhagwan and painted Sita Ram, etc., on the outer and inner walls with Geru (Red loam). Hans Raj on duty asked them to defer but they did not. These persons have already entered the mosque before the available PAC (Provincial Armed Corps) guards

14. *Muslim India*, June 1988, p. 253-54.

could be commanded. Official of the district administration came at the site and involved themselves necessary arrangements. Afterwards, a crowd of 5-6 thousand persons gathered around and while chanting bhajans and raising religious slogans tried to enter the mosque but were deterred and nothing on toward happened thereon because of proper arrangements. Ram Das, Ram Shakti Das and 50-60 unidentified others entered the mosque surreptitiously and spoiled its sanctity. Government servants on duty and several others are witness to it. Therefore, it is written and filed.[15]

Based on the above report, District Magistrate Mr. K.K. Nayar sent a cryptic radio message to the Chief Secretary, Home Secretary and Chief Minister of U.P. The message read as follows :

> "A few Hindus entered the Babri Masjid at night when the Masjid was deserted and installed a deity there. DM and SP and force at spot. Situation under control. Police picket of 15 persons was on duty at night but did not apparently act."[16]

When Nehru was cognizant of the incident, he could immediately foresee the wider implications of these events and urged the United Provinces Chief Minister, Gobind Ballav Pant to personally intervene into the matter and undo the harm done. But Govind Ballav Pant unlike Nehru showed his indifference to this communally explosive issue. Dissatisfied with the inept handling of the situation by the state government, Nehru wrote to Govind Ballav Pant, "I have felt for a long time that the whole atmosphere of the UP has been changing for the worse from the communal point of view. Indeed, the UP is becoming almost a foreign land to me. I do not fit in there......All that occurred in Ayodhya in regard to the mosque and temples and hotel in Faizabad was bad enough.

15. See A.G. Noorani. *Legal Aspect to the Issues in Gopal,* n. 4, pp. 70-71.

16. See S K. Tripathi, "One Hundred Years of Litigation", in Engineer, n. 3, p. 20.

But the worst feature of it was that such thing should take place and be approved by some of our own people and that they should continue. When Nehru realised Mr. Pant's semingly indifference to his pleadings, he at one time had considered to leave all his assignments and launch a crusade against the communal forces. He even strongly felt that prominent Congress leaders have become communally oriented[17] in their political posture.

But despite his deep concern and sincere desire to solve the problem, it remained unresolved. After forty years since Nehru spoke on it, the controversy has become more complex, politicised and intensified. The controversy has alredy come to a situation of a communal cauldron threatening to shatter the peaceful inter-community relations and the secular polity.

The Chief Secretary of U.P. and Inspector General of Police had sent frantic messages to the District Magistrate K.K. Nayar to remove the idols from the mosque but he was not willing to carry out the order on the pretext that it would lead to "bloodshed and man slaughter". The District Magistrate was subsequently forced to resign from his service and later he joined the 'Bharatiya Jana Sangh' (BJS) and played a active part in Faizabad's communal politics.[18]

On 20 December 1949, the Additional City Magistrate of Faizabad cum-Ayodhya instead of removing the idols from the mosque ordered the attachment of the Babri Masjid under section 145 CRPC and appointed a Hindu receiver to take care of the property in dispute till such time as the court decided the right to the ownership of the mosque.[19]

Later on, a suit was filed by Gopal Singh Visharad, a sanatanist Hindu resident of Ayodhya in the Civil Court of Ayodhya

---

17. See S. Gopal's introductory chapter, in Gopal, n. 4, pp. 15-16.
18. See for example, Peter Vander Veer, *Gods on Earth : The Management of Religious Experience and Identity in a North Indian Pilgrimage Centre* (New Delhi : Oxford, 1989). pp. 40-41.
19. S.K. Tripathi, "One Hundred Years of Litigation", in Engineer, n. 3, p. 22.

on 16 January 1950, praying for a declaration to the effect that, he was entitled "to worship and visit without obstruction or disturbance to Shri Bhagwan Ram Chandra and others Installed at Asthan Janambhoomi and 'a perpetual injunction restraining the defendants from remaining the idols......" Total numbers of the defendants in the case were eight, five among them were Muslims and the rest were the state of U.P., Deputy Commissioner and Superintendent of Police of Faizabad. The Civil Judge, Mr. N.N. Chhadha in his judgement on 19 February 1950, ordered that : "The parties are hereby restrained by means of the temporary injunction to refrain from removing the idols in question from the site in dispute and from interfering with the "Puja Prayer, etc. as at present carried on". The interim injunction was later on confirmed by the civil judge in his judgement on 3rd March 1951 but with an important observation, "The undisputed fact remains that on the date of this suit the idols of Shri Bhagwan Ram Chandra and others did exist on the site and that the worship was being perform by the Hindus including the plaintiff, though under some restrictions put by the executive authorities. The High Court confirmed this order on 26 April 1955.[20] (emphasis added).

But once again, the judiciary deliberately ignored the crucial issue of the forcible dispossession of the mosque and through maintaining the *status quo*, the judiciary implicitly approve the illegal occupation of the mosque.

In addition to this suit, three more suits were filed relating to disputes over the receivership and Wakfs in 1950, 1959 and 1961. The leading suit No. 12 of 18 December 1961 was filed by the Sunni Wakf Board before the civil judge, Faizabad seeking a declaration to the effect that the property indicated by letters ABCD in the sketch map attached to the plaint in public mosque commonly known as "Babri Masjid" and that the land adjoining the mosque shown in the sketch map by letters EFGH is a public Muslim graveyard as specified in para

20. See Vinay Chandra Mishra and Paramanand Singh ed, *Ramjanmabhoomi-Babri Masjid* (New Delhi : Bar Council of India, 1991), pp. 241-44.

2 of the plaint, may be decreed." The second relief was sought for the delivery of the mosque and the graveyard in suit and removal of Hindu idols and other articles of worship from the mosque and a decree be passed in plaintiff's favour, against the defendants, Gopal Singh Visharad and others.[20a] On behalf of the U.P. Government, Deputy Commissioner of Faizabad, J.N. Ugra filed a written statement on 24 April 1950 which said in paragraph 14 that, "The property in suit is known as Babri Masjid and it has been for long time in use as a mosque for the purpose of worship of the Muslims. It has not been in use as a temple of Shri Ram Chandraji". In the next para, the Deputy Commissioner stated that, "on the night of 22 December 1949, the idols of Shri Ramchandraji were surreptitiously and wrongly put inside it." In the paragraph 16 it added that, "That as a result of the said wrongful act, a situation imperilling public peace and tranquility was created and the public authorities had to intervene in order to prevent the breach of peace and tranquility.[21]

J.N. Ugra's written statement also disproves the claim of Justice Deoki Nandan Aggarwal (retd.) a V.H.P. leader, that there is no evidence of Muslims' offering namaj during Mogul times or during the reign of Nawabs of Avadh.[22]

From 1951 to 1986, the Ramjanmabhoomi-Babri Masjid dispute largely remained a localized affair free from communal tension except for endlessly unfruitful legal battle. The 1 February 1986, judgement of the Faizabad District Court to throw open the gates of the Babri Masjid was very controversial which revived the sterile controversy. However, the judgement was more political in nature, if we take into account, the undue

---

20. (*a*) See Jafaryab Jeelani, "A Glimpse of Judicial Process on Babri Masjid", 1989-90 in *Radiance*-Babri Masjid special, 25 Nov.-1 Dec. 1990, p. 6.

21. See A.G. Noorani, "Legal Aspects to the Issue" in Gopal, n. 4, pp. 76-77.

22. Justice Deoki Nandan Aggarwal, *Sri Ram Janmabhoomi: Historical and Legal Perspectives* (New Delhi : VHP Publications, n. d.), p. 4.

haste and secrecy in which the legal proceedings were carried on, and the impact of extraneous political events, like the agitation of the RSS and VHP, to open the locks of the Babri Masjid, and the Central government's move to placate the Muslim fundamentalists over the Shah Bano judgement. As it has been argued in the previous chapter, that the Ayodhya controversy surfaced since the opening of the Babri Masjid gates on the order of the District Judge, Faizabad, and the decision to open the locks of the Babri Masjid gates was guided more by political expediency than legal obligation.

For about 36 years the decision given by the District Court and approved by the High Court regarding the maintenance of the *status quo* of the Babri Masjid remained effective and the Hindus continued the 'Akhand Kirtan' to 'liberate' the Sri Ramjanmabhoomi since 23 December, 1949 in front of the Babri Masjid, without any disruption. On 25 January 1986, an application was filed by a Hindu lawyer in the Court of Munsif Sadar, Faizabad, seeking for opening of the locks of Babri Masjid and for permission to all the Hindu public to offer puja and have Darshan of the idol inside the mosque. The Munsif in his judgement dated 28th January 1986 refused to pass the order since the file concerning the main case of 1961 is with the High Court and the orders could be made only in that suit.

It can be mentioned here that the applicant Mr. Umesh Chandra Pandey's name did not appear in any of the previous suits related to the Babri Masjid either as plaintiff or as a diffendant.[23] On 3 January 1986, Umesh Chandra Pandey went in appeal against the order of the Munsif which was filed in the Court of K.M. Pandey, the District Judge of Faizabad. A copy of the appeal was also not give to the defendants, the Muslims. Within a day of this appeal, 1 February 1986, was fixed for final hearing. When the appeal under reference was being heard by the District Judge, per chance, Sri Mohd. Hashim who is plaintiff in suit no. 12 of 1961 came to know

23. M. Mahmud, ***Babri Masijd* : *Facts vs. Fiction*** (Faizabad, n. d.), pp. 3-4.

of the proceedings and at once moved an application through his lawyer for hearing. The District judge heard the arguments of Sri Hashim's application till 3.45 p.m. and rejected the same by 4.15 p.m. At the same time, the appeal of Sri Umesh Chandra Pandey was allowed finally and an order was given to open the locks of both the doors of the mosque. The District Judge also recorded the statements of District Magistrate and the Senior Superintendent of Police on the issue of law and order and at 4. 40 p.m. he passed his order, directing the respondents, the state of Uttar Pradesh, the DM and the SSP to open the locks forthwith.[24] The judge observed :

> "......It is clear that it is not necessary to keep the locks closed at the gates of O and P for purposes of maintaining law and order or for the safety of the idols. This appears to be an unnecessary irritant to the applicant and other members of the community."

The Judge further added that :

> "After having heard the parties it is clear that the members of the other community, namely, Muslims are not, going to be affected by any stretch of imagination if the locks of the gates O and P are opened and the idols inside the premises are allowed to be seen and worshipped by piligrims and devotees. It is undisputed that the premises is presently in Court's possession and for the last 35 Hindus have an unrestricted right of worship as a result of the Court's order in 1950 and 1951. If the Hindus are offering prayers and worshipping the idols, though in a restricted way, for the last 35 years, then Heavens are not going to fall if the locks of the gates O and P are removed.[25]

Within forty minutes of the delivery of his judgement, the gates of the Babri Masjid were thrown open amidst the police security, the T.V. personnel were already at the Babri Masjid

---

24. Mahmud, n. 23, p. 4 ff.
25. See the "Judgement of District Judge, Faizabad, Shri K.M. Pandey 1 February 1986", in Engineer, n. 3, pp. 215-16.

to televise the whole operation and it was given wide publicity in the government media. While the opening of the gates made the Hindu fundamentalists to feel jubiliant, the Muslim fundamentalists reacted the situation by causing a Muslim backlash. Undeniably, the District Judge's order has fanned the communal fires all over India and has given rise to the present impasse. The District Judges' judgement was virtually, in effect, sanctifying the forceful dispossession of the mosque that took place 37 years ago and, indirectly handing over the Babri Masjid to the Hindu chauvinists regardless of the fact is that, the title of the structure is subjudice in the High Court.

Mohd. Hashim, on 3rd February 1986, moved an application before the High Court seeking the stay order of the District Judge Faizabad. The Lucknow Bench of the High Court gave an order on the same day to the maintenance of the *status quo* "as existing today", till its further order. The Sunni Wakf Board on 12 May 1986, also filed a writ petition against the District Judge on 11 December 1987. The state of U.P. moved to the Allahabad High Court on the plea that the two petitions filed by Mohammad Hashim and Sunni Wakf be deterred for hearing the and four civil suits be withdrawn from the Court of Munsif Sadar, Faizabad, and tried by the Court.[26]

It is interesting to note that on 25 May 1990, the special bench of Allahabad High Court framed up several issues which relate neither to law nor historically verifiable facts, rather, most of the issues which the Court will deal fall in the dark areas of history, mythology and religious belief and tradition.[27] Farlier on 7 November 1989, the Special Bench of Allahabad

26. A.G. Noorani, "Legal. Aspects to the Issue", in Engineer, n. 3, p. 79. Here is a sample out of the 43 contentious issues framed up by the High Court on 25 May 1990—which the Court would deal.

"Have the Hindus been worshipping the place in dispute as Sri Ramjanam Bhoomi on *Janamsthan* and have been visiting it as a sacred place of pilgrimage as on right since times (ic) immemorial ? If so, its effects" ?

27. *Ibid.*, pp. 80-81.

High Court, Lucknow, remarked that, "It is doubtful that some of question involved in the suit are soluble by the judicial process."

The legal history of Ayodhya dispute shows that the judiciary as well as the government have utterly failed to solve the controversy. While the state of U.P. has so far been unable to clarify its stand with regard to the Babri Masjid dispute, the judiciary has set the communal ball rolling by attaching the mosque, and giving frequent orders to maintain the *status quo* after the 22-23 December 1949, incident.

The prime reason for the failure on the part of the judiciary to solve the case relating to the right of worship and possession of a particular site is due to the involvement of deeper issues like the faith, popular traditions and beliefs of the two communities, that have contending claims over the Babri Masjid. The legal history of Ayodhya dispute, also unravels some other important aspects to the controversy, like popular myths and history of Ram's Ayodhya and their inter-relationship, which have defied the judiciary's ability to intervene and solve the issue. The failure on the part of the judiciary to solve the dispute which has been pending more than one hundred years has complicated further the prospects of a solution. With the government's inability to solve the contentious issue through negotiation between the AIBMAC and the VHP, it remains to be seen how far the judiciary would be able to deliver a judgement by taking into account various aspects of the controversy, that would be acceptable to both the parties.

II

The differing notions of myth and history and their relations to social practices is an important aspect of the Ayodhya controversy. While the popular beliefs and traditions with regard to the Ramjanmabhoomi are often, constructed or invented and found their acceptance and appeal among the elite as well as mass level, the historical records and facts that challenge such notions become irrelevant.

The events, narratives and the social actors found in a myth are without any concrete historical existence. Yet, it is viewed that myths sometime give clues to reality. Since myths are produced and reproduced in a society and they are also useful in understanding the mind or nature of the social actors or processes which produce the myths and the role that myths played in that society. With the changes in the pattern of ideas and values in the society, myths also undergo changes but at the same time different notions of the same myth exists. The process of mythification and its reproduction and sustenance in the social and political processes has to be understood. Since like traditions, myths also constituted or invented. We can question its 'givenness' or 'eternality' of the myths and also the politics which derives its legitimacy from the mythic discourses.[28]

Myth and history are inter-related. Both are narratives. While myth is a narrative of origins taken place in a time other than that of everyday reality, history is a narrative of recent events extending progressively to include events that are nontheless situated in time. It has been argued that the colonial historiography of India has been projected with a pre-conceived mind. The colonialists model of Indian history which speak communalism in India as 'essential type' of Indian society-"its religious bigotry and fundamentally irrational character" has created a number of "myths" which the modern Indian historians are unhesitatingly following their model of historiography. In the colonialists account of 'essential type' which not only distorts 'reality' but also takes history out of it. Viewed from this context, "Myth is a depoliticized speech.........It deprives of the object of which it speaks of all History. In it history evaporates...all that is left for one to do enjoy this beautiful (or ugly) object without wondering where it come from. Or even better : it can only come from eternity.[29]

But one finds it difficult to accept myth as 'depoliticized speech' in the context of conscious attempt to mythify historical

28. See Neeladri Bhattacharya, "Myth, History and Politics of Ramjanmabhoomi", in Gopal, n. 4. pp. 122-123.

29. Quoted in Pandey, n. 8. pp. 107-08.

monuments and the historicity of the present day Ayodhya. The presentation of some places like Ramjanmabhoomi (birth place of Lord Ram) which even did not exist earlier, are being made through resort to myths.

The process mythification of history occurs when the outdated theories are used for historical analysis and even preconceived conclusions are reached which are used in selecting the historical evidences.[30] Further, concocted evidences are produced by spurious historians to produce history for dubious purposes. In such writing of history, the use of myths become a common tactics.[31] The main purpose for such distorted writing is to contort the historical facts and events and use it for political ends. So, myth should not be viewed as "depoliticized speech", rather it acts as 'archetypal narratives'[32] meant for 'novel purposes'.[33]

Pre-conceived conclusions are used to popularise the idea that, the Muslim rule in India was 'the bloodiest chapter' in Indian history. The problem of Babri Masjid controversy is viewed from the two oft-repeated notions that Muslim rulers in India had destroyed and desecrated innumerable number of Hindu temples and iconoclasm is one of the central tenents of Islam. As one 'historian' writes, "No matter how hard the JNU historians deny it, the old Muslim records and the temples turned mosques keep on testifying with one voice that the 'Muslim period' of Indian history was blood soaked catastrophe, a marathon of persecution and religious was including thousand fold temple destruction.[34] These perverted

30. 'Mythifying History' in *Seminar*, No. 364, December, 1989, p. 12.

31. For example, see, Arun Shourie *et al.*, *Hindu Temples : What Happened to Them* (New Delhi : Voice of India, 1990).

32. Neeladri Bhattacharya, n. 28, p. 123.

33. Eric Hobsbawm, and Terence Ranger eds., Inventions of Traditions" (Cambridge, 1983), p. 6.

34. Koenraad Elst, "*Ramjanmabhoomi vs. Babri Masjid*: *A Case Study of Hindu Muslim Conflict* (New Delhi : Voice of India, 1990), p. 83.

notions are linked with the demands of some bigoted Hindus that all the mosques that stand on the destroyed Hindu temples should be pulled down. Thus, the Babri Masjid at Ayodhya, the Gyanvapi mosque at Mathura and the Kashi Vishwanath temple at Banaras are being viewed as "national shame and the present communal mobilization for Ram temple has been portrayed as the movement for the vindication of 'national honour.'[35] Another aspect of the mythification of history is seen in the recent attempt to suggest that some of the architecturally marvelous monuments like the Taj-Mahal were in origin Hindu so that contribution of medieval period to India's culture and heritage is denied.[36]

Since history plays a crucial role in shaping man's social consciousness in any society, its appropriation is a common phenomenon and a continual process. But the appropriati on of history takes place when it is mythified through a new construction of history. During the pre-independence period Indian history was appropriated by different ways, which are broadly known as nationalist, colonialist and communalist approaches to Indian historiography. The contemporary communal politics can be attributed due to the false representation of the India's past by the historians. The teaching, learning and writing of Indian history has greatly contributed to the ideology of communalism in India.

The nationalist historians while giving an inspiring interpretation of India's glorious cultural heritage have ignored deliberately the contributions of outside races who settled in India and became an integral part the Indian cultural fabric. But the practice of branding them as 'foreigners' has given a new coin to the ideology of Hindu Communal parties.[37]

---

35. Shourie *et al.*, n. 31, preface page.
36. Michael W. Meister, 'Mythifying Monuments', *Seminar*, No. 364, December, 1989, p. 27.
37. R.S. Sharma, *Communal History and Ramas Ayodhya* (New Delhi: PPH, 1990), pp. 6-8, See also, Romila Thapar *et al.*, *Communalism and the writing of Indian History* (New Delhi, PPH, 1987,) pp. 40. ff.

The 'history' of Ramjanmabhoomi originally based on the Valmiki's Ramayana, revolves around several myths : the myth Ayodhya's sacredness and its pre-history character, the myth of rediscovery of Ayodhya to the myth of destruction of the temple and construction of a mosque in its place, the myth of heroic struggle of the Hindus to liberate Ramjanmabhoomi and the myth of miraculous appearance of Ramamurti inside the Babri Masjid.

The important aspect of Ramayana or known as Rama Katha) Ram's story) is that it consists of multiple versions and each of these versions carry a different and sometimes even contradictory meanings and narratives and impossible to give a coherent religious expressions.[38] It is also recognised that since the epic literature is composed of several layers of consciousness and some the layers have already receded into subconscious level, several interpolations have taken place on the epic material.[39] The heroic poem originally composed by Valmiki was inflated with incorporation of several other mythical things, characters and events from time to time and this inflation has not been ceased even to date.[40] Many of the myths also incorporated into the original 'Ramayana' in the post Buddhist age known as the "Age of Brahmanical revival" during which came into existence sacred poems called Puranas.[41] The multiple forms of Ramakatha reflects that they are part of the ongoing diologue over time and at the same time reflects itself to the changing social cultural situations.[42] Historians and archaeologisits working on the Indian epic have not succeeded, to locate the historicity of the text and to

38. Romila Thapar, "A Historical Perspective on the Story of Rama", in Gopal, n. 4, p. 141.

39. Romila Thapar, *Exile and Kingdom : Some Thoughts on Ramayan* (Bangalore : Mythic Society, 1978) p. 1.

40. H D. Sankhalia, *Ramayan : Myth or Reality* (New Delhi : PPH, 1973) p. 15.

41. Donald A. Mackenzie, *Indian Myth and Legend* (London : Gresham Publishing Co., 1972) p. 124.

42. Romila Thapar, n. 38, p. 141.

authenticate the events in the 'Ramayana' after years of research.[43] While it is practically impossible to identify the exact certainity of Ram's birthplace and at the sametime to identify the present day Ayodhya with the Ayodhya city as depicted in the Ramayana, places like Lanka, Kishkindha and Ayodhya are places of poetical imagination and these places have achieved the status of sacred geography because of their identification with the names of cities and towns mentioned in the Ram's story. H.D. Sankhalia, the dozen of Indian archaeology argues that, "The Valmiki's Ramayana is a poetic composition and is the product of a particular time and place. Its historicity can be established only on the basis of critical examination of the events and characters and places described with the help of concrete historical and archaeological sources. Further, this examination must be supplemented by or checked against ethnographical data as well as knowledge of flora and fauna.[44]

Undeniably, the importance of the present day Ayodhya derives from its association with the Ram cult. In the 500 B.C. Ayodhya was identified with Saket during the reign of Guptas. But, "The question of whether therever existed an Aryan settlement in pre-historical India which bore the name of Ayodhya must remain unanswered since it falls beyond the limits of historical investigation.[45] In the 'Ayodhya Mahatmya' (A piligrimage to Ayodhya), Ayodhya is presented to us as the sacred place as well as geography which existed even before the profane world came into being. The 'Ayodhya Mahatmya' was instrumental in mythifying the sacredness of Ayodhya.

---

43. Thapar, n. 39, p. 10.

44. Sankhalia, n. 40, pp. 18-19. Similarly Prof. Romila Thapar views that, "Poems as literary forms, even if they should be dealing with historical themes, can not in themselves be regarded as historical texts. They can at best provide clues to the ways in which people perceived the past or their own times, but are not evidence of historical events unless proven to be so from other contemporary historical sources ; See, Romila Thapar, n. 38, p. 143.

45. Hans Bakker, *Ayodhya* (Gongington : 1986). part-I, pp. 11-12.

The 'Ayodhya Mahatmya' depicts that, a man who has seen (Janamsthan) will not born again even if he does not offer gifts, does not practice ascetism, does not go on (further) piligrimage or does not perform sacrifices : When the day Navami has come a man engaged in the vow will be liberated from the bondage of rebirth due to miraculous power of a bath and a gift. By seeing janambhoomi he shall obtain the result that accrues to one who offers daily a thousand red cows.[46]

Ayodhya's sanctity is attached to the mysterious events related to its recovery. "The Ayodhya Guide" and also several historians have depicted the myth of Ayodhya's rediscovery. The priests in Ayodhya narrate the myth of Ayodhya's rediscovery before the piligrims in similar ways. The myth tell us that at the end of the Treta Yuga, the period in which Lord Ram was born, Ayodhya was gone into oblivion until it was miraculously rediscovered by the king Vikramaditya in 500 A.D. Tired of hunting, king Vikramaditya was taking rest on the bank of river Sarayu. All of a sudden, he observed a darkman taking bath in the river. After having his bath the man was no longer looking dark. When he approached to that man, he came to know that, he was Tirtha Raj Prayag (king of piligrimages) who cleanse the sins of all human beings. When he could no longer bear the burden of other peoples' sin he had come to Ayodhya and purified himself in the holy water of the Sarayu. The above mythic narrative attempts to prove that, if the Tirtha Raj Prayag could come to Ayodhya to purify himself from the sins then Ayodhya is the most holiest place on the earth. Prayag asked Vikramaditya to recover the holy places of worship of Ram in Ayodhya. He advised king Vikramaditya to recover the holy places with the help of a cow and its calf. The king should allow a cow to roam there and he must walk around that cow. Where that cow would halt and milk would flow from its under that place would be the Janmabhoomi the birth place of Ram. Vikramaditya followed the advice accordingly and recovered Ram's birthplace and 360 other places related to Ram's life in some other ways. He built 360 temples in Ayodhya and the most important one was the

46. Bakker, n. 45, Ch. 8, Part-II, p. 128.

Ramjanmabhoomi temple which was based on 84 pillars made of black stone. Being the birthplace of Ram the Ramjanmabhoomi temple become the most important temple and attracted Hindus and Muslims alike. Babur had destroyed the Ram janmabhoomi temple and several other temples in the sixteenth century. With the decline of Muslim rule, temples which were demolished partly were repaired and new temples were built on old places where temples had been destroyed.[47]

Several local myths of Babar's involvement in the temple destruction are also found in the colonial historical records and reports. The local inhabitants, both Hindus and Muslims describe the same circumstances with little variations leading to the construction of the Babri Masjid. Before the arrival of Babur there was a famous place called Ramjanmabhoomi temple in Ayodhya and Mahatma Shyamananda was the saint of that temple. The Mahatma had several disciples even belonging to Muslim community. Two faquirs, Fazl Abas and Musa Ashikan, who were the disciples of Shyamananda, had later on developed vested interests and responsible for the destruction of the Ramjanmabhoomi temple. Impressed by the sacredness and spirituality of the place attributed by the Hindus, the faqirs planned to destroy the temple and erect a mosque which they believed would popularise Islam. When Babur arrived in Ayodhya the faqirs approached and forced him to agree with their proposal of destroying the temple and building a mosque over it. The other side of the story tells that when one of the faqirs was thrown out of the Ramjanmabhoomi temple, he took revenge of destroying the temple. Another facet of the story is that Babur had to destroy the Ramjanmabhoomi temple and ordered the construction of the mosque upon the advice of the two faqirs for the success of his mission against the Pathans in Ayodhya.[48]

47. Srivastava, n. 5. pp. 78-79 ; Veer, n. 18, pp. 19-20. During my field study in Ayodhya-Faizabad towns, I also heard several times the above kind of mythical narratives from the priests and Mahants.

48. Srivastava, n. 5, pp. 70-71.

The myth of destruction of the Ramjanmabhoomi temple by Babur also appear in a popular book[49] which has also been described by Peter Vander Veer.[50] Babur had faced extraordinary problem of constructing a mosque after destroying the temple. Each day, everything that had been built fell down in the night. Babur grew desperate and decided to give up the building of Masjid. Babur was told by the mahantas of Ayodhya that Hanuman would not allow the construction of Babri Masjid unless he make changes in the ongoing construction of the Babri Masjid and incorporates Hindu elements in the construction of the mosque and Hindus are allowed to worship in it. Babur had to follow their advice and the Babri Masjid which stands today is on the birth place of Ram. The above myth al o re-emphasizes, the divine character of the place known as Ramjanmabhoomi and its mysterious power of resisting the barbarities of the outsiders.

Since then, Hindus have been continuously worshipping in that mosque and have never ceased their claim on the Babri-Masjid. The VHP document of evidences of Ramjanmabhoomi argues : "There is no reasonable explanation for this persistent attachment to the site, except that it was in continuation of an older pre-Masjid tradition".[51] It is claimed that in the 'heroic battle' for the 'liberation' of the holy land, over 300,000 Hindus have laid down their lives in the last 400 years.[52]

Time and history are made irrelevant in the above mythic discourses. It is the religious feeling and the spiritual vision of the common man which makes the present apparent. Ayodhya's history is made to transcend all the known historical epochs. By way of visiting Ayodhya, listening mythic

---

49. Ram Gopal Pandey, "*Shri Ramjanma Ka Rakat Ranjit Itihas*" (Ayodhya : 1986), pp. 16-17.

50. See also Veer, n. 18, p. 21.

51. See, *History Versus Casuistry* : *Evidence of the Ramjanmabhoomi Mandir*" (New Delhi : Voice of India, 1991), p. 26.

52. See, the Ramjanmabhoomi Nyas's advertisement, "You can run, but you can not hide, from yourself from the facts," *The Pioneer* (Lucknow), 11 May 1991.

stories from the priests and sadhus and going through popular history books, the devotee is able to realise the eternality and holiness of the place. From this point of view factual histories are irrelevant in understanding the historicity of Ram's Ayodhya. As Peter Vander Veer has succinctly put it, "The piligrim, at least, is not interested in proofs. He comes only for a few days to Ayodhya and want to hear its Mahima, its greatness, its power and not its real History."[53]

The mythic history of Ayodhya does not cease with the destruction of Ramjanmabhoomi temple by Babur. Time and again, myths have been invented to rephrase the divine character of the place where Ram is supposed to have been descended on the earth. The event on December 22-23, 1949 is remarkable on two counts. While it has been reported by the district authorities that the mosque had been surreptitiously occupied and converted into a temple but the RSS mouthpiece Organiser has invented another myth. It reported, "On the historic morning of 23 December 1949, the idols of Shri Ram Chandra and Sita Devi miraculously appeared in the janamsthan. As the Hindu devotees rejoiced over the miracle and thronged in their thousands ; the government proclaimed the promises a disputed area and locked the gates "[54]

To vindicate the above miracle Justice Deoki Nandan Agarwal, a retired judge of Allahabad High Court, describes another myth related to the incident that took place on 22-23 December 1949 in the Babri Masjid. A Havaldar (constable), Abdul Barkat, was on his duty on that night in the police outpost Ramjanmabhoomi. He saw a flash of light inside the Babri Masjid and suddenly that light glown into a golden colour. In that light he saw a "God like child" of 4/5 years old appeared which he had not seen earlier. He, so struck by the incident that he fell unconscious. When he regained senses,

53. Veer, n. 18, p. 11.

54. See 'Ram Janmabhoomi or Babri Masjid' ? in *Organiser*, 29 March 1987. The miraculous appearance of Ram has also been mentioned in the VHP's documentary evidences for Ramjanmabhoomi. See, "History vs. Casuistry", n. 51, p. 28.

he found that the main gate of the Babri Masjid was broken and innumerable number of Hindus gathered and were worshipping the idols in the mosque.[55] But there is no such police record to confirm the incident.[56]

The mythic narratives provide the basis upon which popular communal histories are constructed and communal meanings are also filled in. Even though events and characters depicted in the myths are impossible to imagine but they are carefully invented to strengthen the popular beliefs about the sacredness of the place and its defilement by the Muslim rulers. As the RSS 'historian' Koenraad Elst points out, "........The Babri Masjid is just one out of thousands still existing Muslim building that have replaced the Hindu temples as a part of a violent campaign of Islamization which the more faithful of Indias' Muslim rulers have systematically pursued."[57]

Myths appeal to the masses because they are invented and reconstituted with the changes in the social and political processes and they are part of the Known or accepted tradition. While some sections of the society may accept the mythical truth of Ayodhya other sections my not accept. Those who challenge the mythic history of Ramjanmabhoomi and seek a different historical knowledge, then mythic history is justified on the grounds of faith. On 10 March 1987, at a joint meeting of the VHP and AIBMAC leaders there was a proposal by a Muslim leader to appoint a committee of experts consisting of historians from reputed universities to study the claims of the rival parties and give their opinion but Mahant Avaidyanath, leader of Shri Ramjanmabhoomi Mukti Yanja Samiti said, "with Hindus it is a matter of faith that Bhagwan Rama was born where the Babri mosque is. No government or court can sit on the judgement over it".[58]

---

55. Deoki Nandan Agarwal, Ramjanmabhoomi : *Historical and Legal Perspective* (New Delhi : Delhi : VHP, n. d.), p.8.

56. Srivastava, n. 5, p. 14.

57. Elst, n. 34, p. 90.

58. *Organiser*, 5 April 1987.

But the VHP and RSS show their apparent volte-face with regard to the Ayodhya dispute. On the one hand, they insist that the Babri Masjid is situated on the site called Ramjanmabhoomi and it is 'believed' by the Hindus to be the birth place of Ram' and it is an article of faith and raises the question from their own side. "Is there proof that an old and persistent among the Ram devotees has considered the site as the sacred Ramjanmabhoomi, and that the Ram worship took place in a temple, before and until the Babri Masjid was built" ?[59] K.S. Sudersan an RSS leader unequivocally emphasizes that, "Faith does not ask for proof. We all believe that Ramjanmabhoomi is in Ayodhya, that Ram was born where the mosque structure is there. That is enough".[60] The campaigners of Ram temple maintain that, since the issue of Ramjanmabhoomi is a matter of faith which involves the emotions and unshakable beliefs of millons and it also involves the question of undoing the vandalism of history, the judiciary can not decide the dispute.[61]

On the other side, the VHP claims to have provided a mass of literary, historical, judicial and archaeological records in support of their contention that a temple was destroyed and a mosque was raised on that spot held sacred by the Hindus.

The RSS and its affiliates like the VHP and BJP have been consistently propagating in various ways about the history of Ramjanmabhoomi temple and its eventual destruction by Babur guided by his iconoclastic zeal. The VHP leader Justice Deoki Nandan Agarwal's influential article says, "that there was an ancient temple of Maharaja Vikramaditya's time at Sri Ramjanmabhoomi is a fact of history, which is indisputable, although there is some controversy as to which of Vikramadityas resurrected the place and built the magnificient temple.

59. See, the VHP's document *Evidences for Ramjanmabhoomi Mandir* presented to the Government of India on December 23, 1990, p. 1.

60. *Organiser*, 21 April 1991.

61. See the advertisement—"When can the Courts Decide' issued by Bharatiya Janata Party, *Indian Express*, 29 October 1990.

That temple was desecrated and destroyed by Mir Baqi, a commander of Babur's hordes, after Babar visited to (sic) Ayodhya and a mosque was 'sought to be raised there at, in order to please Fazl Abbas Qualander.[62] (emphasis added)

Interestingly, earlier the BJP leader Atal Bihari Vajpayee in his reply to the open letter of Hiren Mukherjee had viewed that, "it is not possible to pin point the exact spot where Ram was born. But it is known that, Rama, the king of Ayodhya whom most mass of Hindus regard as the reincarnation of the God was born in that historical city and a temple dedicated to him had been in existence since long. This temple was built and rebuilt over the ages.[63] Despite the BJP leader's ambiguous assessment, the Vishwa Hindu Parishad had submitted a coherent write up containing is earlier documents and memorandums to the Government of India in support of its claim over the Babri mosque.[64]

The main contentions of the VHP rest on the following four major claims :

1. Hindus have been for long time worshipping a particular sacred place in Ayodhya known as Ramjanmabhoomi even before the construction of the Babri Masjid. The Babri Masjid had been constructed after the demolition of Ramjanmabhoomi temple.

2. There exist, concrete historical and literacy sources, archaeological evidences and revenue records to prove that, a Ram temple was forcibly pulled down and the Babri Masjid was constructed in its place.

In the paragraph, "Total lack of counter evidence", the VHP document suggests that, the thesis advanced by some quarters that the Babri Masjid did not replace any extent the Ram temple goes against the common sense in may ways. The

62. Deoki Nandan, n. 55. p. 2.

63. *Organiser,* 24 September 1989.

64. See *Evidences for the Ramjanmabhoomi Mandir,* submitted by the VHP to the Government of India on 27 December 1990.

"well attested fact" about the continuance of worship in the mosque courtyard even in the Muslim rule, the findings of pillar bases aligned with the walls in the mosque, black stone pillars with intricate carvings all suggest that, the Babri Masjid had replaced the pre-existent Ram temple. The document concludes that until recently the pre-existence of a Ramjanmabhoomi temple at the Babri Masjid side was a matter of consensus and was supported by the European, Hindu and Muslim sources and all the archaeological findings since the 17th century.[65]

The VHP, in its rejoinder, submitted on 6 January 1991, to the AIBMAC's claims on the Babri-Masjid demands the AIBMAC and the Muslim community at large to recognise the "wrongs of the past", "And we would like the Indian Muslim Community to rise to the occasion of its own free will. After all, two mosques (at Mathura and Kashi) and a Non-mosque (the Babri Masjid at Ayodhya) are very small price for an immense gesture of goodwill, which will convince the Hindu society that the Muslims have effectively broken with the unhappy record of their predecessor. For us these places are no less sacred than Kerbela or the Al Aqsa mosque are for the Muslims. Muslims should understand what kind of message they sending by insisting on the continuing the occupation which was started by fanatics and mass maruders like Babur and Aurangzeb."[66]

The AIBMAC submitted its document on 23 December 1990 to the government as per the resolution taken in the meeting of the representatives of the Vishwa Hindu Parishad and All India Babri Masjid Action committee on 4 December 1990 at the initiative of the Government of India. However, like the VHP's documentary evidences for Ramjanmabhoomi, the AIBMAC documents were a sort of systematic presentation of vast mass of literature consisting all of its earlier claims and documents submitted to the UP government and Government of India.

65. *Evidences of the Ramjanmabhoomi*, n. 64, pp. 18-19.

66. *Evidences for the Ramjanmabhoomi*, n. 64. p. 17.

The AIBMAC has submitted the evidences in support of its claims over the disputed mosque under the following heads :

A. Documents showing the mythological history of Ayodhya.

B. Documents showing the construction of Babri Masjid in 1528 and historical evidence of that period.

C. Documents showing the exclusive possession of Muslims over Babri Masjid in 1528 A.D. to 1885 A.D.

D. Documents showing judicial verdict from the successive decisions in favour of Muslims arising out from the suit of Mahant Raghubar Das, Mahant Janam Asthan, Ayodhya, (*i.e.*, Suit no. 61/280 of 1885) for the construction of a temple over Ram Chhabutra situating infront of the Babri Masjid.

E. Document showing the exclusive possession of Muslims over the Babri Masjid from 1885 to 22nd December 194 .

F. Documents showing the injustice and excesses committed against Muslims in independent India having secular credential arising out of the Babri Masjid—Ramjanmabhoomi controversy since 23rd December 1949 onward.[67]

The AIBMAC stresses specially on the historicity of Ram, rejects the thesis that Ramjanmabhoomi temple was replaced by the Babri Masjid and claims Judicial Judgements in favour of Muslims possession of the Babri Masjid, the VHP on the other-hand, marshalled out evidences in support of its claim from Muslim testimonies and European accounts apart from, resorting to popular traditions that have received the status of facts in the colonialist accounts over the years.

The AIBMAC, unlike the VHP and its allies, has failed to bring out complete historical documents and analysis on its

67. See, the interim List of Documents showing the Claim of Muslims over Babri-Masjid site. Submitted by the AIBMAC to the Government of India.

own. Except the Babur's tesatment and successive judicial verdicts in favour of Muslims, it relies exclusively on the writings and views of 'secular historians' on the Ramjanmabhoomi in Ayodhya and produced these in support of its claim.

What is evident from the controversy over the Babri Masjid is that, behind a facade of historical evidences and dialogue between the rival parties, the dispute has undeniably been vitiated into a question of sentiments and faith of the majority community and the threat to the identity of a minority. The question of ownership of a dilapidated mosque has brought to fore the issues of faith, identity, the nature of Islam, the communalism-secularism debates and the nature Indian nationalism. And the space for a reasoned and objective study over the historicity of Ram's Ayodhya has suffered. The RSS 'historian' writes with his characteristic blind anti Islam attitude, "The debate over the Ayodhya really is a footnote in the fundamental ideological debate about the nature of Islam. No matter what Babur's innermost motivations were...that Islam as an ideology played a crucial role in bringing about wars, plunder, oppression, slavery and destruction of places of worship possibly including Ram temple in Ayodhya."[68] (emphasis added).

The failure of talks for an amicable settlement of the vexed dispute in January 1990, signifies that both the VHP and the AIBMAC have taken mutually antagonistic and irreconciliable position and the possibility of a mutual understanding and settlement of the dispute has appeared remote.

The greatest victim in this controversy has been the discipline of history because of its political appropriation. When the VHP produced false and concocted historical evidences to establish its claim of the Ramjanmabhoomi, the AIBMAC ungrudingly appropriates the secular historiography to disprove the VHP's claim on the Babri Masjid and demands its restoration to the Muslims, which interestingly, the secular historians refrain to speak. In the so called 'debate' over the historicity

68. Elst, n. 57, p. 45.

of Ramjanmabhoomi, the factual history and its analysis provided by the country's reputed historians with unchallenged intellectual honesty, has become irrelevant not because of the issue of 'unshakable faith' of Hindus but the sheer failure of the 'Rambhakta' historians to put forward convincing counter evidence or reasonable arguments against the secular historians.

In this curious controversy over the historicity of Rama's birth place, all those historians and secularists who oppose the political abuse of history and the language of religious bigotry and intolerance are identified as "anti-Hindu", "traitors of Hindus or "anti-mandir" groups responsible for brutal falsification of history, by the Hindu communalists.[69]

It is in this context, the politics of Ramjanmabhoomi is characterized by violent opposition and hatred to those 'pseudo secular' historians who challenge the historicity of Ramjanmabhoomi. "The struggle for Ramjanmabhoomi", we are told, is not primarily with the Muslim Community. The most important opponents of Hindu society today are not the Islamic communal leaders but the interiorized colonial rulers of India, the alienated english educated and mostly left leaning elite that noisely advertises its 'secularism'. It is these people who impose anti-Hindu policies on Hindus society and who keep Hinduism down and prevent it from proudly raising its head after a thousand year of oppression."[70] (emphasis added.)

The Vishwa Hindu Parishad's claims to the Babri Masjid based on the evidences from various sources like European accounts and Mulsim testimonies as well as mythic history and popular belief, have raised serious doubts among the notable historians in India about the validity of the historical evidences. Eminent historians, and archaeologists have refuted the VHP's

69. See, for example, the rejoinder given by the VHP to AIBMAC documents on. Babri Masjid, in *History vs Casuistry*, n. 51, pp. 35-65.

70. Koenraad Elst, "*Ayodhya and After : Problems Before Hindu Society*" (New Delhi, Voice of India, 1991), p. VI.

claims and have linked its historical evidences with mythic history and attempted to separate the two in their recent study and analysis on the history of Ramjanmabhoomi. The historians accuse that the VHP through manipulation of historical data presented the evidence for an 'imagined Ram temple' and converted historical facts into a weapon of contemporary political prejudice.

II

Historical study of Ayodhya is a challenging task for the historians because of the paucity of in historical, archaeological and epigraphic evidences available on the subject. Further, systematic description of the rise of the Ayodhya as a sacred centre of Hindus is even difficult because of the non-existence or lack of chronological records available. The archaeological records often contradict with the information available in the literary sources.[71] Despite popular belief being identified with the present day Ayodhya with Valmiki's Ayodhya but it has been the centre of other religions like the Jainas and Buddhists and has taken different names like Saketa, Vanita, Kosala, Ikshvakumbhoomi and Rampuri in different historical periods.

On the basis of VHP's evidences, the historians have raised several questions about the historicity of Ramjanmabhoomi. Whether it is possible to identify the present day Ayodhya with the Ayodhya of 'Ramayana' ? Whether it is possible, to identify Ram's birth place with the location of the Babri Masjid ? Did Babur destroy the Ram temple and construct a mosque on it ? If Ayodhya is a sacred place for Hindu, then was there any popular belief about the existence of temple on its demolition ?

The epic poem 'Ramayana' was originally told in 'Ram Katha which is no longer available. It is being assumed that most of the characters, events and places are fictional due to several interpolations. In the Valmiki's 'Ramayana' story, Lord Ram, king of Ayodhya was born in the 'Treta Yuga'

71. R.S. Sharma, "Calling the VHP's Bluff", *Times of India*, 27 January, 1991.

which was thousand years back before the arrival of 'Kaliyuga' which was supposed to have started from 3100 B.C. But the archaeological excavations conducted by the Banaras Hindu University s History and Archaeological department in 1975-76 at 3 places in Ayodhya releaved that, habitation in the area had begun with the early phase of Northern Black Polished Ware culture (5th – 8th Centuries). Prof. B.B. Lal, former Director General of the Archaeological Survey of India, had conducted an intensive archaeological studies on Ayodhya and concluded that the earliest habitation in the area had started from the circa 700 B.C. with fairly simple human habitation. But the events narrated in 'Ramayana' had taken place in an highly developed urban setting as the frequent references to and depictions of various places in the epic testify.

Prof. B.B. Lal's more recent statements and writings show that, in the Janmabhoomi area a trench near the south of Babri Masjid brought to light a series of brick built pillars which indicate that the black stone pillars that are used in the Babri Masjid must have come from this preceding pillar bases.[72]

He also suggested further excavation beneath the Babri Masjid in order to confirm the above findings.[73] B.B. Lal's shift of his earlier stand has generated lot of heat and controversy among the historians and archaeologists.[74]

Further, Prof. B.B. Lal is convinced that, Ayodhya of today is the same as the Ayodhya of the epic literature.[75] But, it is

---

72. B B. Lal, "Archaeology of the Ramayan sites Project : Its Genesis and Summary Results "*Manthan*", October, 1990, p 15.

73. *Ibid.*

74 *Times of India*, 10 February 1991 and *Hindustan Times*, 13 February, 1991.

75. B.B. Lal in his recent article in the RSS journal *Manthan* October, 1989 issue has argued that, "Ramayana is not the figment of everybody's imagination but may have had a kernel of truth at its base" which is however generally not accepted by eminent historians and archaeologist, Lal, n. 72, p. 21.

argued by the historians that, Prof. Lal's argument can be weakened if the controversy about the exact location of the Sarayu river and its distance from the city of Ayodhya is considered.[76] The reason for the persistence of confusion over the exact identification of Ayodhya is due to the absence of contemporary text, archaeological or epigraphic evidence about the existence of the Ayodhya city.

According to the Buddhist sources, Saketa and Ayodhya were two different cities and the Saketa was identified on the river Ganges not on the river Sarayu where the present day Ayodhya is situated and Budha's visit to Ayodhya had also been recorded. During the period of later Guptas, the indentification of Saketa with Ayodhya is corroborated by the Jain and Sanskrit literatures like "Brahmadaputra' and Kali Das's 'Raghuvamsham'. The inscriptions of later Guptas have also been found one of which states in 436 A.D, the donees of a gifts as 'Brahmin hailing from Ayodhya'. The town of Saketa had been renamed as Ayodhya possibly during the reign of Skandagupta or Kumargupta-1 when the royal court of Guptas was shifted from Pataliputra to Saketa. By bestowing the name of Ayodhya on the town Saketa the Gupta king was obviously attempting to gain political legitimation since Ram was viewed as one of the 'Avatars' of the vaisnava tradition and most of the royal families adopted the suryavamshi linieage—a line which Ram is said to belong.[77] This view has been complemented further by the myth of Ayodhya's rediscovery by the king Vikramaditya.

The change in the name of Saketa to Ayodhya is also found in the travel accounts of Fa Hisien and Hsuan Tsang during their visit to India, had described Ayodhya as one of the important centre of Budhism and major cities of Koshala. The existing literary sources indicate that, Saket was indentified as Ayodhya only in the late fifth century A.D. "If the present day Ayodhya was known as Saket before the fifth century, then

76. Srivastava, n. 5, p. 54.

77. K.N. Panikkar, "A Historical Overview", in Gopal ed., n. 4, pp. 24-25.

the Ayodhya of Valmikis's Ramayana was fictional. If so, the identification of Ramjanmabhoomi in Ayodhya today becomes a matter of faith, not of historical evidence."[78] Further, the doubt persists with the archaeological report of Prof. B.B. Lall in 1975-76 that, the present day Ayodhya was not rebuilt by the Guptas since no Gupta layers had found in the excavations at Ayodhya.[79]

Ayodhya has been an important centre of major religions like Hinduism, Jainism and Budhism. Among Hindus, vaishnavism and shaivism were existed earlier and more popular than the Rama cult which is of recent development.[80]

According to Hsuan Tsang's accounts, Ayodhya was an important centre of Buddhism and Lord Buddha is said to have visited the city several times. Number of monasteries had far out numbered other temples in 'Ayodhya which proves the dominance of Buddhist sect in Ayodhya.

Like Buddhism, Ayodhya was also an important jaina piligrimage as it is associated with the birthplace of the two founders of Jainism and the Jaina literature also indicate the visit of Mahavira and Parshanath to Ayodhya. A Jain terracota found in excavations belonged to third to fourth century A.D. proves the presence of jainism in the region.

Hans Bakker's comprehensive studies show that the development of Ram cult "worshipped as the supreme form and main mainfestation of Vishnu did not rise into the prominence before the eleventh and twelveth centuries AD. "But there existed very few temples dedicated to Ram in places outside Ayodhya.[81] The cult of Ram became popular and established

78. See the pamphlet, ***Political Abuse of History*** published by the Centre for Historical Studies, JNU, in Engineer ed , n. 3, p. 233.

79. See the report on result of Ayodhya excavation, 1976-77 in ***Indian Archaeology 1976-77—A Review*** and reproduced in Engineer ed., n. 3, p. 208.

80. K,N. Panikkar, n. 77, pp. 25-26.

81. Bakker, n. 45, Part-I, pp. 65-66.

itself only from the 18th century with the rise of Ramanandi sects in Ayodhya.

Ayodhya's evolution as an important centre of Hindu piligrimage is however of later growth. W.C. Benet, the compiler of first Gazetteer of the Province of Avadh wrote in 1877 that Hindu revivalism in Ayodhya occurred in modern times. While other sacred places of Hindus like Gaya, Puri kept their reputation as, piligrimages, 'Ayodhya became a wilderners and famous hunting ground". Further, several treatises on the Hindu piligrimages also support the view of the late evolution of Ayodhya as a piligrimage centre.[82] Peter Vander Veer wrote after his intensive studies, "Ayodhya's rise as a supra-regional place of piligrimage is relatively recent. Only during the eighteenth century did the Ramanandi sadhus start to build their institutions here while many of the buildings we see today were built in the second half of the nineteenth century or the first half of the twentieth century. In a civilisation a where traditions and antiquities are seen as respectable, these facts do not recommend a sacred place. This problem is evaded by an anti-historical examination."[83]

The Ramcharitmanas of Tulasi Das became instrumental in the deification Ram worship and chanting the glories of Ram became the most popular form of Vaishnavism and by the sixteenth century Ram cult become the most popular form of Vishnu. In the eighteenth century many events related to the life of Ram were celebrated and the 'Ram Navami' (Birth day of Rama) become the most popular festival in Avadh.[84] It was only during the reign of Nawabs, Ayodhya became the centre of Ram cult and controlled by Ramanandi order.[85]

The Vishwa Hindu Parishad has failed to produce any literary sources upto eighteenth century that speak about the destruction of temple at the birthplace of Ram. Even in the

82. Srivastava, n. 5, p. 39.

8 . Veer, n. 18, p. 36.

84. Veer, n. 18, p. 11.

85. Srivastava, n. 5, p, 42.

Vaishnavaite texts there would have been reference to the Ram's birthplace in Ayodhya. The VHP's reference to the 'Ayodhya Mahatmya' which is of later addition and insertions have been made at the end of that text. The 'Ayodhya Mahatmaya's reference to Ram's birthplace do not take us to the Babri Masjid because of the existence of two identical place *viz.*, Janamsthan and Janambhoomi. Further, the text gives more importance to the 'Swargadvara tirtha' and lesser importance to the 'Janamsthan tirtha'.[86] The first European visitor William Finch in 1838 had given in his account, the existence of a fort said to be the birthplace of Ram at Ayodhya and a cave where Ram is said to have left for heaven. But he did not mention about the existence of Ramjanmabhoomi temple.[87]

No place in Ayodhya is associated with Ram's birth either in the eleventh century or even six centuries after. When a place is associated with his birth possibly in the late eighteenth century, its location given in various Mahatmyas does not tally with the present Babri Masjid. It would be a mistake to view that, on the basis of an old Hidu belief, that the Ramjanmabhoomi temple was situated at the same site as is now occupied by the Babri Masjid.

In 1902, a local citizens committee under the leadership of Mahant Bara Asthan (birth place of Dashrath) had put up a number of stone pillars marking the birthplace of Ram and other places related to his life. The committee put up a stone pillar marking "No. 1 Ramjanmabhoomi" near the east gate of the Babri Masjid and another marking "No. 5, Ramjanmabhoomi" in front of the 'Kaushalya Bhavan' without giving reasons. It is being argued that the 'faith' in the local traditions made the committee to put up a stone pillar near the Babri Masjid but the location of Ram's birthplace mentioned in the Mahatmya forced them to put another stone pillar near the 'Kaushalya Bhavan.'[88]

---

86. R.S. Sharma *et al.*, ed., "*Ramjanmabhumi-Baburi Masjid : A Historians Report to the Nation* "(New Delhi : PPH, 1991), pp. 5-6
87. Srivastava, n. 5, pp. 100-01.
88. Srivastava, n. 5, pp. 101-04.

The most important contemporary source which points to the construction of Babri Masjid by Babur, is the inscription written in Persion verses inside the wall of the mosque. According to the inscription in the mosque, Mir Baqi, the commander of Babur had built the mosque in 1528. The English translation of the Persion verses are as under :

"By the command of emperor Babur, whose justice is an edifice reaching upto the very heights of the heavens" ;

'The good hearted Mir Baqi built this alighting place of angles' ;

'May his goodness last forever'. (The year of the building was 935 A.H. or 1529 AD)[89]

On the basis of the above inscription, it is being believed that, Babur was responsible for destroying the Ramjanmabhoomi temple.[90] But the inscription on the Babri Masjid does not give a slight hint of temple destruction to pave the way for constructing the Babri Masjid. Moreover, the inscription does not tell us how the mosque was built there and whether a temple was existed there earlier. It is also difficult to accept the assumption that the temple was destroyed by Mir Baqi due to his fanatical mind. Had he been guided by his iconoclastic zeal then he could have got this recorded in the inscription to add his reputation.[91] It would be very simplistic to argue that Babur did not mention about the destruction of a temple. Since he was a visionary ruler and afraid of the posterity.[92] The details about Babur's expedition to Avadh and his stay are not available in 'Babur Nama' (Memoirs of Babur) because pages in his memoirs from 2 April 1528 to 18 September 1528 are missing. In the absence of these pages, a local myth has been developed about Babur's involvement in the destruction of Ram temple. But in his memoirs Babur had not mentioned his visit' to Ayodhya rather he had mentioned his brief stay in

89. Quoted in Srivastava, n. 5, p. 85.

90. See, *Evidence for the Ramjanmabhoomi*, n. 39, p. 14.

91. Sharma *et al*, ed, n. 87, p. 15.

92. Irfan Habib, Ayodhya Dispute-II, *People*'s *Democracy*, 14 April 1991.

the north of Avadh on the junction of the two rivers.[93] Despite the gap in Babur's memoirs the parallel sources, a multiplicity of chronicles as well as texts in the regional languages are silent about the Babur's involvement in the destruction of Ramjanmabhoomi temple.[94]

A close reading of Babur Nama by the historians suggests that Babur was not a religious fanatic and in a no way associated with the destruction of temples.[95] He had even praised the Hindu arts and architecture and scriptures though he had ridiculed the life of ascetics and ordered the destruction of nude idols in other places. In his 'Will' to his son Humayun, he had advised him to rule India with all fairness and justice to the natives, to respect their religious beliefs and sentiments and to give up the practice of cow slaughter in order to win over the hearts of Hindus.[96]

It was on the basis of Persian inscriptions inside the mosque, Mrs. A.S. Beveridge in her translation of Babur Nama has mentioned in the appendices of her book that, since Babur was an obedient follower of Prophet, so he was intolerant of other faiths. He, therefore, might have regarded the demolition of a place of worship of the infidels as the religious duty. However, she had mentioned that she has no evidence to prove that Babur was involved in the destruction of the temple. Mrs. Beveridge arrived such a spurious conclusion on the basis of her biased notion as stayed in Ayodhya for some months.[97] Hans Bakker, despite his authenic interpretation has accepted Mrs. Beveridge's assumption and wrote that, the "temple was destroyed by the first Mogul prince Babur in A.D. 1528 and replaced by a mosque which still exists".[98]

---

93. Srivastava, n. 5, p. 71.
94. In the name of history, *Indian Express*, 1 April, 1990 reply of JNU historians to A R. Khan's critique to their pamphlet, "Political Abuse of History".
95. Sharma, n. 37, pp. 29-30 and also Srivastava, n. 5. pp. 27.
96. R.L. Shukla and Nilofar Ahamad, "*Babri Mosque or Ramjanam Temple* ? (New Delhi : (rescent. 1986), pp 6-7.
97. Srivastava, n. 5, pp. 86-87.
98. Bakker, n. 45, Part-I, p. 44.

Abul Fazl, a prominent chronicter of medieval period and author of Ain-i-Akabari and Akabar Nama had referred Ayodhya as the residence of Ramachandra but existence of a temple commenorating the birthplace of Lord Ram and its replacement by the Babri Masjid was not mentioned by him.

Tulasi Das, who wrote his masterpiece Ramcharitmanas in 1575-76, was belong to that region and a great devotee of Ram, yet he did not mention about the existence of Ramjanmabhoomi temple and its subsequent replacement by a mosque.[99]

The Hindu belief about the existence of a Ramjanmabhoomi temple is further buttressed by the Muslim communal historians. The statement that Babri Masjid stands on the Ramjanmabhoomi was not first made by the Hindus but by the Muslim communal bravado and this is the reason why the VHP produces 'the Muslim testimony in its evidences for Ramjanmabhoomi temple. For nearly 150 years the Muslim communalists have engaged in the construction of the myth of the Ram temple destruction in their writings. 'Hadisa-i-Shuhada' (1855-56) by Mirza Jann, Azmat Ali Alvi in his, 'Amir Ali Shaheed wa Morke-e-Hanumanghari (1853), in 1909 Mohammad Najmul Ghani Khan in his 'Tarikh-i-Awadh' and particularly Maulana Abdul Hai in his book—'Hindustan-Islami Ahed Mein' had suitably mentioned about the destruction of the Ram temple by Babur and construction of Babri Masjid on that side.[100]

While no ancient Sanskrit text has given any information about the demolition of a Ramjanmabhoomi temple in Ayodhya, the VHP has based its evidence on the reports of Proof. B.B. Lal and Dr. S.P. Gupta which are as follows :

1. In the 11th century there existed a large structure on the pillars on the site popularly known as Ramjanmabhoomi on that very spot, the Babri Masjid stands today.

99. *Political Abuse of History* in Engineer ed., n. 3, p 235.

100. Habib, "Ayodhya Dispute", n. 94 pp. 6-7.

2. Most of the pillars of the 11th century temple were removed in the early sixteenth century, while some pillars still lie in their original placements and few other pillars are removed.[101]

But the VHP's archaeological evidences have been seriously challenged by the leading historians and archaeologists of India.[102]

The historians are of the view that it is necessary to be established, the fact, as to whether the pillars used in the Babri-Masjid are from a destroyed temple existed on that very spot. Even if the pillar bases indicating the existence of a structure are found but a correlation can not be established between the pillars that might have been used in the mosque, and the pillars that were used in the preceding structure which also necessarily may not be a temple.

In the Indian Archaeology, 1976-77, B.B. Lal had mentioned about the existence of "later medieval brick and kankar lime floors in the trenches near the Babri Masjid which belong to 17th 18th centuries."[103] On the basis of his findings, it is impossible to prove the existence of an eleventh century temple

---

101. *Evidences for the Ramjanambhoomi*, n. 59, Annexure-29.

102. Twenty eminent historians in a joint statement accused Prof. B.B. Lal of distorting archaeological evidences, under the current impetus of '*Hindutva*' campaign", (see, *Hindustan Times*, 13 February 1991, Prof. B.B. Lal in his earlier papers on the archaeological excavations in Ayodhya and his contributions to *Indian Archaeology—A Review, 1978-79 and Encyclopaedia of Indian Archaeology, Vol. 2* (Edited by Arun Ghosh) did not mention about the existence of pillar bases in the trench near Janmabhoomi area. Nor did he mention about the discovery of pillar bases in his site-note book and registrar of antiquities connected with the Ayodhya excavations. Dr. S.P. Gupta who claims his association with the Ayodhya excavation is not corroborated by the official records of ASI and despite the historians' plea to make public the relevant materials relating to B.B. Lal's excavation for its scrutiny and analysis, the Government of India has chosen to ignore their plea. (see sharma *et al.*, ed., n. 87, p. 10. and also *Peoples Democracy*, 29 march 1991.

103. Sharma *et al*, ed., n. 87, p. 12.

temple and its demolition in the Sixteenth Century. Further, the existence of Islamic glazed ware pottery proves the Muslim habitation on that place from thirteenth, Century onwards and they might have needed a mosque for offering prayers. The black pillars used in the Babri Masjid and lying elsewhere in Ayodhya and Faizabad are not common stratigraphically and their structure for example, diameter and style varies. Further, the blackstone pillars that have been used in the Babri Masjid might have transported from other places since in medieval times it was a common practice to use transported materials for the construction of a place of worship.

The full blown local myth about the demolition of Ramjanmabhoomi temple received its historical basis only in the nineteenth century colonial historiography. In the colonial historiography, religious communities and their mutual antagonism held the centre stage" as it was perceived as essential feature of Indian society. Such type of distorted interpretations of Indian history had ignored other categories of 'reconstructing' history.[104] John Leyden who translated Babur's memoirs in 1813, had pointed out the missing pages of Babur's memoirs. The revelation followed by the claim of Montogomery Martin in 1834 that unislamic elements are used in the Babri Masjid to which he had visited upon. When William Erskine published his translations of Babur's memoirs in 1854, he also contended that, Babur was in Ayodhya on 28 March 1528. In 1860, P. Carnegy made a direct reference to Babur having destroyed the Ram temple in Faizabad Gazetteer and in 1873 T.S. Elliot also repeated this view in his book "History of India as told by its own Historians. In 1877, W.C. Benet also supported Carnegy's findings. Whatever the British historians had viewed was once again repeated in the archaeological survey of Cunningham in 1865 and A. Fuher in 1891.[105]

The explanation that Muslim rule in Ayodhya is connected with the rise and fall of Ayodhya as a piligrimage of Hindus[106]

104. K.N. Panikkar, in Gopal ed., p. 29 and Pandey, n. 8, pp. 24 ff.

105. Srivastava, n. 5, pp. 81-84.

106. Elist, n. 57, pp. 75-77.

is however not supported by the historical records. The attitude of Muslim rulers vary from the demolition of certain temples by Aurangzeb, to the active promotion and help to the construction and maintenance of Hindu temples in Ayodhya. There is certainly no evidence of total suppression of Hinduism in Ayodhya. Hindu worship remained possible in the compound of newly built Babur mosque and the activities of Brahman Pandas are recorded by the first European to visit the place, William Finch between 1608-1611.[107]

In the eighteenth century, Nawabs of Avadh (oudh), succeeded the Mughal rulers as the most powerful ruler in the Northern India. The first Nawab of Avadh, Sadat Khan's (1 22-39) reign witnessed the expansion of Ayodhya as a major centre of Hindu piligrimage which was continued during the regime of his successor Safdarjung (1739-54). The success of Nawabi rule depended to a large extent the mutual co-existence of Hindus and Muslims. Nawab Safdarjung's and Nawab Asaf ud-Daula's diwans in Ayodhya were Hindus. While the Nawabı administration was controlled by Kayastha Hindus the military force was dominated by shaivaite Nagas. As it has been argued that exercise of royal patronage was crucial in the development of Ayodhya as Hindu piligrimage Centre as well as legitimising the Nawabi rule.[108]

The peaceful co-existence of Hindus and Muslims in Ayodhya was threatened due to the decline of Nawabi rule and rise of British influence in Avadh. In 1855, Muslims of Ayodhya led by a Sunni leader Ghulam Husain claimed that there had been a mosque within the precincts of Hanumanghari temple and it should be reopened to the Muslims. However it was resisted by the Bairagis of the Hanumanghari temple and this led to a violent conflict in which Muslims had suffered many casualities. The event could not stop the Sunni leaders to make further attempts to Hanumanghari temple. Under the leadership of Amir Ali, armed Muslims once again marched towards Ayodhya

107. Veer, n. 18, p. 37.

108. Veer, n. 18, pp. 37-39 and see also, *Political Abuse of History* in Engineer ed., pp. 236-37.

to reclaim the Masjid but were prevented by the intervention of British troops.[109]

An important dimension of the Hindu-Muslim conflict in 1855 was that, originally the dispute started over the control of Hanumanghari temple but subsequently it was shifted to the Babri Masjid. As a counter claim to foil the demands of orthodox Muslims to gain possession over Hanumanghari temple the Bairagis made claim that the Babri Masjid stands on the Ramjanmasthan. It is believed that the local traditions about the existence of Ramjanmasthan temple, did not appear to be current in 1855.[110]

In 1855, Hindu-Muslim clash took place over the possession of the Babri Masjid. The Muslims forcibly recaptured the Babri-Masjid which was occupied by the Bairagis in the earlier clash with the Muslims near the Hanumanghari temple. But the Hindus led by the Bairagis of Hanumanghari temple again reoccupied the Babri Masjid after a bloody conflict with the Muslims in which seventy five Muslims were killed and buried near the Babri Masjid known as Ganj-i-shahidan (martyr's resting place).[111]

In February 1856, the British annexed the Avadh region on the pretext of growing hostilities between the two communities and the general decline of law and order situation in the region. After the Sepoy Mutiny in 1857, the British perception to the Babri Masjid was changed. Soon after the revolt, the Mahantas of Hanumanghari temple occupied a part of the Babri Masjid and raised a Chhabutra' (platform) for worship of Lord Rama. The local Muslim protested against the move of the Mahant to the British magistrate.[112]

In 1856, the British intervened in the dispute over the Babri Masjid and decided to erect an iron grill to physically separate the structure of the Babri Masjid from the 'chhabutra' in front

109. Veer, n. 18, pp. 37, 38, see also Srivastava, n. 5. p. 45.
110. K.N. Panikkar, n. 77, pp. 32-33.
111. Srivastava, n. 5, p. 24.
112. K.N. Panikkar, n. 77. p. 33.

of the mosque (eastern side). The 'Mahantas' continued to occupy the eastern side of the Babri Masjid but, the Britishers chosen to overlock, despite the entire land in Ayodhya declared as 'nazul' (government) land.[113] In the twentieth century, as we have argued earlier, the political development and intercommunity relations in Faizabad was determined by the larger political changes that took place in the colonial North India.

The historical facts shown that the claims of Muslim communal forces and Hindu communal forces over the history of Babri-Masjid finds no sanction from history over the centuries, Ayodhya has been developed into a 'market for religion'[114] and different religious communities attach their own sacred meanings to it though the importance of Ayodhya derives its association with the Ram legend.

III

POLITICS OF RAMJANMABHOOMI

The present agitation for the 'liberation of Ramjanmabhoomi' at Ayodhya, as we have argued earlier, emerges from the widespread communalisation of Indian political process. While the historicity of Ram's birthplace occupies central to the understanding the nature of the dispute but the issue is a symbolic of deeper crisis faced by India's plural social order.

The present controversy over the Babri Masjid, it has been argued by the protagonists of Ram temple, is not a political problem rather, it is integrally related to the 'cultural' and 'historical' aspects of Hindu society and the restoration of Ramjanmabhoomi is claimed as a 'national demand' which must be respected.[115] The demand for the construction Ram temple at the disputed mosque, it is claimed as cultural right

113. Srivastava, n. 5, p. 46.

114. Veer, n. 18, p. 28.

115. See Shri Ramjanmabhoomi Mukti Yanja Samiti's Open Letter to all MPs, reproduced in *Muslim India* (58) October 1987, p. 445.

even though it involves causing affront to the sentiments of other community, while the construction of a magnificient Ram temple by demolishing the Babri Masjid is viewed by the Hindu chauvinists a the assertion of Hindu' cultural right, the existence of Babri Masjid has been described as the 'national shame' not only for Hindus but also Muslims because both Hindus and Muslims have a common cultural history and identity. By mixing the Hindu religious sentiments with their cultural rights, Hindu religion is interpreted as the quintessence to culture. Further, Hindu culture is accepted as the national culture. Lord Ram has been symbolised not only as Hindus hero[116] but also as national hero, as he is the quintessence of Indian culture and the "Muslims and other pseudo secularists must understand that Indians culture is Hindu culture and the "Sarva Dharma Samabhava" is the mark of Hinduism."[117] The Hindu Communalists argue that, the Ramjanmabhoomi is not an election issue, since the construction of Ramjanmabhoomi is a matter for millions of Hindus, the issue is concerned with the Hindus faith and the government must respect the sentiments of Hindus.[118] The Hindus want to construct the Ram temple" to revive the memory of Ram" because 'Ram' is the supreme manifestation of the divine and his birth place at "Ayodhya is the holiest of the holy."[119]

The politics of the Ayodhya dispute seeks to erase the diversities of faith and pluralities of cultural traditions and speaks the language of cultural assimilation. The movement for Ramjanmabhoomi has been interpreted as not against the Muslim community rather it is an attempt to reintegrate the Muslims into the 'mainstream' of Indian culture and 'national' identify.[120] The Indian Muslims must not identify with Babur who was an invader, rather they should accept 'Maryada Purushottam' (supreme man) Ram as the national hero since

116. See L.K. Advani's statement in *Organiser*, 12 July 1987.
117. *Organiser*, 15 October 1939.
118. *Organiser*, 8 July 1990.
119. *Organiser*, 27 August 1989 and 29 October 1989.
120. Elst, n. 70, p. v.

the Muslims in Indian are not a separate community because their ancestors are the same as of Hindus.[121] The Babri Masjid in Ayodhya is projected before us as the symbol of 'foreigners victory over Indian Hindus and Indian Muslims. Thus it is insulting both alike."[122]

The present conscious effort by the RSS and its affiliates to mobilise the entire spectrum of Hindu society on the Ram Symbol is fraught with the danger of streamrolling the plural traditions and diversities of social cultural life among the Hindus. While the Dalits in South India venerate Ravana, the Ram cult has never been accepted as the popular culture among the Hindus in regions like Orissa and Bengal. But nevertheless, the campaigners for Ram temple project Ram as the ideal man and national hero which the protagonists of Ram temple believe, would help them in their quest for achieving a homogeneous Hindu community.

The controversy over Ramjanmabhoomi plays an important role in the present search for an "imagined Hindu community".[123] The need to create the idea of a single Hindu community appears to have been a concern of more recent times which is sought to be justified by the recourse to a particular construction of history, and, now sought to be projected as a religion of this community which is in many ways a departure from the earlier religious sects.[124]

---

121. *Organiser*, 16 April 1989.

122. *Organiser*, 27 October 1989.

123. However the quest for a Hindu community is not a new political and social phenomenon, rather its root can be traced back to the pre-independence days and it received, momentum, after the partition. The concept of Hindu community was not a culturally given rather 'constructed, and 'reconstructed' from the colonial experience. See, Pandey, n. 8, pp. 259-61.

124. Romila Thapar, 'Imagined Religious Communities : Ancient History and Modern Search for a Hindu Community", *Modern Asian Studies* 23 (2), 1989, pp. 228 ff. Nirmal Mukherji and Ashis Banerjee, "Neo-Nationalism," *Seminar* No. 313 (1985), pp. 26-28 ; Rajni Kothari, "Fundamentalism is not the Essence of Hinduism, *Illustrated Weekly of India*, 7 December, p. 16.

The new Hinduism which is being currently propagated by the RSS and its affiliates in their mobilization of Hindu for the Ramjanmabhoomi temple is meant to build a uniform and homogeneous Hindu community and to redefine Hindu identity on the lines of other semitic religions. The heterogeneous and amorophous nature of Hinduism are being perceived as their sign of weakness in the face of growing assertion of India's religious minorities. The present weaknesses of Hindus would be over come when Hindus are united in a spirit of fellowship and share similar religious world views. Behind the ongoing search for a Hindu community, deeper social and political forces are at work. The concern for constructing a Hindu community comes not from the subaltern level of the society rather from the upper castes, urbanised middle classes and politically sanskritized OBCs among the Hindus. The anxiety for a Hindu identity derives its sustenance from those identity conscious Hindus who have been losing their hegemonical social status due to the growth of political consciousness, economic development and social mobility.

The contemporary search for a Hindu community purely mobilized on religion, meant for securing political power and asserting majoritarianism, marks a fundamental departure from the earlier concept of Hinduism. The term 'Hindu religion' or 'Hindu community' is alien to Hinduism because of its open and flexible nature and absence of any fundamental tenents and belifs. Its pluralities of sects and beliefs and diverse customs and social practices, its spread over diverse geographical regions, its unequal caste hierarchies and a "deepening inner awareness and commitment to compassion form the essence" of the majority community known as Hindus.[125] While the present quest for a Hindu community coined as "Syndicated Hinduism" that claims to reestablish the old spirits and ideas of Hinduism but in fact it reestablishes and consolidates its position and in the process, it destroys the diverse and open nature of Hinduism.[126]

125. Gopal ed., n. 4, p. 14.

126. Romila Thapar, "Syndicated Moksha" in *Seminar* No. 313 (1985) January, pp. 29-32.

Religious symbols and rituals and their manipulation in the political arena play an important role in constructing the imagined Hindu community. The cow protection movement in 1890's and 1910's in Northern India succeeded in forging a new unity and awareness among the Hindu upper castes, backward castes and lower castes. The mobilization around a sacred symbol (mother cow) had brought a dramatic success to the Hindu organisations trying to form an "identifiable community". The cow protection movement not only brought to diverse and antagonistic sections within Hindu society to a common platform but also forged a bridge between the urban cultures and rural ethos of social life.[127] The struggle for Ramjanmabhoomi in this process, contributes immensely as a symbolic issue which have been used as powerful emotive issue in the mobilization of Hindu community against the Muslims. The present 'liberation' movement for Ramjanmabhoomi has demonstrated its potentiality of 'attracting various Hindu groups which may have different even antagonistic interests in other fields of political and economic action."[128] The Ekatamata yanja (sacrifice for unanimity), the Ram Janaki Rath, the distribution of 'sacred water of the river Ganga' worship of bricks (Ramshila Pujan) in every village, 'Rath yatras' public display of 'Trishuls' and massive display of religiousity in

---

127. Sandria B. Freitag, "Sacred Symbol as Mobilizing Ideology : The North Indian Search for a Hindu Community" *Journal of Comparative Study of Political and History*, 22 (4), 1980, pp. 600. See for example, Clifford Geerts sees sacred symbols as possessing a unique double quality, on the one hand, they provide a representation of the way things are—a Cosmology or metaphysics. On the otherhand, they provide a representation of the way things are—a Cosmology or metaphysics. On the otherhand, they provide a guide or program for human action—on ethics or aesthetics. Thus sacred express both an 'is' and ought'. A religion consists of Cluster of such symbols that make up an ordered Whole, a Symbolic system that bestows meaning on human actions.........(Michael Banton, London : 1966)

128. Peter Vander, Veer, "God must be Liberated" A Hindu Liberation Movement in Ayodhya", *Modern Asian Studies* 21, (2), 1987, pp. 284, 304.

various transregionalized festivals like Ramnavami and, Ramlila celebrations are newly invented symbols of "Rambhakti" (devotion to Ram). Further, the invention of new ritualistic activities like the holding of periodic 'Sant Sammelans' and 'Dharma Sabhas' in the piligrimage centres like Hardwar and Allahabad synchronising their with other religious festivals like "Kumb mela" and laying the Shilanyas' for Ram temple on the day of Devo Utthan Ekadeshi (a day when Gods awake from their 9 months of sleep to undo wrongs) and taking out the Astikalash processions of the dead Kar Sevaks in the length and breadth of the country are some of the ritual symbolisms invented to not only deny the communal and anti Muslim character of the movement but also to generalise the appeal of the VHP within the Hindu society and in the process provide sanction to the VHP for furthering the cause of Ram's 'liberation.' In this whole process of mobilization around Ram and the liberation of Ramjanmabhoomi, the image of Ram has also been changed. Today's 'Maryada Purushottam" and "national hero". Ram is not the Ram of Gandhiji, Tulasi Das or Mohammad Iqbal, for whom the Ram symbolised as inter-religious harmony." Ram is being given a new face an unusual coat of war paint. The present Ram symbol is not the familiar peaceable examplar of tradition, "his bow is unstrung his right hand held up in the "nirbhaya", gesture of forgiveness, but a new commer warrior impatient to fight and punish".[129]

While these new ritual symbolisms have succeeded to a large extent mobilizing Hindus as a religious community, these symbols of mobilization can be inevitably seen as symbols of confrontation. The BJP/RSS/VHP's isolation of the Babri Masjid as the symbol of the cultural contest between the Hindus and Muslims is an essential part of its project of identifiying Hindu honour and Symbolism of Ram with Indian civilizational and cultural honour. Thus, L.K. Advani categorically asserts, "If the controversy in Ayodhya are simply one between a temple and a mosque it would not have been

129. T.N. Madan, "Rambhakti or Power Play : Politics of Hindu Fundamentalism, Times of India, 16 May 1991.

that intractable. Those campaigning for Babri Masjid should realise that they are wanting the country choose not between a Masjid but they are pitting Babur against Ram".[130] Horrific communal riots have broken out in the wake of aggressive campaign for Ramjanmabhoomi, new areas have been identifeld as communally sensitive, communal passions of the people have risen over the issue of protecting the Masjid and constructing temple. Devotion to Ram and acceptance of Ram's historicity is being regarded as synonymous with patriotism and nationalism.

The campaigners for Ramjanmabhoomi even explicitly admit the importance of Ayodhya dispute, in the resurgence of 'Hindutva' (Hinduness). Thus, K.S. Sudershan, the sahasarkaryawah of the RSS in his speech at the massive VHP rally on the 4 April 1991 observed, "The laying of bricks for the 'Shilanyas' of Ramjanmabhoomi temple was not merely a matter of temple, it was symbolically laying the foundation of the Rashtra. It was shilanyas of the manifestation of an awakened non-uniformity . . The 'Shilanyas' could be performed because Hindus are united, 'Bhagwa' (saffron flag of the VHP) was unfurled on at Ayodhya because Hindus are united. Therefore, if the Hindus unite, the coming history will be Hindu history. And coming century will also belong to the Hindus. So, move ahead with this determination."[131] The Hindu resurgence in the Ramjanmabhoomi movement also promises a new begining for the proponents of Hindutva. The shilanyas (laying the foundation stone for the Ram temple). On 9 October 1989, for the Hindu communalists has played a great role in the awakening of the Hindus. "This date is as important as the 15th August 1947. It makes a second phase, perhaps a more important phase of recent struggle for independence. ...But let Hindus remember that Ayodhya is the symbol of greater things ahead. It is neither the begining nor

---

130. L.K. Advani, *Ramjanmabhoomi* (New Delhi : BJP Publications, n. d. reproduced in Mishra and Singh eds., n. 20, pp. 136-141.

131. K.S. Sudershan, 'Historical Significance of Resurgence of Hidutva and fall of Communism", *Organiser*, 7 May 1991.

the end. The important thing is that Hindus recover their Atma sanskriti, their self identity, their confidence." (emphasis added).[132]

A recurrent theme behind the politics of Ramjanmabhoomi is that it not only speaks the language of assertion and unity of Hindus but also the language of venegeance and retribution. After centuries of foreign occupation and oppression now the time has come for the Hindus to assert themselves as the majority community in their "own country", their "fatherland". They must undo all the medieval barbarities that have been perpetrated on them. If the Muslim rulers destroyed the Hindu temples, now it is the time for the Hindus to "liberate" or "restore" these temples.... "For centuries, tells Rajmata Scindia, "the injustice to the Hindu community by Babur's hordes can not be allowed to perpetuate".[133] Further, so long as Hindu temples are remain in the hands of the progeny of Muslim invaders even after independence in 1947, India's freedom movement can not be treated completed.[134] In short, the liberation movement for the Ramjanmabhoomi seek to re-enact the politics of medievalism and undo the realities of history.

CONCLUSION

The Ramjanamabhoomi—Babri Masjid controversy at Ayodhya unfolds an interesting and complex relationship between the myth, history and politics.[135] While myths and history in their specific relationship provide sanction to the communal politics which in turn seeks its legitimacy as well as

132. Ram Swarup, "Ayodhya is a Symbol of Greater things Ahead". *Organiser*, 30 June 1991.

133. "Time for Hindus to Assert themselves as Religious Majority", *Organiser*, 6 July 1986.

134. Jay Dubashi, 'Hindus must Assert their Nationhood", *Organiser*, special issue, 26 January 1988 see also, P.C. Asdhir, "Let India be a Hindu Commonwealth'. *Organiser*, 17 May 1987 and *Organiser*, 20 July 1986 ; 25 February, 1988.

135. Neeladri Bhattacharya, n. 28, pp. 132 ff.

articulation through the mythic history. The communal historiography on Ayodha is intrinsically related to the politics of Ramjanmabhoomi because it is the kind of communal history which gives communal meaning and character to the Ayodhya controversy. In otherway, the mythic history of Ramjanmabhoomi not only provides rationale for the present communal politics but also denies its communal character.

The Babri Masjid—Ramjanmabhoomi controversy is presented before us by the self styled spokesmen of Hindus, as a struggle between 'Hindus' and 'Muslims' a historic battle between the Hindusim (sanatan Dharma) and iconoclasm Islam. Historical facts and records are twisted in careful manner and presented before the Hindu laity to convince them the barbarities and heinous crimes committed by the medieval rulers. The motive behind such a distorted interpretation of history by the Hindu communal forces, has a long term perspective. The present generation of Hindus and the posteriority would realize the dark age and evils and of medieval rule and come forward to redress the historical humiliation on Hindus. The (present liberation) movement for Ramjanmabhoomi derives its legitimacy from the mythic history which tell us the violent struggles waged by the Hindus to restore the sancitty of Ram's birthplace. "For centuries, we have been fighting for Ramjanmabhoomi. It is not a new thing of today. Not thousands, but lakhs have perished for the sake of Ramjanmabhoomi", claims Rajmata Scindia. The myth of heroic struggle is played on in the speeches and writings to convince the Hindus of the sacred nature of the struggle. The sacrifice for the sacred cause by the ancestors would oblige the Hindus of the present generation who must follow the heroic deeds of their ancestors. As the writing in the VHP showroom near the Babri Masjid and 'Shilanyas' site (the place where foundation stone for the temple has been laid) exhorts the Hindu youth—

"Beware that our Ramjanmabhoomi is not lost to us again. Arise, Accept the challenge,

Youth ! It is your turn Today ;

Wipe out these wick folk from this world, become the world conquerers".

4

The Politics of Communal Mobilization : Ayodhya Dispute and Ninth General Elections

I

The opening of the gates of the Babri Masjid had first its impact on the Faizabad-Ayodhya townships which were known for maintaining communal harmony and amity among the two Communities. The order of the District Judge and the role played by the UP government, in opening the gates of the Babri Masjid and the reaction of the Vishwa Hindu Parishad (VHP) and its affilliate, the Shri Ramjanmabhoomi Mukti Yanja Samiti, to Faizabad District Judge's order embittered the relationship of Hindus and Muslims in Faizabad and other parts of North India.[1] While the Hindu Communalists celebrated the opening of the gates of the Babri Masjid as their "victory" the Muslims in Faizabad dismayed by the sudden developments over the disputed mosque reacted in an aggressive manner under the leadership provided by various fundamentalist and communally oriented organisations like Jamait-e-Islami and Muslim Majlis-e-Mushawarat. Frequent communal riots broke out in various parts of Uttar Pradesh when Muslims came out to the streets with protest rallies and agitational measures. The day locks were removed communal riots broke out in Rudauli and in Barabanki where a victory procession of

1. S.K. Tripathi, Competition in Bigotry in, Asghar Ali Engineer edited, *Babri Masjid-Ramjanmabhoomi Controversy* (*Delhi* : Ajanta, 1990), pp. 119-23.

Hindu communalists were attacked. On February 14, black day call was given by the Muslims and communal violence broke out in many cities. On April 30, a protest rally, called by the Babri Masjid Action Committee turned into violent mob where the state police overreacted and gunned down 14 persons.[2]

As we have argued in the first chapter, the capitulation of the Rajiv Gandhi Government to the Muslim fundamentalist leaders had emboldened these forces to rake up Babri Masjid dispute as another useful strategy for their survival and consolidation of their leadership position. The victory over the Shah Bano case led, those Muslim fundamentalist and communal leaders to organise and rally round the poor and illiterate Muslim masses behind a common unifying and powerful cultural symbol—the Babri Masjid. The Muslim fundamentalist and communalist leaders sought to harp on the theme that the "de-facto" conversion of the historic Babri Masjid has given great shock to the Muslims in Indian and for all practical purposes the Indian state has been converted into a Hindu state and this transformation is underway under the facade of secularism.[3] In order to protect his socio-religious identity and "survive in a hostile environment, the Muslim India has to change his way of life, his approach to problems, his style of politics and adopt the enlture of defiant survival."[4] On 24 February 1986, Babri Masjid Action Committee was formed by those Muslim fundamentalists who led the Muslims in countrywide agitation against the Supreme Court verdict on the maintenance of a Muslim divorcee. This was followed by a countrywide mourning by the Muslims in protest against the opening of the Babri Masjid gates for the Hindus. Throughout the country, local action committees were formed by the Babri Masjid Action Committee leaders to mobilize

2. P.K. Roy, Ayodhya Dispute : Challenge to the Doves, *The Hindu*, 26 March 1986. All the reference to *The Hindu* in this *dissertation* are from the Madras edition of that paper.

3. *Muslim India*, March, 1986, p. 100.

4. *Muslim India*, April 1987. p. 147.

Muslims in a powerful way against the 'surrender' of this mosque to the Hindus by the government and to initiate agitational programmes to force the government to handover the Babri Masjid to Muslims.

Despite many suggestions and appeals from the distinguished personalities of from both communities and secular political parties on solving the sensitive Babri Masjid-Ramjanmabhoomi controversy, the Rajiv Gandhi Government at the centre and the Congress ruled government in UP, turned a blind eye to the issue as both the state and central government neither have shown their sincerity in expeditions the judicial wrangles nor initiated any move to involve the disputant parties to solve the dispute, through a mutually acceptable formula. The subsequent effect has been the enhancement of the credibility of Muslim and Hindu fundamentalist leaders among their communities and sharpening of their aggressive and mutually antagonistic posture over the Ramjanmabhoomi-Babri Masjid dispute.[5]

On 22 December 1986, the All India Babri Masjid Conference in its declaration reaffirmed its commitment to free the Babri Masjid through a democratic and peaceful movement and gave a call to the Muslim, not to participate or associate with the observance of the Republic Day, except those on public duty, and called upon observance of bandh on 1 February 1987 and mass rally in Delhi on 30 March 1987 to be followed by a march to Ayodhya and pressing for a settlement through dialogue, negotiation, arbitration[6] or adjudication. The call to Muslims to dissociate from the Republic Day ceremony was given in protest against the indifference of the government to solve the Babri Masjid controversy and its failure to "defend the rule of law and constitution". Despite frequent clarifications by Sayed Shahabuddin, the moving spirit behind the boycott call, that the non-participation of 'Muslim Indians' is

5. Nikhil Chakravorty, 'The Wages of nation', *Times of India*, 11 January, 1987. All the references to the *The Time of India* this *dissertation* are from the New Delhi edition of that paper.

6. *Muslim India*, February, 1987, p. 517.

different from boycott and obstruction and that the decision has been taken collectively by the committee out of the growing sense of frustrations and insecurity of Muslims to their life and property over the Babri Masjid dispute,[7] the call was reacted negatively from various quarters.

The boycott call was strongly condemned by all the political parties and the Muslim MPs strongly denounced the obstinancy of the Babri Masjid Movement Coordination Committee (BMMCC) on the boycott call. Interestingly, except the All India Muslim Majlis-e-Mushawarat headed by Sayed Shahabuddin, no Muslim organisation endorsed the call and prominent citizens belonging to Muslim community vociferously opposed the boycott call. Amidst mounting condemnation, the Babri Masjid Action Committee (BMAC) finally decided to withdraw its proposed boycott call but it went ahead with its plan to organise the nationwide 'bandh' on 1 February 1987 (the day on which the Babri Masjid gates were thrown open in 1986), to protest against the government's inaction on the Babri Masjid-Ramjanmabhoomi dispute but the 'bandh' call evoked mixed response throughout the country.

Though the boycott call was withdrawn, the aggressive posture by the Muslim leaders brought the dispute to the political arena and aroused stong communal passions among the middle class educated Hindus who perceived the call as an attempt by the Muslim leaders to promote separatism among the Muslims in the name of restoring a dilapidated mosque.[8]

Communal tension built up following the BMMCC's call to Muslims for a 'March' to Delhi for a demonstration before Parliament on 30 March to demand the return of the Babri Masjid. The RSS and VHP as a counter move to the former started preparation for 'UP Bandh' on 29 March to "protest against the communal hatred being preached by the Muslims" in the name of the Babri Masjid and demand the transfer of Ayodhya shrine to the Ramjanmabhoomi Trust which planned

7. *Muslim India*, March, p. 106.
8. *Indian Express*, 25 January 1987 and 2 February 1987.

to construct a temple complex at the cost of 25 crores rupees.[9] The RSS and VHP also engaged in mobilizing the Hindus for participation in their Ayodhya Chalo (March to Ayodhya) programme on 5 April where they would renew their pledge to 'liberate' the supposed Ramjanmabhoomi and resist any move to turn the mosque into a national monument.[10]

The rally of Muslims in Delhi was unprecedented in Independent India's political history[11] as for the first time Muslims turned up in lakhs on the call of fundamentalist leaders. Shahi Imam of Jamma Masjid, Sayed Abdullah and many other Muslim leaders delivered very objectionable and inflammable speeches. The rally was communally charged which could be seen from the tenor of speeches and response of the Muslims to the rally. A memorandum to the Lok Sabha Speaker was adopted in the rally which read : "The rally regards the Babri Masjid as a national heritage and as historic monument but above all as place of Islamic worship whose sanctity must be universally respected by all right minded persons, whatever their religion and whose violation should be regarded not only as an offence to the religious sentiments of the Muslims but also the secular order......The rally reiterates the determination and resolve of Muslims of India to regain their Masjid, howsoever long and hard the struggle may be."[12]

The by and large peaceful 'bandh' organised by the Ramjanmabhoomi Mukti Yanja Samiti throughout Uttar Pradesh on 29 March and on 30 March, the Muslim rally in the capital served to underline the deepening crisis and communal feelings of Muslims over the Ramjanmabhoomi-Babri Masjid controversy. Both the agitations had displayed a tinge of fantasy as Hindus without any historical certainity of Ram's supposed birth place but made to perceive the controversy as a 'symbol'

---

9. *Hindustan Times*, 13 March 1987. All references to *The Hindustan Times* in this *dissertation* are from the New Delhi edition of that paper.

10. *Indian Express*, 22 March 1987.

11. *Times of India*, 31 March 1987.

12. *Muslim India*, May, 1987, pp. 195-05.

of the perpetuation of alien precepts, while for the so called custodians of Muslim interests, the crumbling Babri-Masjid symbolised a grim battle to preserve their religious freedom and indentity. The success of the rally highlighted the growing resentment among the Muslims over the vexed problem and a growth of new form of assertiveness among them. The BJP which had so far not taken any concrete position with regard to the Ramjanmabhoomi issue, moved by the unprecedented Muslims' response, reacted by calling the rally as "an unabashed attempt to intimidate the nation by threats of violence. For the generation that has gone through the trauma of partition and the bloodbath that accompanied it, yesterday's speeches had sinister and ominous ring."[13]

The VHP responded to the 30 March rally of Muslims by organising a mammoth rally of Hindus on 5 April on the bank of the Sarayu river in Ayodhya and took a pledge not to let the birth place of Lord Ram be used as a mosque.[14] Later, thousands of Hindus participated in a massive Rathyatra and rally on the occassion on Ramnavami festival in North Delhi organised by the Vishwa Hindu Parishad and its affiliates to strike a show of solidarity for "securing the freedom of Ramjanmabhoomi". The rally concluded with an oath of affirmation by the participants which said : "we affirm an oath and vow of Lord Ram that we would build a temple on the Bhoomi."[15] The vicious communal mobilization by the communalists of the two communities had fouled up Hindu-Muslim relations in the Meerut city of Western Uttar Pradesh and resulted in serious communal riots in the city in April 1987. The proliferation of militant lumpen youth organisations like the Bajrang Dal, Shiva Shakti Dal, Adam Sena, Ali Sena, also played active role in killings, lootings and arson of property that went on for several days despite heavy presence of the security forces. The Provincial Armed constabulary not only watched the occurrence of the riots but also joined with the

13. *Hindustan Times*, 1 April 1987.

14. See, *Hindustan Times* and *Indian Express*, 6 April 1987.

15. *Hindustan Times*, 8 April 1987.

murderers in looting and killings of innocent Muslims as the massacre in Maliana serves as grim reminder of police brutalities. The communal holocaust in Meerut which subsequently spread to Modinagar, Muzaffarnagar, Hapur and Delhi, served a grim warning to the state that it may overwhelm on the wake of nationwide mobilization of Hindu and Muslim Communal forces on Ramjanmabhoomi-Babri Masjid dispute.[16]

On 24 January 1988 the Babri Masjid Movement Coordination Committee (BMMCC) decided to give a call to all Muslims and secular forces for a 'march' to Ayodhya on 12 and 14 october, on the ground that negotiated settlement of the Ayodhya dispute has failed to achieve any result and despite many appeals and petitions to the government by the Muslims the government ignored their problem. Commenting on the proposed "Ayodhya March" Sayed Shahabuddin, chairman of the Babri Masjid Movement Coordination Committee and the All India Muslim Majlis-e-Mushawarat and the Janata Party M.P. wrote, "The Ayodhya March does not imply violence. It is a quest for truth, campaign for righteousness, as an assertion of freedom, a test of fundamental Rights and of human rights...The Babri Masjid movement has enabled the Muslim Indian to maintain his dignity, to hold his head high. He has not surrendered to the forces of violence fanaticism and chauvinism."[17]

The success of the Boat Club rally convinced the campaigners for the Babri Masjid that more confrontationist and strident posture on the Babri Masjid would force the government to intervene in the Babri Masjid dispute and hand over the Masjid to Muslims. So, the call to the Muslims for a "march to Ayodhya" in large numbers and offer namaz (Prayer) in the disputed Babri Masjid complex came closely after the

16. M.J. Akbar, 'Meerut's Politics of Communalism' in his *Riot after Riot* (New Delhi : Penguin, 1988), pp. 153. ff.

17. Sayed Shahabuddin, "Ayodhya March : Are Muslims Fighting Fascism", *The Statesman*, 12 May 1988. All the reference to *The Statesman* in the *dissertation* are from the New Delhi edition of that paper.

good response to Muslims to the rally. But the Hindu Communalists saw the "Ayodhya march" call as a clever strategy to undo the Faizabad District Court's order of 1 February 1986 on the Babri Masjid. On 4 July, the Ramjanmabhoomi Mukti Sangharsha Samiti at its emergency meeting in Hardwar decided to prevent the proposed march of the Muslims to Ayodhya and offer prayer at the Babri Masjid. The Meeting held the view that the proposed march on 14 october and 12 as "a direct attack on Hindu Samaj" and decided to observe 9 August as Ramjanmabhoomi Mandir Raksha Diwas (save the Ramjanmabhoomi temple day) throughout the Uttar Pradesh to coincide with the date on which the Quit India movement was launched, so as to give 'nationalist' colour to the 'liberation' movement for Ramjanmabhoomi.[18]

Despite the fatwa issued by the renowned Islamic centre of learning, Darul Uloom, Deoband, in declaring the 'Ayodhya March' as unislamic as it would foment communal trouble and violence, the BMMCC later in its Lucknow meeting on 24 July rejected the fatwa issued by the ulemas and decided to go ahead with its proposed march to Ayodhya on October 12 and 14. It clarified that their march call as, "the undiputed established right of the Muslims to offer prayers in the mosque." The Bajrang Dal (The militant wing of lumpen youths formed by the VHP and RSS with a professed aim of 'liberating' the supposed birthplace of Lord Ram and other Hindu places of worship) in order to counter the move of the Muslim leaders' March plan to Ayodhya announced to storm into the Jamma Masjid in Delhi and offer Hanuman chalisa inside the mosque.[19] Alarmed by the threat to March to Ayodhya and the counter March (to Ayodhya by the BMAC, the VHP and Bajrang Dal and imminent threat to communal harmony, the Central government expressed its willingness to mediated between the disputant parties and invited both the Babri Masjid Action Committee and Ramjanmabhoomi Sangharsha Samiti for a dialogue to solve the dispute. On 8 August, the Babri Masjid

18. *Times of India*, 6 July 1988.

19. *Patriot* (New Delhi), 9 July 1988.

coordination committee decided to postpone its call for "Ayodhya March" by four weeks as a gesture of goodwill and as a part of the initiative taken by the Union Home Minister for solving the dispute through negotiation.[20]

The Union Home Minister Buta Singh having succeeded in pursuading the Babri Masjid movement leaders to postpone their 'Ayodhya March' plan, initiated a series of negotiations with the leaders belonging to Hindu and Muslim organisations including the Muslim MPs in the Congress (I) to evolve a "consensual" approach to solve the Babri Masjid dispute.[21] Later, the Shri Ramjanmabhoomi Mukti Yanja Samiti delegation met the Union Home Minister and demanded in its memorandum to the government the handing over the disputed mosque to Hindus without delay and further urged the government to respect the 'sentiments' of the majority community and allow the samiti to construct a magnificient temple. The memorandum further clarified that the question of handing over the mosque to the Hindus is not negotiable.[22] The Union Home Ministry failed to bring the two rival parties to a tripartite talk since the two contending parties took rigid and confrontationist posture and "no meeting grounds" could be evolved. The Vishwa Hindu Parishad as per its earlier decision ruled out further talks with the Muslims and started preparation for 'forcibly prevent' the proposed 'Ayodhya March' call given by the Babri Masjid Action Committee leaders.[23]

After the failure to hold a tripartite tale the central government again renewed its effort to bring a mutually negotiated settlement plan to the contentious Babri Masjid dispute while the BMMCC leaders engaged in organising their rescheduled 'Ayodhya March' on 12 and 14 October. The Babri Masjid movement leaders also urged the government to refer the dispute to a special three member sitting judge of the Allahabad High Court for the expeditious settlement since no common

20. *Times of India*, 6 August 1988 and 9 August 1988.
21. *Times of India*, 1 September 1988.
22. *Patriot*, 2 September 1988.
23. *Indian Express*, 21 September 1988.

grounds could be evolved for holding a negotiation.[24] But due to the intervention by the UP Chief Minister N.D. Tiwari and Union Home Minister Buta Singh and their assurance to activate the judicial process for the speedy settlement of the cases relating to the title over the disputed mosque, the BMMCC chairman Sayed Shahabuddin called off their rescheduled 'Ayodhya March' plan.[25] The Babri Masjid movement received a set back following a split in the Committee over the postponement of March call to Ayodhya by Shahabuddin.[26] The split only highlighted the bane of Muslim leadership in India. The clash of ego among the Muslim leaders over the issue of taking leadership on the Babri Masjid-Ramjanmabhoomi controversy arose because it would provide wider acceptability to them among their community members. The 'Ayodhya March' threat and its subsequent withdrawal by the lovers of the Babri Masjid indicated that they used it as a gambit to pressurise the government to give in their demands.

Serious communal riots broke out in Aligarh, Muzaffarnagar and Khatauli due to the 'bandh' call given by the VHP and

24. *Patriot* (New Delhi), 6 October 1988.

25. *Indian Express*, 9 October 1988, *Times of India*, 13 October 1988.

26. The postponement of 'Ayodhya March' for the second time by the BMMCC chairman Sayed Shahabuddin created dissidence in the committee. The hardliners in the committee like Shah Imam Syed Abdullah Bukhari, Zafarayab Jillani, Azam Khan, Sultan Salauddin owaissi and Maulana Muzaffar Hussain Kichhauchavi came out from the BMMCC and continued their association with the BMAC. The BMMCC formally split on 26 November 1988 when the hardcores of the committee led by Imam Bukhari hold an all India 'conference of political and Muslim leaders defying the directive issued by chairman of the BMMCC. The meeting was successful as it was attended by five members out of the 10 members in the BMMCC and a host of opposition party leaders. The splinter group also decided to form AIBMC (All India Babri Masjid Action Committe) to spearhead agitation including a March to Ayodhya. See *Hindustan Times*, 27 November 1988; *Times of India*, 28 November 1988 and 13 Ooctober 1988.

Bajrang Dal and the "Ayodhya March" call given by the Babri Masjid Action Committee leaders. The threats to March to Ayodhya and offer prayers in the Babri Masjid by the Muslims and the determination of the VHP and its affiliates to prevent the Muslims proceeding to railway station for taking trains to Ayodhya had aggravated communal feelings of the two communities in Uttar Pradesh. The communal riots in Muzaffarnagar, Aligarh and Khatauli in october 1989 are the offshoot of the intensive communal mobilization by the Hindu and Muslim communal forces and the political calculation of the Congress party.[27]

The VHP took an important decision to hold three day religious conference in Allahabad to approve its earlier decision to lay the foundation stone at the Ramjanmabhoomi which threatened the prospect of arriving an amicable settlement to the dispute.[28] On 27 January 1989, third religious conference of the VHP opened for three days at Allahabad to coincide with the 'Kumbh mela' there. The 'Kumbh mela' was successfully turned into a rabidly communal platform by the VHP, Bajrang Dal and RSS to whip up the communal passions of pious Hindus about the retrieval of Ramjanmabhoomi in Ayodhya. The 'Kumbh mela' of 1989 therefore assumed more political than religious significance. On the third day of the conference a resolution was passed for the 'liberation' of Ramjanmabhoomi and the resolution was moved by the Adi Sankaracharya of Kanchi Kamkoti Puram Swami Jayaendra Saraswati from South India and supported by the famed Deora Baba of Vrindaban. The appeal of the two revered figures from North and South India made the proposal acceptable to the large gatherings of Hindus. In the conference it was decided that Hindus would not abide by the court verdict or any executive decision on the Babri Masjid dispute and to initiate a sustained campaign which would culminate in the

27. Asghar Ali Engineer and K.S. Durani, 'Communal Riots in Muzaffarnagar, Khatauli and Aligarh, *EPW*, 7 January 1989, pp 22-24.

28. The *Statesman*, 2 March 1989.

laying of 'Shilanyas' (foundation stone) of the Ramjanmabhoomi temple in Ayodhya on 9 November 1989. For the construction of Ram temple it was also planned to bring "Ramshilas" (bricks consecrated in the name of Lord Ram) from every village of India and collect funds from Hindus for the construction of temple.

In that conference, the VHP demonstrated its remarkable strategy of mobilizing diverse sections of Hindu Society for the cause of Ram temple construction : "There are six lakh village and 80 crores of Hindus. If every villages donates one brick and every Hindu devotee donates just one rupee the battle for Ramjanmabhhoomi will be half over. This programme has to be taken from village to village."[29]

The last meeting between the rival parties, was held on 28 December 1988 but it was boycotted by the VHP in protest against the matter being handed over to the courts. At that meeting the Home Minister had assured the AIBMAC leaders of the Central government's willingness to go in for a judicial settlement.[30] It was clear that when both the central and state governments failed to bring the two parties to a negotiated settlement the centre was left with no option but to move to the High Court for its settlement. But both the governments were not interested to act on their own to settle the communally explosive Ayodhya issue as the ruling Congress party was well aware of its repurcussions on the next elections. The Lucknow Bench of Allahabad High Court admitted the transfer application of the state government and summoned five suits relating to the disputed mosque. The government had to move for the transfer of these cases as per the assurance given by the

29. Bharati Sadasivam, "A Communal Time Bomb" in Engineer, n. 1. p. 136. See also, "Communal contagion at the kumbh", *Link*, 19 February 1989, pp. 4-8. Since the decision taken at the Kumbh mela for the construction of Ram temple the VHP and RSS have been holding Virat Hindu Sammelans in various parts of the country with the construction of Ramjanmabhoomi temple by demolishing the Babri Masjid as the chief objective. *Blitz* (Bombay). 27 May, 1989.

30. *The Telegraph* (Calcutta), 30 April 1989.

Government of India to the AIBMAC and demands from the opposition leaders for speedy disposal of these cases as the cases as the scope for negotiated settlement of the dispute become impossible due to the rejection from the VHP. On 14 August 1989 five cases relating to Babri Masjid were clubbed together and the High court gave an interim in order to maintain the *status quo* of the nature of property in question.[31]

Earlier the Bharatiya Janata Party (BJP) in its national executive committee meeting in Palampur (Himachal Pradesh) adopted a very crucial resolution of much political significance. The meeting was significant on the ground that the BJP despite its pro-VHP posture on Ayodhya dispute had retrained from taking any clear stand on the Ayodhya controversy. The Palampur resolution of the party clearly enunciated the BJP's stand which was in line with the stand taken by the RSS and VHP. The resolution reads—"The BJP holds that the nature of this controversy is such that it just can not be sorted out by a court of law. A court of law... can not adjudicate as to whether Babar did actually invade Ayodhya, destroyed a temple and built a mosque in its place. Even where a court does not pronounce on such facts it can not suggest remedies to undo the vandalism of history[32] (emphasis added)." It further reads :

"The BJP calls upon the Rajiv Government to adopt the same positive approach in respect of Ayodhya that the Nehru Government did, with regard to Somnath. The sentiments of people must be respected and the Ramjanmasthan be handed over to Hindus, if possible through a negotiated settlement or else by legislation. Litigation is certainly not the answer."[33] (emphasis added). Since the adoption of the BJP's resolution on Ramjanmabhoomi at Palampur the party has been con-

31. *Hindustan Times*, 13 July 1989 ; *India Today*, 15 December 1989. p. 156.

32. See, Report on Bharatiya Janata Party's National Executive Meeting, June 9-11, 1989, Palampur (H.P.), pp 15-17.

33. *Ibid.*, p. 17.

sistently maintaining its position at all levels and forums and has been accusing all other parties for "betraying the sentiments of majority community "and pursuring the policy of minority appeasement' on the Ayodhya dispute and thus reduced secularism into "an allergy, of Hindulism". The BJP's stand on Ramjanmabhoomi-Babri Masjid dispute is clearly opposite to the stands taken by other centrist and lest parties. In contrast to other issue like the demand for abrogation of Article 370 of the constitution and Minority Commission, the BJP's stand on the Ayodhya dispute and identifying it with the issues of pseudo-secularism, nationalism and national unity, is the single most important cause of the party's uneasy relationship with other parties.

On the otherhand, both the BMMCC and the AIBMAC responding to the demands from the RSS, VHP and BJP and some otner quarters to transfer or shift the Babri Masjid physically to some other place, made it clear that they would oppose any move to shift the Babri Masjid to another place since according to Islam, once a site on which a mosque consecrated and has sanctity in Islam can not be shifted away in any circumstances. The BMMCC resolution says, "It is not the question of the structure of the mosque rather the site on which the mosque stands that is important."[34] The aggressive communal mobilization by the VHP, RSS, Bajrang Dal and BJP combine had resulted in widespread communal riots and tension in North and Western India which created a sense of insecurity among the Muslims and the of Babri Masjid movement leaders failed to rally round the Muslims at par with the VHP. On the otherhand the VHP organised an impressive "Virat Hindu Sammelan" to mark the conclusion of the its five day long "Indraprastha Dharma Yatra" in Delhi.[35] The main purpose of this programme was to create mass awareness

34. *Hindustan Times*, 7 September 1989. See also, "The place of a mosque Per Se has a Sanctity in Islam" Shahi Imam in *Radiance* "Babri Masjid Special", 25 November—1 December 1990, p. 15.

35. *National Herald*, 23 July 1989.

about Ramjanmabhoomi movement and build up pressure on the government to succumb to the VHP's demands.

In accordance with the decision taken by the VHP sponsored third religious conference in Allahabad, the VHP with the help of RSS, Bajrang Dal and BJP started "Shilapoojan Samaroh" (consecration bricks ceremony) from 30 September in 5.75 lakh villages in India for the proposed Ram temple construction at the place called Ramjanmabhoomi. "Sanctified bricks" were taken out in colourful processions from villages and were carried by the volunteers to Ayodhya. Each Hindu family was asked to contribute a nominal Rs. 1.25 paisa for the construction of the temple. While the VHP and its saffron allies organised massive mobilization of Hindus across the country and aroused their communal passions through holding the "Shilapooja" ceremonies and collection of funds for Ram temple, the AIBMAC threatened to organise "hifazati Dastas" (defence squads) to resist the "Shilapoojan" programmes.[36]

Shortly before the announcement of the Ninth General Elections, the BJP in its national council meeting at Bombay adopted a far more strident stand on the Ramjanmabhoomi issue. It decided to extend open support to the VHP's 'Ramshila' campaign. The party leader L.K. Advani clarified that the BJP would desist from making Ayodhya an election issue if the Congress and left parties criticise the BJP for supporting the VHP's movement for Ram temple in Ayodhya. The BJP leader asserted that since there are supporters of Ramjanmabhoomi within the Congress (I), the JD and the TDP, 'the BJP does not want to confine the movement to itself by electioneering on the issue.[37] Later it was reported in the organiser quoting L.K. Advani that, "BJP will not be a party

---

36. *Times of India*, 4 August 1989, *Hindustan Times*, 15 Septmber 1989.

37. *The Statesman* (New Delhi), 26 September 1989. All the references to *The Statesman* in this dissertation are from the New Delhi edition of that paper.

to the division of the country on this issue though it would not adopt an apologetic stand on it either."[38]

Following the crucial talks held between the VHP leaders and the central and state governments on 27 September 1989 at Lucknow where in an agreement was reached about the VHP's Shilapoojan programmes and carrying up the consecrated bricks to Ayodhya for laying the foundation stone of the Ram temple on 9 November 1989, an inevitable confrontation between the VHP/RSS/BJP/Bajrang Dal combine and the central and state governments was avoided. According to the agreement, the VHP would abide by the High Court order of 14 August 1989 and ensure that peace and communal harmony are maintained and the government would provide cooperation and protection to the Ram Shila processions carrying sanctified bricks to Ayodhya. In its memorandum to the Home Minister, the VHP demanded that the dispute can not be solved by the courts since last four centuries Hindus have been treating the site as the hollowed spot.[39] The VHP memorandum also made clear its opposition to any move to divide the Janambhoomi area between the Hindus and Muslims or declaring the Babri Masjid as national monument.[40] While the VHP leaders turned down the Union Home Minister's plea to shift the site of their proposed foundation laying ceremony on 9 November 1989 or abandon the programme altogether till the dispute is solved by the High Court, the Home Minister misled the country by saying that both the sides had agreed to abide by the High court decision and "they had no objection if the temple was constructed outside the boundary of the disputed place of worship.[41] On the otherhand, Mr. Ashok Singhal Secretary

38. See, "BJP will not make Ayodhya a poll issue", *Organiser*, 1 October, 1989, p. 15.

39. *The Hindu*, 29 September 1989. See also, the Text of the agreement between the VHP and UP state Government in *Radiance* (New Delhi,) 25 November—1 December, 1990, p. 33.

40. Report on Shri Ramjanmabhoomi, presented by Shri Ashok Singhal, Secretary General (VHP Publications, n. d.), p. 10.

41. *Indian Express*, 3 October 1989.

General of the VHP asserted in his press conference that there had been no agreement to abide by the court verdict and accused the government creating confusion on the score.[42]

The Vishwa Hindu Parishad's sponsored "Shilapoojan" programme generated unprecedented public support from the broad sections of Hindus and become instrumental in unleashing the communal frenzy among the Hindus. Serious communal violence also broke out in various part of the country in the wake of 'Ramshila' processions particularly in UP, Bihar, Gujrat, Madhya Pradesh, Rajasthan, and Karnataka. The Chief Ministers of Madhya Pradesh and Rajasthan publicly admitted that taking out 'Ramshila' processions in the communally sensitive areas and raising of provocative slogans in the procession were mainly responsible for communal riots in their states and charged the BJP and its allies for instigating riots in their states for narrow political purpose.[43] In Bhagalpur, horrific communal riots broke out over the Ramshila processions and subsequently it also spread to rural areas in which nearly a thousand people were killed in the prolonged riots. The Ramshila procession was just the "spark necessary to ignite" the smouldering communal and political rivalry in Bhagalpur.[44] Communal riots in three Madhya Pradesh towns of Ratlam, Mhow and Khargone was the direct offshoot of Ramshila processions which were mechanised to invite confrontations between the Hindus and Muslims which could be exploited politically in the election year. The Ramshila processions provided immediate contexts to the outbreak of Communal riots in many parts of the Northern and Western India because the Mandir-Masjid dispute in Ayodhya had been projected by both Hindu and Muslim communalists in their

42. *News Time* (Hyderabad), 6 October 1989.

43. *Hindustan Times*, 8 October 1989, *Times of India*, 7 October 1989.

44. Asghar Ali Engineer, "Grim Tragedy of Bhagalpur riots", *EPW*, 10 February, 1990, p, 305 ; Bharat Dogra, Bhagalpur : Communal Riots spreads to village, *EPW*, 24 January, 1990, p. 145.

sustained mobilization, as one which involves the religious sentiments and identities of the two communities.[45] Through Ramshila Poojan ceremony and the massive fund collection drive the BJP, RSS and VHP had evolved a well thought out strategy to ruralise the cause of Ram temple that would help them in achieving "Hindu consolidation" and ultimately the development of Hindu vote bank for the Ninth General Elections. Unlike in the past where the BJP workers were not participating actively in the activities of the RSS but in the Ramshila pooja ceremony and Ramshila processions the distinctions between the RSS and BJP had vanished. Powerful and emotive slogans like Saugandh Ram Ki khate hein/Hum Mandir Wahin Banayenge (we swear by Ram that is where we will build the temple). Bachha Bachha Ram Ka, Janambhoomi Ka Kamka (every child of Ram will work for the Ram temple) Chate Pant anek Hain/Hindu Hum Sub Ek Hain (The Sects are many, but Hindus are one) were given on the way of Ramshila processions to arouse the religious fervour of Hindus[46] around the Ram symbol and demonstrate the killing determination of attaining the noble aim of constructing a temple dedicated in the name of Lord Ram in place of a mosque despite of all the odds, and to the frighten away the Muslims. In September-October alone 55 communal riots had taken place in different parts of the country all in connections with the Ramshila processions.[47]

The National Front leaders met the BJP leaders and pursuaded them to call off the Ramshila processions in view of the deteriorating communal situation in the countryside but failed in their attempt. On the otherhand, the President of the Shri Ramjanmabhoomi Mukti Yanja Samiti met the National Front leaders and conveyed the VHP's firm decision the go ahead with the Shilapoojan aud Shilanyas programmes.[48] In Parliament, Minister of State for Home, Mr. P. Chidambaram

---

45. *EPW*, 18 November 1989, p. 2520.

46. *Indian Express*, 11 October 1989.

47. *EPW*, 18 November 1989. p. 25-30.

48. See, the VHP's Report, n. 40. p. 7.

announced the 'government's determination to uphold the 14 August order of the High Court and not to allow any attempt to 'alternate' the disputed structure and property go by the name Babri Masjid.[49] But the VHP's firm determination to go ahead with the Shilanyas programme on the eve of Ninth General Elections had forced the government to captulate to the pressure of Hindu fundamentalists. Union Home Minister Buta Singh approached to Deora Baba and requested him to cancel the Shilanyas programme. The famed Baba who had blessed the VHP's Ramjanmabhoomi temple construction plan in the 'Kumbh' festival in Allahabad took the decision that Shilanyas must be held as scheduled after consulting with the VHP leaders.[50] On 19 October 1989 at a press conference in Ayodhya, Mahant Avaidyanath of Shri Ramjanmabhoomi Mukti Yanja Samiti announced the VHP's decision to call off its proposed Ayodhya March on 9 November. But reiterated its determination to go ahead with the Shilanyas programme.[51] The VHP's sudden decision to call off its 'Ayodhya March' programme was based on the political and electoral compulsion of the BJP since the Janata Dal had threatened the BJP of snapping its poll alliance in case the November 9 Ayodhya March programme of the VHP was not cancelled. So, the VHP and BJP leaders had to work out a face saving formula as the latter could not afford to defeat the Congress (I) without an alliance with the Janata Dal.

As per the agreement with the VHP by the Central and state government in September, about 1.5 lakh of consecrated Ramshila arrived in Ayodhya on the first week of November which strengthened the VHP's bargaining power. The Vishwa Hindu Parishad threatened of mass Satyagraha in Ayodhya and other parts of the country if there is any obstruction put to its foundation stone laying ceremony by the government in Ayodhya.[52] Earlier the Sunni Wakf Board in its 1961 suit

49. *Times of India*, 13 October 1989.

50. See, the VHP's Report, n. 40. p. 12.

51. *Times of India*, 20 October 1989.

52. *The Telegraph* (Calcutta), 4 November 1989.

before the Civil court of Faizabad District had claimed 23 plots adjoining the Babri Masjid but did not mention plot no. 578 which is in the same area. The Uttar Pradesh government requested the VHP to lay shilanyas on plot no. 578 which the VHP agreed to put backtracked later no. The VHP on 2 November, with the help of its "learned pundits and persons of Ayodhya" fixed the exact spot where the Shilanyas should take place and decided to conduct Shilanyas from a distance of 192 feet from the eastern side of the Babri Masjid. On that day, the Bajrang Dal activists hoisted a safforn flag in plot no. 586 where they intended to lay the foundation stone of their proposed Ram temple.[53]

The Vishwa Hindu Parishad went ahead with its elaborate preparations at Ayodhya for laying the foundation of the proposed Ram temple at the place earmarked by it earlier and the stage was set for a confrontation untill the state government and Central government relented from their earlier decision not to allow the Shilanyas ceremony at the disputed place. The VHP leader S.C. Dixit declared, "We can have the foundation laying ceremony anywhere but neither the dimensions of the temple nor its sanctum sanctorum of the temple (which would be build on the very heart of Babri-Masjid which stands today) would be altered which would be the same where the idols of Lord Ram present inside the mosque.[54] On 6 November the state government moved to the High court for seeking a "clarification" on the matter whether plot No. 586 where the Bajrang Dal hoisted a flag was disputed or not. But the state government pleaded before the High court that plot no. 586 is a disputed area as it included in 23 plots claimed by the Sunni Wakf Board. The court on 7 November 1989 clarified that the piece of land which was barricaded for the foundation laying of a Ram temple is a "land of dispute" and directed that the *status quo* of the disputed place should be maintained and the parties should not be allowed to disturb the *status quo*. The court ruled that, "the order of August 1989 was in respect of the entire

53. *India Today*, 15 Decembor 1989; VHP's Report, n. 40, p. 15.

54. *Indian Bxpress* and *The Hindu*, 7 November 1989.

property mentioned in the suit including plot. No. 586 in so far included within the boundary described as in the site plan."[55] On the same day, Prime Minister Rajiv Gandhi, Union Home Minister and Chief Minister of Uttar Pradesh met Deora Baba and prayed him to get the Shilanyas site changed. The Deora Baba having consulted with the VHP leader on 7 November decided that the Shilanyas should be held at the same place where the saffron flag had been hoisted by the Bajrang Dal.[56] The Court's clarification had put the state government in a dilemma. The court had left it to the state government to find out whether the site earmarked by the VHP for Shilanyas falls exactly within the disputed land or not. The court's clarification left the decision of allowing the Shilanyas to the state government. While the VHP had already identified the Shilanyas site from the disputed plots, the government tried to wriggle out through finding a lacunae in the Suni Wakf Board's petition. The state Advocate General interpreted that plot no. 586 was of two parts disputed and undisputed. The later part was the site where the Bajrang Dal had hoisted a flag.[57]

The swift move by the government to allow the VHP to conduct Shilanyas ceremony was surprising as the day before the government had argued before the high Court that plot No. 586 was included in the 23 plots of disputed land and hoisting of saffron flag in the said plot was "in clear violation of court's interim order dated 14 August 1989." The government clearly took a very ambivalent stand with regard to the nature of disputed property as it was vary of antagonising Hindus on the election eve and decided not to question the Vishwa Hindu Parishad for backtracking from its agreement with the government. The state government avoided taking tough posture against the combine assault of the BJP-VHP-RSS-Bajrang Dal

55. *Times of India*, and *The Hindu*, 8 November 1989.

56. A. G. Noorani, "Congress Agreed to Ramshilanyas" in Engineer. ed., n. 1, p. 152. See also, The VHP's Report, n. 40 p. 156.

57. *India Today*, 15 December 1989, p. 156.

and Shiva Sena and ultimately appeased the Hindu bigots in allowing them to hold Shilanyas ceremony in the disputed site and at the sametime the government sought to hoodwink the Muslims by maintaining that it was is committed to maintain the *status quo*.

On the day before the scheduled Shilanyas was to take place Buta Singh rushed to Lucknow and hold discussions with the VHP leaders. The VHP leaders after their meeting with the Union Home Minister reaffirmed their scheduled programme for Shilanyas ceremony. The Home Ministry issued a press release which claimed that the VHP was agreed to comply with the clarificatory order of the High Court while executing its Shilanyas programme and would extend full cooperation to the government.[58] The Shilanyas ceremony began on 9 November at 9.30 a.m. and the Bhoomi Poojan (land worship) at 10.02 a.m. amidst tight security. Shortly afterwards, Mahant Avaidyanath, President of the Shri Ramjanmabhoomi Mukti Yanja Samiti declared that this amounted to the laying the foundation of a "unified Hindu Society". On the other hand the VHP Secretary General commented, "This was an unparalleled achievement in the fulfilment of cherished expectations of Hindu Samaj.[59] On 11 November morning when thousands of sadhus and Ram Bhaktas (devotees of Ram) marched to Babri Masjid to dig up earth for the construction of the temple it was announced by the VHP leaders that the 'Kar Seva' (Voluntary labour) work had been postponed to a latter date. S. C Dixit, the VHP leader told: "We realise it is not going to be easy to begin the construetion, that is why we need to perpare for it. And we want to give the government and the courts sometime to perpare the way for us."[60]

The smooth manner in which the VHP could undertake its programme confirmed the secret political deals with the government. The government sabotaged the judicial settlement and

---

58. A.G. Noorani, n. 54, p. 153.

59. *Times of India*, 10 November 1989. See also, the VHP's Report on Ramjanmabhoomi, n. 40. p. 18.

60. *Indian Express* and *Hindustan Times*, 12 November 1989.

virtually ignored the court's injunction and set motion to a process which would exacerbate the communal situation apart from making the site where the foundation stone was laid the focal point of permanent Hindu-Muslim tension. The sudden decision of the VHP to put off its temple construction plan definitely suggest the secret deal between the Union and state governments and the VHP about the Shilanyas programme. The government desired the VHP to lay the Shilanyas for Ramjanmabhoomi temple during the election compaign which could be used for securing Hindu as well as Muslim votes.

The Congress (I) leaders wanted to garner Hindu votes without coming under the pressure of the VHP. They used Deora Baba as a via-media for the purpose. Buta Singh met Deora Baba on 17 October and on the sameday evening dates for the Ninth General Elections were announced. The Baba not only directed the VHP leaders to go ahead with its Shilanyas programme but also advised the Prime Minister not to obstruct the programme.[61] The Central government as well as UP government despite being aware of the VHP's massive communal mobilization and its serious repurcussions on the intercommunity relations choose to remain as a mute spectator and even agreed to provide full cooperation and security to the Hindu communalists aggressive Ramshila processions which were mechanised to frighten away the Muslims. Surely if the purpose was not play the 'Hindu card' then the government should have banned the shilanyas processions and communal propaganda at a time when communal prejudices between the Hindus and Muslims were running high. The UP Government earlier declared Urdu as the second official language and later allowed the VHP to undertake shilanyas to keep the communalists of both the communities content.[62]

---

61. *Patriot*, 13 November 1989.
62. But Rajiv Gandhi in his interview to *The Hindu* soon after the fall of V.P. Singh Government maintained that the government had to allow the *Shilanyas* on the ground that the obstruction or interference in the shilayatra could have led to bloodshed and violence. He argued that events on October

(*Contd. on next page*)

With the General Elections barely three weeks away, the Congress could not afford to lose the Hindu caste votes who had emotionally attached themselves to the agitation for the Ram temple construction and provided leadership to the agitation. The VHP leaders were not willing to believe when Union Home Minister Buta Singh told them that Prime Minister Rajiv Gandhi be allowed to lay the foundation for a "new" Ram temple on 9 November which they haughtily rejected. In his Nagpur election meeting Rajiv Gandhi claimed that the credit for 'peaceful' conduct of shilanyas ceremony must go to Congress (I). For having allowed the shilanyas peacefully the Congress party also become the beneficiary of Hindu Votes. Mahant Avaidyanath. Sri Ramjanam bhoomi Mukti Yanja Samiti, leader declared the Congress (I) the Hindus' "Rally No. two". He announced, "our people would work for the Congress (I) in this General Elections wherever we do not have the BJP candidates."[63]

Despite all his vociferous claims and utterances about fighting against the forces of communalism, obscuratism and disruptive forces, Rajiv Gandhi as in the ignonimous Shah Bano case, objectively bowed to the Hindu fundamentalists' pressure in allowing the shilanyas in the disputed site. The manner in which Home Ministry and the UP state government responded to the VHP's Ramshila campaign programme tells the story of relentless prevarication and the search for politically expedient deals. The symbolic shilanyas for Ramjanmabhoomi

---

(*Contd. from previous page*)

30 and 2 November 1990 in Ayodhya had vindicated his decision. He said "when the VHP announced 9 November as the date of *Shilanyas* we had to take decision to hold elections after the *Shilanyas*, so that it would give us the benefit of being able to explain whatever problem or complication that might happen on that day." *The Hindu*, 26 November 1990.

63. Yubraj Ghimire, "A Stone with Many Ripples". *The Telegraph*, 12 November 1989 ; Praful Bidwai, Appeasing Hindu Bigotry" in Engineer ed., n. 1, pp. 139-42 ; Bisakha De Sarkar and Prabhu Jaganathan, "Foundation for Trouble". *Sunday Observer*, 12 November 1989.

temple near the Babri Masjid was not merely meant for the construction of a temple rather it was laying the foundation of what the RSS called Hindu Rashtra and also foundation of unending communal strife. The events on 9 November 1989 in Ayodhya will undeniably go down as a black chapter in the history of India's secular polity as the secular' political elites commanding the levers of secular state apparatus failed to stand up to the challenge posed by the Hindu communal forces.

The Shilanyas ceremony on 9 November caused a strong Muslim backlash in Northern and Western India and some parts of Eastern and Southern India. The Muslim leaders protested strongly of what they believed the VHP—Congress 'complicity' in performing the foundation laying ceremony of Ram temple in Ayodhya. Thousands of Muslims and few non-Muslims courted arrest in Faizabad on the day of Shilanyas ceremony. In sharp reaction to the development, the AIBMAC called upon all Muslim to give a befitting lesson to the Congress in the elections so that no other party dare to adopt such a communal strategy in future. The Shilanyas ceremony further deepened the Hindu-Muslim divide over the Ayodhya dispute.[64] The Congress (I) was not the only party which played the 'Hindu card' by taking a favourable stand for Hindus on the Ayodhya dispute but among the opposition parties the BJP was not lagging behind. Eversince its Palampur resolution, the party had been in the forefront in mobilizing of public opinion in favour of the VHP's demand for building a Ram temple at Ayodhya. The VHP in its press release appealed the Hindus irrespective of their caste and creed to support the BJP candidates in the General Elections and wherever the BJP candidate was not in the fray to vote those candidates who support the construction of Ram temple in Ayodhya at the same place whe.e Garb Griha (Sanctum Sanctorum) of the temple exists."[65]

---

64. H.V. Seshadri, "Shilanyas : What it Signifies," *Organiser*, 17 December 1989.

65. *News Time* (Hyderabad), 19 November 1989.

II

These background political events invariably influenced the Ninth General Elections which was held in the last week of November. It has been undeniably accepted that in the Ninth General Elections communal issues deeply influenced the voter's behaviour. The pre-elections communal mobilization on the Ramjanmabhomi-Babri Masjid controversy by Hindu and Muslim communalists had brought a sterile local dispute into the wider arena of party politics and tended to polarise two major religious communities. The government's failure to solve the dispute either through a mutually acceptable formula or expenditing the judicial process of settlement also provided grist to the mill of communal forces. The Ayodhya dispute was complicated further after the opening of the Babri Masjid gates and the government found in a helpless situation in what is essentially a problem of its own making. The government was in a precearious situation as it neither could appease both the parties nor could antagonise to any party at the same time. The ruling Congress party was unable to launch a counter mobilization strategy and wean away the people from the clutches of communal forces because it also wanted the stalemate over the Mandir-Masjid dispute to continue as any decisive action would hamper the party's poll prospects. Thus, the pre election communal mobilization of the Ayodhya dispute had inevitably drawn the issue into the arena of electoral politics.

The Vishwa Hindu Parishad's 40 day long shilapooja programmes in over 5 lakhs of villages accompanied with horrific communal riots in the Northern and Western India and the Shilanyas within the disputed property of Babri Masjid barely three weeks before the General Elections had made the Ayodhya dispute as an election issue and the major political parties responded to in their election manifestoes. Commenting on the Shilanyas programme the organiser remarked, "Hindutva is no longer a dirty word in Indian politics. Despite vilification campaign by the Janata and Left leaders, the VHP's Ramshilapoojan programme had

The major issues in the Ninth General Elections that influenced the voting behaviour of the Indian electorate are non-performance of the ruling party and anti-establishment feelings resentments against corruptions and scandals in the top levels and growing consciousness for the ethnic, caste and community identities. But the election results showed that majoritarianism and anti-minorityism are the most significant features that have emerged in the Indian politics.

Congress (I) on the eve of Ninth General Elections sought to play both the Hindu and Muslim card in a desperate bid to retain power in the face mounting Opposition challenge. The frequent recrudescence of communal riots in U.P. and the ruling Congress party's inability to check the spread of riots had led to the steady erosion of the party's Muslim support base. The move to introduce legislation by the Uttar Pradesh government for giving Urdu as the second official language status in September last week was guided by the electoral compulsion of securing Muslim votes. It was obviously the political game of retaining the Muslim votes who were alienating and to create a hurdle in the JD and BJP's electoral alliance since the latter strongly opposed the granting of Urdu as the second official language by the UP government.

The introduction of Urdu language by the U.P. government just few months before the General Elections and UP assembly elections established the fact that the Congress party can stoop to any level to secure the votes of the minorities. The BJP reacted to the government's political move by organising violent protests and agitations at a time when the communal passions had already reached a feverish pitch in the state which was already besieged by the Ayodhya imbroglio.[70]

The Congress party's exclusive reliance on playing the 'Hindu card' as well as 'Muslim card' in the elections was evident from the attitude of the Congress ruled state govern-

70. Kuldip Nayar, "Tne Communal Cauldron" in Engineer, n. 1, p. 138. See also, P.K. Roy's article in *The Hindu*, "The Intrighning Urdu Bill", reproduce in *Organiser*, Special Issue, 1989, pp. 45-47.

ments to the Shila processions organised by the VHP. Interestingly, most of the communal riots that took place in the wake of VHP's month long Ramshila programme were in the Congress ruled states. Despite some disimilarities in the pattern of riots in the states, Congress (I) used these riots to secure both Hindu as well as Muslim votes and turn these riots against its political adversaries. While allowing the provocative Ramshila processions it sought not to alienate caste Hindu votes who were in the forefront of Ramjanmabhoomi temple campaign and at the same time its criminal negligience in controlling the riots and killings of innocent people and accusing the BJP and opposition parties for engineering riots it tried to cultivate an impression in the minds of panicky Muslims that only the Congress has "the guts to fight communalism"[71] and under the Congress rule the minorities are safe. It was believed that Congress (I) on the eve of Ninth General Election engaged in "controlled communal tension" with the help of the VHP and Bajrang Dal to create in secure feelings among the Muslims who would run for protection of their lives and property. When the raging controversy over the Babri Masjid had vitiated the inter-community relations all over the country, Rajiv[72] Gandhi could have successively met the challenge of Hindu fundamentalists by joining hands with the National Front and the Left Front leaders and isolated the BJP/RSS/VHP combine and thus, in turn, could have created a crisis in the Opposition alliance. But the Rajiv Gandhi Government adopted a very soft attitude to

71. *Times of India*, 20 November, 1989.

72. During the election campaign, the Janata Dal leader V.P. Singh declared in an unscheduled press conference that he had definite and reliable information that the Congress party was hatching a 'diabolical plot' to fan communal violence in Ranchi, Baroda, Meerut, Bareilly, Delhi and Ayodhya by using agent provocateurs. Once communal riots would breakout in such a massive scale the party would be free to use either the Hindu or Muslim card or even postpone the elections on the ground of law and order problem. He said, "this political plot is aimed at polarisation of votes and drowning of all other issues" in the elections. See, *Times of India*, 26 October 1989 ; Madhu Limaye, "Staying Away", *Illustrated Weekly of India*, 3 December 1989, p. 24.

the VHP and RSS and their pernicios communal mobilization for Ram temple in the election campaign. The Hindu communalists also perceived the Congress (I) as lesser evil and extended their support to it where the electoral battle had been polarised between the Congress and Left or Janata Dal. For example, in Faizabad Lok Sabha constituency in eastern Uttar Pradesh, the Congress (I) Lok Sabha candidate who played a crucial role in extending cooperation to the VHP's Shilanyas programme on behalf of the Congress party, was supported by the BJP and VHP in the Lok Sabha elections against his CPI rival.[73]

Emphasising that the major issue in the election was the future of secularism, the Congress party's election manifesto reiterated its pledge to uphold the secularism and its determination to continue the struggle in cooperation with like minded forces to eradicate all communalism in the body politic. On the Ayodhya dispute, the party's election manifesto does not explicity says about the party's stand. It only says, "the sensitive issue of Ramjanmabhoomi-Babri Masjid need to be looked at from broader perspective of maintenance of communal harmony and goodwill. The case is before a bench of Allahabad High court and both sides are parties to the case.[74] The party manifesto also makes deceitful claim about its commitment to promote secularism in India. It says, "For the Congress (I) there can be no diluting of its secular heritage. While communal forces engaged in spreading the seeds of discord, the Congress (I) has never wavered its determination to fight against the forces of communalism and sectarianism."[75]

---

7 . Balraj Puri, "Can Caste, Religion and Ideology stem Hindu Wave", *Teaching Politics*, Vol. xv, No. 3 & 4, 1989, p. 62; Narendra Sharma, "Some observations on 1989 General Elections" *Mainstream*, 9 December 1989, p. 4; Nicholas Nugent, *Rajiv Gandhi : Son of a Dynasty*, (London, BBC books, 1990) pp. 191 ff.

74. See the full text of the Congress (I)'s election Manifesto for the Ninth General Elections in *National Herald* (New Delhi), 7 November 1989.

75. *Ibid.*,

On 3 November 1989, when Prime Minister Rajiv Gandhi launching his party's election campaign for the Ninth General Elections from Faizabad, he called upon the people to vote for the Congress (I) and promised to usher "Ram Rajya". In his speech he said, I am proud of being Hindu which echoed the slogan that has been popularised by the RSS and its affiliates :

"Garv se Kaho hum Hindu hain" (Say with Pride that we are Hindus). Thus, while appealing to the Hindus through the voice of Hindu chauvinists from a place where the Mandir-Masjid dispute has lit the communal fires across the country, he was explicity playing the Hindu card. It was evident that the BJP was not solely playing the Hindu card. The Congress (I) also competed with the BJP for cashing on Hindu Votes.[76] The fact is that the Congress government opened the Babri Masjid gates for Hindus and widely published it through the official media, sabotaged the speedy judicial settlement of the dispute, allowed the 'Kumbh mela' to be used as a communal platform by the VHP, permitted the consecration of bricks for Ram temple in every village and Shilanyas of Ram temple to take place within the disputed plot, speak in volumes the complicity of the party to aid and abet the Hindu communal forces and to play 'Hindu card' over the Ayodhya dispute. The reason for Rajiv Gandhi's flirtation with 'Ram Rajya' and appeasement to Hindu and Muslim communal forces is not far to seek. The growing disillusionment of the people to Rajiv Gandhi's economic policies and the party's inability to fire the imagination of the masses with anything more than gimmicks and rhetorics, the party was determined to go to any extent for retaining its power.

In contrast to the ambivalent attitude of the Congress party to the Mandir-Masjid dispute, the Janata Dal took an unambiguous stand with regard to the dispute but at the same time implicitly tried to woo the Muslims who had been disenchanted with the Congress party for its failure to guarantee security

---

76. Harish Khare, "Sparring with the Communalism : Why the Sadhus Determine the National Agenda", *Times of India*, 20 October 1989.

to their lives and property and its dubious role in the Babri Masjid dispute. But like the Congress party, the Janata party and its new incarnation the Janata Dal after the merger of small centrist parties failed to launch a political and ideological struggle against the fundamentalist and communal upsurge and confrontation over the Ayodhya dispute. V.P. Singh, the Janata Dal President joined with the left forces in unequivocally condemning the bogey of "Hindu Rashtra". But given his ambivalence to the left and right at the early stage of his political career as opposition leader, it was difficult for him to condemn openly and stridently the communal politics of the BJH. The credit for forcing V.P. Singh to break his silence on communal issues undeniably goes to the left forces.[77]

The Janata Dal's approach to Ayodhya dispute was based on both political expediency and electoral compulsion. The party was in dilemma in its relationship with the BJP whose commitment to building of a Ram temple at Ayodhya and installing a non-Congress government was equally important. Nevertheless, the Janata Dal made a cautious tight rope walking over the Ramjanmabhoomi Babri Masjid dispute like the Congress (I). The Janata Dal while careful not to alienate the Muslims who had tilted towards the party, sametime could not afford to antagonise the sentiments of Hindus by taking a tough posture with regard to the VHP's claim over the disputed masjid. Rajiv Gandhi's accommodation of VHP's demands through 'negotiation' and secret political deals and declaration of Urdu as the second official language by the Congress ruled Uttar Pradesh state were meant to serve the party's electoral interests. The Janata Dal by joining hands with the left and distancing from the BJP on issues like growing communal menace, support to Minortiy Commission and Art. 370 and at the same time entering formal alliance and seat adjustment

77. See the editorial, "Communalism and the Janata Dal" in the *Telegraph*, 11 May 1989.

with the BJP indirectly followed the same strategy of the Congress.[78]

Shortly before the announcement of the Ninth General Elections and when the VHP sponsored Ramshila campaign was playing havoc throughout the country, the Political Affairs Committee of the Janata Dal took an unanimous and unambiguous stand with regard to the volatile Mandir-Masjid dispute. In its resolution it said, "Now that the issue is in the midst of Judicial process and all concerned must await the final verdict of the court. This is how all the controversial and explosive issues should be settled in a democratic society. The Janata Dal accused the Congress party for its manipulative and divisive politics and instigating communal riots for its political purpose. It called upon its members to launch campaign against the mechanisation of the ruling Congress party.[79] The Janata Dal top leadership was split over their attitude to the BJP because of their differing notions of political expediency. While the party's leadership from North India believed that the alliance with the BJP would alienate the Muslim votes because of the BJP's uncompromising pro-Hindu stand on the Ayodhya dispute and opposition to Urdu language party's other leaders were strongly in favour of electoral alliance with the BJP as they believed that Congress party can not be defeated without a united opposition. They believed that even if the party's alliance with BJP would cost the party of its Muslim votes but it would be make good of by the shift of Hindu votes from the Congress (I).[80] When the Vishwa Hindu Prishad was engaged in organising its Ramshila campaign and Ayodhya March plan on 9 November 1989 to lay the Shilanyas for the proposed Ram temple, the Janata Dal strongly urged the VHP and particularly its politically ally the BJP to reconsider their proposed plan of Ayodhya March. The Janata Dal's resolution adopted by its Central Parliamentary

78. Arun Sinha, "Election, Parties and the Political Void", *EPW*, October, 1989, p. 2413.

79. *Indian Express*, 9 October 1989.

80. *Times of India*, 1 October 1989.

Board emphasised the need to respect both Hindu-Muslim sentiments in Ayodhya and said that, "While Hindu sentiments to have a temple dedicated to Lord Ram in Ayodhya should be respected no act should be undertaken that would cause apprehension in the minds of Muslims that there is a design to demolish the mosque."[81]

In a symbolic gesture to appease the Muslim sentiments and thus put a dent on the Congress party's traditional vote bank, the JD leader V.P. Singh undertook his courageous "political piligrimage" to Ayodhya to prevent the VHP from changing the *status quo* of the Babri Masjid dispite the risk of alienating some sections within the Janata Dal and National Front, which even threatended to break the much negotiated and bargained alliance with the BJP. His visit to Ayodhya along with the left leaders to resist the BJP's programmes was not successful as the local administration prevented him to proceed from Faizabad to Ayodhya.[82] The Janata Dal under the leadership of V.P. Singh gave importance to the issues of corruption at high places, economic mismanagement and the Congress party's failure to curb the growing communal violence in its election campaign. V.P. Singh consistently refused to share election platform with the BJP and repeatedly declared that the JD would not share power with the BJP in the event of Congress party's defeat. In Maharashtra the Janata Dal made no truck with the BJP as the latter entered a poll alliance with the Hindu chauvinist party—the Shiva Sena. The Janata Dal decided to fight the Lok Sabha and subsequently the assembly elections in Maharashtra in alliance with the Left and other progressive parties. The Congress was the loser of Muslim votes as the Muslim in the Northern India and Western India felt jittery over the virulent of communal riots and allowing the shilanyas near the Babri Masjid. The Janata Dal without antagonising the Hindu sentiments garnered Muslim votes. Even compared to its lose of Hindu votes the

81. *The Telegraph*, 24 October 1989.

82. S.K. Chaube, 'Election Campaign for the Ninth Lok Sabha Election', *Teaching Politics*, Vol. No. 3 & 4, 1989, pp. 40-47.

unsolicited gain it received from the Muslim brightened its poll prospects.[83] In addition, the Janata Dal received its main support from the UP and Bihar where it worked out a caste combination known as AJGAR (Ahir-Jath-Gujar and Rajput) which successively stemmed the "consolidation of Hindu Votes" over the Ayodhya dispute.[84]

Shahi Imam of Jamma Masjid who weilds considerable influence among the Muslims declared publicly his support to the Janata Dal and other partners of National Front. Shahi Imam who is known for his aggressive communal politics announced to the press that the Janata Dal had agreed to the "conditions of his support and commented, "Mr. V.P. Singh's stand on the Babri Masjid issue and Shilanyas is fair.[85] The JD's spokesman immediately responded to Imam 'fatwa' to his coreligionists and stated that, "The help of Imam is something we welcome at all times but in this difficult situation when communal flare-ups have gripped Bihar and other parts of the country, his assistance will be particularly useful.[86] Having secured the support from the Muslim community, the Janata Dal had also entered alliance with the BJP and demonstrated its remarkable sense of purpose and earnestness in adjusting almost all the seats in eight states—UP, Bihar, Rajasthan, Gujrat, M.P., Haryana, Himachal Pradesh, Jammu & Kashmir and Union Territories of Delhi and Chandigarh involving 262 constituencies."[87]

Despite the Janata Dal's hobnobbing with the BJP, the party's stand on Ramjanmabhomi-Babri Masjid dispute shows that it seeks to maintain its centrist secular image but it utterly failed to keep a respectable distance from both the Hindu and Muslim communalist forces. For sheer electoral

83. *The Tribune* (Chandigarh), 14 November 19.9.

84. Balraj Puri. "Can Caste, Religion and Ideology stem Hindu Wave, *Teaching Politics*, Vol. xv, No. 3 & 4, 1989, p. 63.

85. *Times of India*, 12 November 1989.

86. *Hindu*, 13 November 1989.

87. *Organiser*, 12 November 1989.

expediency it did not hesitate to secure the support of Muslim communalists for defeating the Congress and capturing power. In short, the politics of Ayodhya dispute came as a cropper to the party's electoral success.

The left parties as represented by the CPI and CPI (M) in particular, took a sharp ideological posture with regard to the communally sensitive Ayodhya dispute. Unlike the Congress (I) and the Janata Dal's vacillation with Hindu and Muslim communal forces for narrow electoral gain, left parties are in the forefront of struggle against fundamentalism and communalism of all varieties. The glorious struggle that the Left wedges against the communal terrorism in the Punjab is an eye-opener to all the politically conscious citizens in our country. The Left's approach to Ayodhya dispute was not based on narrow electoral calculation, rather determined by the larger interests of national unity, communal harmony and secularism.

The left parties, strong opposition to the Muslim Women's Bill in Parliament and its unequivocal denouncement of the RSS's espousal of 'Hindu Rashtra' theme prove they oppose the politics of both Muslim and Hindu communalism and fundamentalism. Realising the unprecedented growth of communal forces in the body politics the left parties took initiative to organise a national convention against communalism and separatism at 'Delhi and appealed to all patriotic forces to take up in right earnest the crusade against the dark forces of communal reaction and separatism. Because of the Left's marginal presence in the Indian politics, it has on every stages of its struggle against the communal forces sought the cooperation and help from the progressive and secular forces in society. The left parties had organised various rallies and meetings and tried to educate the people against the dangerous politics of communal and fundamentalist forces.[88]

The CPI and CPM have got a similar understanding of the Ayodhya dispute. These parties see the linkage between Rajiv Gandhi's appeasement of Muslim Fundamentalists over

88. *New Age*, 18 October 1987.

the Shah Bano Case and its subsequent decision to open the gates of Babri-Masjid due to the pressures of Hindu fundamentalists. The two left parties hold the Congress (I) responsible for its supreme indifference to the Ayodhya dispute which stimulated the growth of rabid communal elements and consequent, hardening of their attitude to the Babri Masjid dispute. The left parties believe that the Muslim 'agressiveness and exclusiveness' on the Ayodhya dispute had provided teeth and strength to more aggressive Hindu communalism.[89] The secular political parties, the left parties accuse, for having given political legitimacy to the all kinds of communal forces by entering formal alliance with them purely on electoral grounds and short term political gains which has weakened secularism and undermined to the cause of communal harmony and national integration. The Left perceive the growth of communal and fundamental forces in the political process due to the failure on the part of the ruling party to separate religion from politics in the public affairs.

The left parties prepared for the Ninth General Elections with the two main objectives of defeating the Congress (I) and at the same time isolating the communal forces. The Left paid equal importance to both the objectives : "Rajiv Gandhi and Congress (I) has to be thrown out of power. Otherwise the country would be plunged into communal strife all along its length and breadth, India's unity and integrity demands that Rajiv Gandhi must go and the vicious communal chauvinist RSS-BJP-VHP must be thoroughly isolated."[90] The joint statement of the left parties view that the paramount task of defeating the Congress (I) is jeopardised if any understanding is reached with the communal forces like the BJP, Shiva Sena and the

89. Shameem Faizi, "Irony of Muslim Politics," *New Age*, 23 April, 1989 ; *People's Democracy*, 23 April 1989 ; C. Rajeswar Rao and Shameem Faizi, "Babri Masjid—Ramjanmabhoomi Controversy" (New Delhi : PPH, 1989), p. 3 ff ; H.K.S. Surjeet, *Babri Masjid-Ramjanambhoomi Issue* (New Delhi, National Book 1989) 2 ff. Is 2.

90. *New Age*. 12 November 1989.

IUML.[91] It criticised the Janata Dal ling for an alliance with the BJP for achieving its short term political objective and ignoring the long term opposition unity. The joint statement of the Left Front on the eve of General Elections viewed : 'The coming elections instead of being utilised as an opportunity to strengthen secularism, democracy and communal amity and safeguarding the unity of the country, is being turned into a battle ground for communal massacres." The BJP's strident support to the VHP's Ram temple campaign, opposition to giving Urdu as official second language status, demand for abrogation of Minority Commission and Art. 370 of the constitution had convinced the Left of the BJP's communal face.

The CPI and CPM had frequently urged the Janata Dal to join in the anti Rajiv, anti-communal front which can defeat the Congress (I) as well as isolate the BJP. E.M.S. Namboodripad asserted, 'We the Left, though a small political force, in alliance with Janata Dal and National Front can be able to defeat the Congress (I) and help the emergence of a united Front of all left democratic secular forces".[92]

As the Ramshila processions gained momentum with the alarming rise of communal riots the left parties' election campaign in the latter phase concentrated mainly against the BJP and the Congress party's communal politics : "There is no doubt that the main cause of the present wave of communal violence is the highly provocative and agressive communal campaign launched by the RSS/BJP/VHP combine over the Ramjanmabhoomi-Babri Masjid dispute. Through Ramshila processions the BJP is trying to spread its tentacles..."[93] Accusing the Congress (I), the CPM's weekly organ People's democracy wrote that, "the ruling party members actively played ignoble role in organising and inciting communal riots and it was difficult to draw the line between the BJP and

91. *New Age*, 8 October 1989.

92. E.M.S. Namboodripad, "BJP Tie up : Fatal For Opposition", *Times of India*, 12 October 1989.

93. *New Age*, 22 October 1989.

Congress (I) in Bihar"[94] The Left was of the view that Rajiv Gandhi courted Hindu communalists over the Ramjanmabhoomi-Babri Masjid dispute as witnessed in the part'y refusal to ban the Ramshila processions and allowing the VHP to lay Shilanyas for Ram Temple within the disputed property near the Babri Masjid.[95]

In their election manifestoes, both the CPI and CPM had expressed concern over the unprecedented threat to India's secular democracy from the fundamentalist upsurge. The CPI manifesto says, "Today the country is faced with menacing spectre of a communal holocaust. In the name of Ramjanmabhoomi-Babri Masjid issue, unprecedented communal violence has been unleashed all over the Hindu heart and Gujrat. Because of the pandering which the Rajiv Gandhi Government had done to the religious fundamentalists of both sides, (on one side the Shah Bano case and on the other side breaking open the locks of Babri Masjid complex) communal forces have gained new leverage during the last few years."[96] While the CPI's manifesto is silent about the party's stand, the CPM manifesto clarifies its stand on the Ayodhya controversy, 'On the Babri Masjid/Ram Janambhoomi dispute, the CPM is of the firm opinion that it should be settled through a court verdict. This is the only way such explosive dispute in society can be settled. Pending the court verdict there should be no agitation and procession which are likely to break communal peace."[97]

Despite all its sincerity in fighting against the communal forces the left parties could not successively mobilize people against the aggressive communal politics of the RSS/VHS/BJP combine even in areas of its strong influence. Though the West Bengal government could not allow the Shilapoojan

94. *People's Democracy*, 19 November 1989.

95. *Ibid.*

96. See, the full text of the CPI's manifesto in *New Age*, 5 November 1989, p. 7.

97. *People's Democracy*, 29 October 1989, p. 5.

programmes in the Community Puja pandals in every village of the state, but the government faced the challenging tasks up banning the Shilapooja programmes throughout the state. The Left campaign on the Ramjanmabhoomi issue very often took the form of exclusive exhortation to the National Front and Janata Dal leadership to stay away from the BJP's communal politics.

As we have explained earlier, the BJP as the political affiliate of the Rashtriya Swayamsevak Sangh played a leading role in the VHP sponsored month long Ramshila processions throughout the country. The party's association with other members of the RSS family in recent years is so close that it is difficult to draw a dividing line between the RSS/VHP/BJP and Bajrang Dal workers. For example, then BJP Vice President, Rajmata Vijay Raje Scindia who was also the Vice President of the Vishwa Hindu Parishad, took active role in the VHP's sustained communal mobilization. L.K. Advani and his party leaders despite their denial, kept the Ramjanmabhoomi-Babri Masjid dispute alive in the elections and during their election campaign they accused the Rajiv Gandhi Government for practising minorityism in the Ayodhya controversy.[98]

But despite its aggressive pro-Hindu image and call to the government to handover the Babri Masjid to Hindu the party surprisingly refrained from including Ramjanmabhoomi issue as its man agenda in the Ninth General Elections.[99] The most important reason for non inclusion of the party's stand on the Ayodhya dispute was due to its lock of confidence in securing the mass approval of its stand from Hindus. But nevertheless, the BJP with the help of its allies exploited the Ramjanmabhoomi controversy to a hilt in their election campaign. The BJP leaders despite pressures from the Janata Dal and left parties, refused to appeal to its sister organisation

98. B. Ramesh Babu, "Opportunity for the Opposition" *Seminar*, No. 365, April 1990, p. 21.

99. See, the BJP manifesto for the Ninth General Elections 1989.

leaders appeal to the VHP and it was also apprehensive of BJP's active support in its temple construction plan.

The ministerial committee set up by the Union government to find a solution of the dispute achieved little after two months of its formations due to the uncompromising posture taken by the Vishwa Hindu Parishad and the All India Babri Masjid Action Committee.[7] In the four months of time only one meeting could be held between the Central government and the contending parties without any success. The Central government's deferment of time was a tactical move to buy time but at the same time the state government can be credited for taking the firm stand against the Sankaracharya of Dwarakapeeth[8] who went to Ayodhya on May 7 to lay the second Shilanyas and start the temple construction work. Before the seer could precipitate communal tension in Northern India, the state government arrested him. Despite outright denunciation of the Dwaraka Seer's move by the Vishwa Hindu Parishad which branded him a "Sarakari-Sankaracharya" for his closeness with the Congress party, the VHP Secretary General condemned his arrest as an attack on the devotees of Bhagwan Ram and two senior RSS leader decried the arrest as an "insult to Hindu society".[9] Dwaraka Sankaracharya's liasion with some sections of Congress leaders was seen when Congress (I) leaders of U.P. and Madhya Pradesh Strongly protested against his arrest.[10] The belated denial by the Congress (I) about its links with the proposed second Shilanyas on May 7 failed to carry conviction. By encouraging the Dwaraka Seer and obscurantist Sankaracharya of Puri to set themselves up as alternative to the VHP inspired Sri Ramjanmabhoomi Mukti Yanja Samiti. the Congress (I) tried to divert the attention of

---

7. *Sunday Observer*, 29 April 1990.

8. The Sankaracharya decided to lay the second *Shilanyas* for Ram temple at Ayodhya on 7 May as he rediculed the VHP for having started the construction of Ram temple in inauspicious time and violation Shastras, *Times of India*, 27 April 1990.

9. *Deccan Herald*, 6 Mav 1990.

10. *Patriot*, 8 May 1990.

Hindu chauvinists into their internal bickering. It was indeed ironical to say that the political party which explicitly claims and professes secularism could stoop to such an incredibly low level in encouraging Hindu chauvinists merely to embarrass the National Front Government and take political milage from it.

As the VHP took adamant attitude on the Ram temple at the disputed site, the governments's move to seek a solution to the Babri Masjid dispute in asking the Muslim leaders to agree on to the proposal of shifting the Babri Masjid from its present site also failed. The VHP despite deferring its temple construction plan continued to maintain its aggressive stance besides giving regular threats and tis activists had staged a dharna outside Prime Minister's residence reminding of him the government's inaction in finding a solution to the dispute. It appeared that both the state and union governments were not clear about the nature of the disputed land adjoining the Babri Masjid because the Union Home Minister while maintained in Parliament that the Shilanyas was conducted in undisputed site the Uttar Pradesh government took the position that the Shilanyas was taken place in a disputed plot.[11]

The strong determination exhibited by the Uttar Pradesh Chief Minister to maintain the *status quo* of the Babri Masjid and putting the Sankaracharya behind the bar failed to restraint the BJP/VHP/RSS/Bajrang Dal combine from their aggressive communal mobilization.[12] Rather, in a stepped up rhetoric the VHP leaders announced that the matter has now gone out of the hands of the Prime Minister and is now to be decided by the religious leaders."[13] On the other hand, the leaders of Indian Union of Muslim League attacked the National Front Government for its "lack of firmness" in dealing with the VHP's threats on the Ramjanmabhoomi-Babri Masjid issue and

11. *Patriot*, 12 May 1990.

12. *The Telegraph*, 10 June 1990. Interview with Mulayam Singh Yadav.

13. *The Statesman*, 9 June 1990.

demanded an outright ban on any form of campaign to interfere with the mosque and its site till the final judicial verdict is made.[14] Thus, with the failure on the part of the government to seek a solution to the dispute within four months of time, the contending parties were back to the square and the dispute again moved to a dangerous drift. During its four months of reprieve to the government, the LHP formed throughout the country the Balidani Dastas (suicide squades) and recruited lumpen youths into a massive scale who would be used in its Kar Seva programme for the temple.[15]

The VHP and Sri Ramjanmabhoomi Mukti Yanja Samiti in the Sant Sammelan at Hardwar set October 30 as the final dead line for the construction of the temple. The conference planned to set the communal passions of Hindus alight by literally using the fire symbolised Ram Agni and Ram Jyoti which the volunteers would carry the blazing torches from Ayodhya on September 19 to different parts of the country and would begin to retreat Ayodhya at the end of the month. The Kendriya Marga Darshak Mandal (Central Advisory Council) of the Vishwa Hindu Parishad passed resolution according to which batches of volunteers led by saints religious luminaries would leave from 100 religious places in Vijay Yatras (victory processions) for Ayodhya where the Kar Seva for the proposed Ram temple would be started from the scheduled dated. The resolution further read : "There would be no change in regard to the place where the temple will be constructed under any circumstances. "The VHP leader Ashok Singhal later clarified that they had no plan to "demolish" or 'remodel' it. This

14. *Hindustan Times*, 24 June 1990.

15. *The patriot*, 6 June 1990. In recent years, the term Kar Seva which means 'voluntary service' has gained currency particularly after the 'Operation Blue Star' in Punjab in 1984. But the term '*Kar Sewa*'' for Ramjanmabhoomi temple has been conveniently borrowed and misappropriated from the Sikh tradition. While the Sikhs organise their *Kar Seva* for such operations as the disilting of the lakes at the Golden Temple in Amritsar, the VHP/BJP/RSS/Bajrang Dal combine ask for *Kar Seva* for blatantly unlawful acts like forcefully demolishing a disputed mosque on sheer force of being in majority.

clarification assume significance considering the storming into the Babri Masjid by the VHP supporters on the end October.[16]

The Sant Sammelan while fixing the date of temple construction it had in effect extended another four months to V.P. Singh Government to seek a solution to the dispute though already the VHP had expressed its disapproval of any talks. By setting such a firm date of temple construction the VHP demonstrated not only its firmness of going ahead for temple construction but also left no scope for tis escape. The BJP responded the VHP's Hardwar meeting positively after its initial vacillation. The party while reiterating its earlier stand on the controversy rejected the growing demand from various quarters to maintain the *status quo* as it considers the Babri Masjid as "the symbol of slavery" for the Hindu society.[17] The BJP's strategy was reported in the RSS's mouthpiece : "The party's gameplan was to launch agitations and join movements started by like minded organisations like the VHP on these issues while continuing to support to the government in Parliament."[18]

Eversince the arrest of Sankaracharya Swaroopanand Saraswati oı Dwaraka the difference between the state government and the Hindu fundamentalists came wide open and also demonstrated the state government's determination to uphold the judiciary. Mulayam Singh Yadav's Government in Uttar Pradesh adopted a two pronged strategy of mixed caution with aggression. While he frequently appealed the VHP to reconsider its decision to start temple construction at the same time he warned them of his government's determinations to uphold the rule of law. Subsequent to the Hardwar Sant Sammelan, the massive communal mobilization initiated by the RSS/VHP/BJP and their allies particularly in North India was indeed a fight between the Lok Shakti (the people's power, *i.e.*, the Hindus) vs. Raj Shakti (the state power) as described by a BJP leader in U.P.[19] It was a pure and simple method of challenging the

16. *Times of India*, 24-25 June 1990.
17. *Deccan Herald*, 16 July, 1990.
18. *Organiser*, 8 July 1990.
19. *Times of India*, 7 June, 1990.

secular state apparatus and assert in a crude way the majoritarianism despite the chauvinists loud claim of commitment to the rule of law and uphold the cherished values of the Indian Constitution.

The ascendancy of Hindu communal forces after the Ninth General Elections had emboldened them to go ahead with their arm twisting tactics and exerting pressure on the National Front Government at the Centre and the Janata Dal Government at the state to succumb to its demand. The National Front Government was virtually reduced to a prisioner of indecision and remained under perpetual siege over the Ayodhya dispute. The main factor that compounded any initiative of the government to solve the dispute was the minority character of the National Front Government and its dependence on the BJP for tis survival, whose main concern was to keep the communal cauldron boiling over the Ayodhya dispute and thus effect a communal polarisation (between Hindus and Muslims. The recalcitrant attitude of the VHP/RSS/BJP to 'liberate' the presumed birth place of Lord Ram and the insistence of the Babri Masjid movement leaders to restore the mosque to its original shape was the most important reason for the failure of the government's initiative to solve the dispute. Since the struggle over a dilapidated mosque raises the deeper question of changing the very nature of a polity it would be surprising to except that both the parties would agree or comply with other's demand. Contrary to the wide-spread criticisms that were levelled by the print media against the National Front Government for its indifference to solve the dispute it must be understood that apart from inherent weakness of the Government, the most important factor that forestalled and move from the government to solve the controversy is the fact that both Hindu and Muslim communalists were more interested to exact maximum political milage from the controversy. When the Ramjanmabhoomi-Babri Masjid controversy is made into a powerful mobilizing ideology by the Hindu communalists for homegenising and unifying the Hindus and consolidating Hindu sentiment over the dispute and thus creating a Hindu vote-bank which would in the long-run change the nature of the Indian polity, the possibility of evolving a mutually acceptable solution is, nonetheless, remote. Despite all the pretensions and emphatic declarations to solve the Mandir-Mosque controversy through negotiation, the VHP is neither interested in holding negotiation with its Muslim counterpart nor prepared to accept the judicial verdict.

I

The failure of the National Front Government's initiatives to solve the Ramjanmabhoomi-Babri Masjid problem and the subsequent communal build up for a confrontation in Ayodhya on October 30 assumed a frightful dimension when on August 7 the Prime Minister announced the much awaited and neglected Mandal Commission Report's implementation. Soon after the government's declaration Babri-Masjid-Ramjanmabhoomi issue became the bone of contention between the National Front and BJP though the letter had never made the Ayodhya dispute as a condition of tis support to the National Front Government. After the announcement of the Mandal Commission Report's implementation and reactionary outburst of the so-called forward castes against the reservation policy, there had been rising crescendo from the BJP and its sister organisations spawned by the RSS that they were not prepared to relax their determination to build the Ram temple at the site where the Babri Masjid stands today.[20]

The reaction to the Mandal Commission Report by the upper caste Hindus created a deep social turmoil and threatened to polarise the society into "forward" and "backward" castes. L.K. Advani's decision of taking leadership from the VHP for mobilization of mass support for the temple construction and to undertake a motorised Rathyatra (journey

20. D.R. Goyal, "What Price the BJP Crutch", *National Herald*, 15 December 1990.

through chariot) covering 10,000 k.m. long route passing through 10 states was based on the post Mandal realities.[21]

When V.P. Singh attempted carefully to build up a formidable political support base for him through underprivileged OBC minority alliance the BJP could discern the incompatibility of V.P. Singh's strategy with its own. The BJP despite its promises in its election manifesto to support the implementation of the Mandal Commission Report backtracked and purturbed by the determination of the government to implement the report. The decision to implement the Mandal Report affected the party in two ways. Firstly, the party's strategy of forging Hindu unity and consolidating Hindu support base was brought to the naught by the anti and pro-Mandal agitation as it threatened to devide the Hindu society by pitting the backward castes against the reactionary forward castes and attacked directly the BJP and its saffron allies sustained mobilization for consolidating Hindu votes. Thus the polarisation of society on caste lines posed a formidable challenge to the campaigners for Ramjanmabhoomi. The BJP responded to such a situation by assuming the leadership of the BJP's campaign for Ram temple as the party leadership sought to arrest the growing caste cleavages by creating "alternative focal points of national consolidation". Secondly, the party and its ideological family organisations like the RSS, VHP, ABVP, BMS and its other frontal organisations' upper caste and urban middle class moorings were threatened by the

21. L.K. Advani time and again views that his decision to take out 'Rathyatra' had been conceived by him in June and not related to the government's decision to implement the Mandal commission Report in any way. See for example, his interview with the *Times of India*, 14 October 1990. But his actual decision to undertake *Rathyatra*, came on September 12 much after the announcement of the MCR's implementation. Advadi himself admits in his party's 'souvenir' : The *Ram Rath* Yatra not only cooled tempers raised by Mandal, it united the people in the name of Sri Ram. But, the government was blissfully ignorant of national mood." See L.K. Advani's interview in *March on* released in Jaipur (New Delhi, 1991), p. 7.

growing assertions of Backward and under-privileged caste over the implementation of Mandal Commission Report. The upper caste Hindus had a great stake on the BJP as their political front and the main crutch of the minority National Front Government. Though the BJP leadership carefully avoided to express explicity against the Mandal Commission Report and strongly advocated economic criteria of providing job reservation for all sections of society but its frontal organisations and affiliates were in the forefront of the violent anti-Mandal Commission agitation.

The BJP's decision to give leadership to the Vishwa Hindu Parishad's nationwide massive mobilization for Ramjanmabhoomi came as a double edged weapon. While the Rathyatra was carefully directed against the government's policy of so-called "minority appeasement" and indifference to the just cause of Hindus which in turn created communal antagonism among the cross-sections of Hindus at the same time it also diverted the attention of the socially, economically and educationally underprivileged sections from the V.P. Singh Government's job reservation policy for them. It has been rightly put that... "the anti-Mandal agitation is a reflection of the attempt to perpetuate casteist plutoarchy and the Mandir issue is one of the irrational, socially divisive, aggressive and ritualistic "Hindutva". The two are in effect the backward movement of the socalled forwards."[22]

While the BJP President on September 12 announced his Rathyatra programme from Somnath to Ayodhya "to mobilize public opinion and canvass support for the BJP viewpoint on Ramjanmabhoomi."[23] The top BJP leaders Atal Behari

---

22. Ariving N. Das, "Pathology of Uncivil Society : Ritualism Unites Mandal-Mandir Mover", *Times of India*, 5 October 1990. T.V. Satyamurti, "State and Society in Changing Political Perspective", *EPW*, 9 February 1991. p. 307 ; Swapan Dasgupta, "Nationalist in Dissarry : Renewed Importance to Ayodhya", *Times of India*, 10 November 1990 ; Invoking Ram to Fight Mandal", *Times of India*, 14 October 1990.

23. A.G. Noorani, "Ayodhya and Advani", *Mainstream*, 13 October 1990. p.6.

Vajpayee and L.K. Advani in a sudden reversal of their earlier stand in the meeting for Promotion of Communal Harmony agreed to abide by the Court verdict on the Ayodhya temple issue. But subsequently L.K. Advani denied having reversed party's stand on Ramjanmabhoomi temple as adopted in Palampur session.[24] The BJP did not attend the NIC meeting called by the government in protest against the alleged leakage of the resolution adopted in the sub committee of the National Integration Council (NIC) on the Ayodhya dispute. A resolution was adopted unanimously in the NIC meeting which called for a continuing dialogue to consider and decide the site of temple at Ayodhya and allied problem to the satisfaction of all concerned with a view to reaching an amicable settlement.[25]

L.K. Advani started his much published 10,000 k.m. long Rathyatra from Somnath to Ayodhya on 25 September. During the trail of his journey Advani maintained that his purpose of using the Rathyatra programme as a tool to bring about "a resurgence of national spirit" in much the same manner as Gokhale did while reviving Ganapati festival, Gandhiji in his movement against cow slaughter and Sardar Patel by building Somnath temple.'"[26] Instead of attacking the Babri Masjid move-

24. *Indian Express*, 19 September 1990.
25. *Deccan Herald*, 23 September 1990.
26. Saibal Das Gupta, "The BJP's Yatra; Roping in Ram and Patel", *The Statesman*, 5 October 1990. The BJP leader's equation of his Rathyatra (popularly known as *Vote Yatra*) with party's election symbol on the *Rath* with *Patel's* initiative in building Somnath temple is utterly frivolous and distortion of facts while it is undisputable that the fabulous Somnath temple had attracted the foreign invaders from time to time to enga e in the acts of vadalism and one questions the historicity of these facts, the claim that Babur or his General had replaced a Ramjanmabhoomi temple with the Babri Masjid on that spot is baseless and it not corroborated by concrete archaeological, stratigraphical, historical or literary facts and evidences Even the BJP leaders have very often maintained that it is not possible to pin point the exact place of Ram's birth but, the belief

(Contd. on next page)

ment leaders Advani chose carefully to attack the political parties for their policy of 'minorityism' and 'pseudo-secularism'. In most of the public meetings he criticised the political parties for treating the Hindu sentiments with contempt and continuing their policy of appeasing the minorities. The tremendous popular response which Mr. Advani received during his Rathyatra mark him to take unyielding posture and he turned down the appeals. National Front Government and various other political parties. Rather he maintained that the yatra had been peaceful throughout its routs.[27]

L.K. Advani's Rathyatra was an ingenious device to create a consciousness among the Hindus on the basis of some powerful cultural and symbolic issue—'the liberation of Ramjanmabhoomi'. The Rathyatra succeeded in evoking Hindu symbolism and inducing unprecedented militant religious sentiments among the Hindus and serious communal riots broke out in many parts of the country during the course of Rathyatra and after Advani's arrest on 23 October. The message that Advani sought to give to Muslims was clear : The Hindus comprised of 80% majority in the country. It is a matter of their right to build the Ram temple and their sentiments must be honoured by Muslims. The Muslims, ought to recognise this and remove the 'historical wrongs' heaped on the majority community by their forefathers.[28]

The Bajrang Dal workers who were in the forefront of Advani's Rathyatra had given a totally aggressive and com-

---

(Contd. from previous page)

that Babri Masjid stands on the Ramjanmabhoomi is a matter of faith. So, the Somnath temple does not offer any paralled on precedent to the construction of Ram temple by demolishing a mosque. See, for example, Sikander Bakhat, 'Let us Go Back to Somnath Spirit' in, *March On* (BJP Souvenir, New Delhi : 1991). pp. 10-12.

27. L.K. Advani's interview with the *Times of India*, 10 October 1990 and 14 October 1990.

28. Based on my study, Attitude to *Rathyatra* : A Study of Jamia Milia Islamia University Students", New Delhi, in November 1990.

munally surcharged nature of Advani's journey. Provocative slogans like :

Babar ki Santan Jayegi Kabarsthan, (Offsprings of Babur will go to the graveyards). Sougandh Ram Ki Khate hein hum Mandir Wohin Banayenge (We swear in the name of Ram that we will build the temple there only). Ek Dhakka Aur Do Babri Masjid Tor Do (Give one more push and break the Babri Masjid), Tel lagao Dabar ka naam mita do Babar Ka (use Dabur's oil and erase the name of Babar) and display of swords and trishuls in the processions accompanying the Rathyatra and given an impression that the purpose of yatra was to assert majoritarianism and create hatred against the Muslims for not identifying with Ram— "the national hero." [9]

Barbaric ritualism formed a part of Advani's blood strained Rathyatra, while a BJP worker tore up his hand with a trishul (trident) and applied blood on Advani's forehead, in Jaipur 101 Bajrang Dal workers offered a pot of blood to him. After Advani's Rath passed Baroda, communal riots broke out. It was not just coincidence that communal riots should have broken out in Karnataka within days of Advani's Rathyatra passing through Solarpur, near the Maharashtra border with Karnataka. On October 3, communal riots claimed more than 20 lives in Kolarpur, Chennapatna, Ramnagram towns and 12 people killed in a few days later when the riots spreaded to Devangare town. In Rajasthan also, several cities like Udaipur, Jaipur, Hamirgarh witnessed communal riots on the trail of Rathyatra.[30]

The response of the political parties to the Vishwa Hindu Parishad's unnegotiable temple construction plan from October 30 was guided essentially by the political considerations. The Janata Dal in Uttar Pradesh with left parties organised series of anti-communal rallies throughout Uttar Pradesh. But these

29. See "Advertising Discord" written by a group of academics of JNU in *Mainstream*, 26 January 1991, p. 51.

30. *The Telegraph*, 14 October 1990.

rallies in turn vitiated the communal feelings among the Hindus and Muslims. Uttar Pradesh Chief Minister Mulayam Singh Yadav's open advocacy for the cause of Muslims like defending the Muslims to keep illegal fire arms in public exacerbated the communal feelings of Hindus. In his desperate bid to emerge as the saviour of frightened Muslims and secure the Muslim votes, Mulayam Singh Yadav's excessive pro-Muslim posture in public prompted a CPM MP in U.P. to say that, so long there is a person like Mulayam Singh Yadav to speak for them, the Muslims need not come to the streets. The BJP/RSS/VHP Bajrang Dal combine counter mobilized solely on communal lines. In asking the Hindus to choose between 'Ram and Babar', organising Pravat Pheris in several parts of Uttar Pradesh for Ram temple, successfully organising 'bandh' in places where Mulayam Singh Yadav and left parties were scheduled to address anti-communal rallies and mobilizing Hindus in rural areas against those who were 'preventing' the construction of Ram temple, the Hindu communalists whipped up communal hysteria among the large sections of Hindus.[31]

The announcement of 10,000 k.m. long Rathyatra by the BJP President L.K. Advani was obviously meant to send a sharp and critical message to the Janata Dal led National Front Government at the Centre for frustrating the BJP's ambition of Hindu unity by announcing the caste-based reservation policy. On 17 October, the Bharatiya Janata Party's National Executive Committee issued a strong warning to the National Front Government : "The executive calls upon the Union Government to honour the sentiment of the people and allow a temple to be built at the Janamsthan. The executive warns the Government that if it fails to do so or it disrupts the Rathyatra which has come to symbolise the sentiments, the BJP would be constrained to withdraw support to this Government.[32] The Janata Dal on the other hand decided to firmly deal with the law and order situation in the wake of Advani's Rathyatra and not to allow the construction of Ram temple in

31. *Times of India*, 6 October 1990, *News Times*, 12 October 1990.

32. *Times of India*, 18 October 1990.

Ayodhya in violation of the Court orders. The JD's spokesman maintained : "Our commitment to the rule of law is sacrosanct political principle and an inescapable legal duty. There is no political monoeuverability where court order is concerned."[33]

Despite the confrontationist posture take by the National Front Government against the VHP efforts were made at various levels by the government to avoid a showdown. In the last minute bid to save the government from threat of the BJP's withdrawal of support, the National Front Government called on meeting at all levels, hold discussions behind the bars and made persistent efforts to secure an amicable settlement to the dispute through negotiation with parties concerned as well as religious leaders and public men. But all efforts were revolved around the Janata Dal's firm stand that the *status quo* of the disputed mosque would be maintained at all costs. The government finally brought out a compromise formula in the form of Presidential Ordinance which envisaged the government's takeover of the disputed land at Ayodhya and provision to make available to the VHP for temple construction in the adjoining areas barring such disputed land at Ayodhya, reference to the Supreme Court for the speedy solution of the temple-mosque wrangle and maintenance of *status quo* till the case is decided by the Supreme Court. However the compromise formula evolved by the government failed to take off as both parties to the dispute rejected the Ordinance forthwith though the BJP gave a lukewarm response.[34] While the VHP reaffirmed its decision to go ahead with the Rathyatra programme the AIBMAC charged the Prime Minister for "breach of assurance" by promulgating Ordinance and even gave a call for all India bandh in protest against the Ordinance.[35]

The Government by acquiring the disputed land as well as its adjoining area apparently cleared the way for the VHP to construct a Ram temple at a site which was not disputed and

33. *Times of India*, 18 October 1990.
34. *The Hindu*, 20 October 1990.
35. *The Hindu*, 21 October 1990.

thus the VHP could have achieved its objective of starting the construction of the temple which it had promised to Hindus. But the VHP in rejecting the government's offer shown its determination to go ahead with its objective in gross violation of the rule of law and judiciary. With the failure of the Chief Ministers' conference to evolve an immediate solution to the dispute the stage was, then, set for a showdown with the BJP Bajrang Dal/VHP/RSS combine. The Union government left with no other option but to uphold the judiciary and the constitution to prevent an explosive communal situation even though this entailed the inevitable downfall of the government. Prime Minister V.P. Singh on 22 October in his address to the nation made clear : "What we face is not just a new problem, a wew crisis : the nation is being tested as never before. The challenge we face is not only to the rule of law, not only to our political system and our Constitution... If it is a question of saving the nation or saving the government then the nation will come first. Government come and go, but the nation must remain."[36]

The Government prevented Advani's Rathyatra by arresting him in Bihar which touched off communal riots in several parts of country and about fifty people lost their lives in the communal violence and police firings in Bihar, Rajasthan, Gujarat, U.P. and West Bengal in the wake of an nationwide 'bandh' called by the BJP in protest against its leader's arrest.[37] Mulayam Singh Yadav's pro-Muslim posture backfired. Indiscriminate arrests, restrictions on the movement of vehicles and political activity and deployment of army and police for facing the communal challenge of the VHP and his anti-communal rallies where his public outburst against the BJP/BJP became provocative for them. Both the Uttar Pradesh Chief Minister and the BJP and its saffron allies were responsible for queering a pitch for communal confrontation over the Ayodhya dispute.

36. See "V.P. Singh's Historic Speech on Babri Masjid Issue", *Radiance*, 25 November-December 1990, p. 19.

37. *Times of India*, 24 October 1990 and *National Herald*, 26 October 1990.

Despite multilayered security arrangements and elaborate precautionally measures to prevent the entry of the Kar Sevaks to Ayodhya, thousands of Hindus converged on the twin cities of Ayodhya-Faizabad even much earlier to the day of Kar Seva to begin. The Kar Sevaks in defying curfew and threat to the punitive action by the administration could assemble in Ayodhya in thousands which amply proves the police administration complicity to the VHP's cause. The Kar Sevaks who thronged in Ayodhya were determined to strom into the Babri Masjid. A bloody confrontation between the security forces and the Hindu bigots became unavoidable.[38] At least a dozen of people were gunned down when the socalled Ram bhaktas forced their way into the Babri Masjid complex, damaged its outer walls and hoisted a saffron flag on the domes of Babri Masjid. Mulayam Singh Yadav's rhetorical assertion that a winged bird would not be able to enter the Babri Masjid and not a brick of the Babri Masjid would be allowed to touch, sounded hollow when the Kar Sevaks thanked the police after performing a symbolic kar Seva and fled away.[39]

As the news of "symbolic conquest" of the Babri Masjid by the VHP spread almost the entire Uttar Pradesh experienced mounting communal tension and surcharged feeling. Curfew continued to be clamped over 30 cities of the state with army controlling the law and order situation in several cities of the state to prevent the flare up of communal clashes. At least hundred people were killed in communal riots throughout the country following the incidents in Ayodhya.[40] The storming into the Babri Masjid had also its ominous fall out on the minority Hindus in neighbouring Bangladesh and Pakistan. The Muslim fundamentalists in these country destroyed some Hindu places of worship which in turn provided a campaign point to the RSS and its affiliates in the country.

38. *Times of India*, 29 October 1990 : *Tribune* 30 October 1990.

39. *The Hindu*, *The Statesman*, and *Telegraph*, 31 October 1990.

40. *Times of India*, 31 October 1990, *The Telegraph*, 2 November 1990.

The event on October 30, 1990 was indeed a high-water mark in the Ramjanmabhoomi-Babri Masjid Controversy. All those who stand for the values of composite social and cultural life, secularism and rule of law must have hanged their head in shame over the incident.[41] A premier national daily observed : "It is indeed a dark day for the nation. Never before since partition has there been an assault on this scale and significance on secular India as witnessed in the gory triumph of Hindu fanatics who braved bullets and lathis (sticks) to enter the disputed Babri Mosque determined to perform kar seva.[42] The event was not merely a challenge to the very basis of India's secular apparatus but exposed the real face of the Hindutva and dangers that are posed against the very core values of Hinduism which has come so far the mean more than a religion of faith. Another prestigious daily remarked : "When the kar seva entered the Babri Masjid, hoisted the saffron flag and even attempted to damage the structure they were not only dealing a blow to the secular principles enshrined in the Constitution. What was under attack at Ayodhya was centuries old traditions of tolerance, assimilation and respect for religious diversity which characterised Hinduism as the pre-eminent religious cultural entity of the people of India."[43]

While the leaders of Ramjanmabhoomi Mukti Yanja Samiti went undergound after evoking hysterical religious frenzy among the lumpen youths who fought pitched battle with security forces in Ayodhya and the bloody showdown whetted the BJP/VJP's quest for blood. The firing incidents on October 30 and November 2 in which a number of kar sevaks killed gave a powerful emotional campaign point to the campaigners for Ram temple. The VHP-Bajrang Dal decided to postpone their kar seva programme and carry urns containing the ashes of those kar seva died in police firing (Asti kalash) on a Bhasmi Yatra (journey for immersion of ashes) through every state. This switching of strategy from demolishing the mosque which

41. *Times of India*, 7 November 1990.
42. *The Hindu*, 31 October 1990.
43. *The Tribune*, 1 November 1990.

was localised in Ayodhya was meant to spread the campaign to every part of the country and give the issue an emotional and national overtone.[44] The entire Asti-Kalash exercise from carrying the urns from Ayodhya to different parts of the country and finally their immersion in Allahabad was undeniably a powerful propaganda weapon for the VHP.[45] The dead kar sevaks were lionised as the "martyrs" and "patriots" who made "86 attempts" to liberate the birth place of Ram.[46] The idea of martyrdom which gained critical political currency for the Congress (I) after the assassination of Mrs. Indira Gandhi also came as handy for the BJP/VHP. The dead kar sevaks also preceived as exploitable commodities for securing power. So, the purpose of transporting the urns containing the ashes of the kar sevaks to various parts of the country was aimed at to muster sympathy of those sections of Hindus who had not fallen in the trap of Hindutva. The purpose of Asti-Kalash programme was to generate an elemental hatred among the Hindus against the state which killed them as well as against the Muslims for their refusal to hand over the Babri Masjid to Hindus. The Asti kalash programme was yet another powerful symbol invented by the Vishwa Hindu Parishad intended for mobilizing the Hindus and the rallying them for a common cause.

When the communal fires stoking across the country in the wake of Advani's Rathyatra and its aftermath, the Janata Dal was caught up in the internal squabbles. The ruling Janata Dal steadily alienated from the Hindu middle classes over its stand on the Mandal Commission Report and the refusal on the part of the Janata Dal led National Front Government to cow down to the pressure tactics of the BJP also threatened its very survival in the office. Instead of standing by the ruling Janata Dal and the beleaguered Prime Minister from the combined onslaught of Hindu leader Chandra Shekhar despite all his mumbo-jumbo of value based politics and secularim, engaged in a desperate scramble for power and hobnobbed with dis-

44. *Times of India*, 8 November 1990.
45. *The Week*, 3 February 1991, p. 8.
46. *Times of India*, 1 November 1990.

gruntled opposition leader, Rajiv Gandhi, to cause the downfall of the V.P. Singh Government.

The V.P. Singh Government fell because the BJP withdrew the support from the National Front Government over the arrest of L.K. Advani and impounding his Rathyatra. It is undeniable that the main reason for the V.P. Singh Government's fall was the Ramjanmabhoomi-Babri Masjid controversy[47] and not the internal cleavage of the Janata Dal. When the BJP withdrew the support from his government, V.P. Singh instead of resigning from the Prime Ministership rather decided to face Parliament solely on the issue of Ayodhya dispute and threat posed by the Hindu communalists against the secular democracy in the hope that the National Front Government would survive by the surprise support of the Congress (I). The Congress (I) led by Rajiv Gandhi which swears by secularism and committed itself to fight against the communal and fundamentalist forces of all kinds once again played a shabby role not only in engineering defection in the ruling Janata Dal but also joined hands with the BJP in throwing out the V.P. Singh Government.

II

Mr. Chandra Shekhar soon after assuming power at the Centre had shown his desire to solve the already complicated the Ayodhya dispute. Though Chandra Shekhar Government succeeded in bringing the two parties to dispute to a negotiating table for evolving a mutually acceptable solution to Ramjanmabhoomi-Babri Masjid controversy but it did not yield any result despite holding of several rounds of talks between the rival parties. The talks between the VHP-AIBMAC broken down due to the refusal of the Vishwa Hindu Parishad to the All India Babri Masjid Action Committee experts' demand for more time to verify the VHP documents.[48] The Chandra

---

47. See "Why BJP withdrew support from V.P. Singh Government", speech delivered by L.K. Advani on 7 November 1990. See also, the text of the V.P. Singh's address to the nation in *Mainstream*, 17 November 1990, p. 15.
48. *Times of India*, 7 February 1991.

Shekhar Government while continuing the policy pursued by its predecessor regime, gave emphasis on out of court settlement and acted as a mediator between the contending parties. What was worse in the government's approach to the Ayodhya dispute was that it asked the two parties to submit "proof" in support of their claims to the Babri Masjid. Though both the parties rejected each other's claims it was strange to expect the VHP to submit "proofs" on Ramjanmabhoomi temple when it was already prepared "preliminary survey" of 3000 temples that have supposedly been destroyed by the Muslim rulers and erected mosques on their sites.[49] The Chandra Shekhar Government also involved Chandraswami—the controversial God man in the Ayodhya dispute. The main purpose of Chandraswami's vistit to Ayodhya and organising of a parallel meeting of religious heads at Allahabad with the help of state government was, to create a dissension among the Mahantas and Sadhus of Ayodhya, who already peeved at the VHP's leadership over their campaign for Ramjanmabhoomi, and thus reduce the influence of the Vishwa Hindu Parishad. But Chandraswami's strategy of wooing religious heads to his favour failed.[50]

Congress party's role in the Ayodhya dispute was dubious one during Chandra Shekhar's regime. Rajiv Gandhi in an apparent move to satisfy the pro-mosque demolition group within the party and to buy time to clarify his party's position proposed a three point formula which envisaged the setting up a judicial inquiry consisting of the Supreme Court judges to examine whether a Ram temple existed on a particular site and replaced by a mosque which should be completed within three months and to stipulate a legislation that would maintain the *status quo* of any place of worship from the January 26, 1950. The proposal was devious in the sense that while other non-BJP parties are not in favour of demolition of Babri Masjid in the

---

49. Praful Bidwai, "Counting Majoritarianism : Another Approach to Ayodha Dispute", *Times of India*, 6 January 1991.

50. "Avodhya : Exploiting the Issue", *India Today*, 31 December 1990, p. 83.

process while allowing the construction of Ram temple Rajiv Gandhi's objective was to shift the Babri mosque if it was established that it was built after destroying the temple. Even if it is proved that a temple had been replaced by the Babri Masjid on that particular site more than 400 years ago, it would still make the act of demolishing a mosque shocking. Further, this formula would set a precedent for other 3000 mosques that are originally claimed to be 26, 1950.[51] The Congress (I) in order to vindicate its controversial decision in allowing the Shilanyas in the disputed site the party extended its support to Mulayam Singh Yadav's Government in Uttar Pradesh when the latter had to accept the Congress party's position that the Shilanyas had been conducted at the place and allowed the second phase of kar seva for Ram temple, but as precautionary measure the state government the kar sevaks were arrested when they offered peaceful satyagraha.[52]

The Vishwa Hindu Parishad shortly after the assumption of Chandra Shekhar's Government announced its decision to launch the second phase of kar seva to construct the Ram temple. The VHP's decision was amply clear of its determination to keep alive the Ramjanmabhoomi-Babri Masjid controversy. Significantly the VHP's decision came after the BJP issued directives to its party cadres to prepare for mid-term elections.[53]

The Vishwa Hindu Parishad and Rashtriya Swayamsevak Sangh combine participated the government mediated talks with the AIBMAC as a delaying tactics to buy time till they reorient their fresh strategy of mobilization. The fact that the VHP and RSS were not interested to solve the Ayodhya dispute through a negotiated settlement could be seen from their preoccupation with the launching of second phase of kar seva at Ayodhya while at the same time continuing dialogue with the

51. *Times of India*, 4 December 1990 ; *Hindustan Times*, 9 December 1990.

52. *Financial Express*, 24 November 1990.

53. *Times of India*, 13 November 1990.

AIBMAC.[54] Despite the appeal made by the political parties at all party meeting to the Vishwa Hindu Parishad to postpone the second phase of kar seva but it went ahead with the plan. But in contrast to the violent showdown in October-November the VHP leaders resumed their Kar Seva in a peaceful manner from December 6 in the form of offering Satyagraha.[55] Having hyped the religious frenzy of its supporters in October-November the VHP leaders realized the futility of openly challenging the state and the rule of law by recourse to violent path. The changed political circumstance in which the BJP was no longer in a position to bully the government at the Centre and the possibility of growing disillusionment among the so-called 'kar sevaks' and 'Rambhaktas' prompted the VHP to launch their kar seva programme in peaceful and low key manner.

During the negotiation with the AIBMAC, the Vishwa Hindu Parishad's Kendriya Marga Darshak Mandal (Central Advisory Committee) at its meeting in Allahabad on January 15 as well as the subsequent Sant Sammelan reiterated its resolve to construct the Ram temple but affirmed that since the government is the main obstacle for construction of the temple, the construction would not be possible without the change of the government. Hence, the new battle strategy of much political importance that evolved was to change the government.

The VHP decided to hold a mammoth rally on April 4 and lay siege to Parliament which would be culminated after months long Jan Jagran Abhiyan (mass awakening programme) throughout the country. Ashok Singhal said, "Thus our objective now is to launch such an agitation that the government is forced to listen to us. We will paralyse its functionings. Either the government bends to our will or it breaks. And when it breaks we will certainly try our best to see that a government which supports the temple construction comes in."[56] The decision at

54. *The Statesman*, 6 December 1990.
55. *The Statesman*, 8 December 1990.
56. *The Week*, 3 February 1991, p. 8 ; *Indian Express*, 17 January 1991.

Allahabad had much bearing on the political process as the VHP now embarked itself in the political arena while its hitherto mobilizations were primarily meant to pressurise the government to succumb to its demands. The October 30 and November 2 incidents in Ayodhya changed the VHP/RSS strategy altogether. With the BJP as its political front the VHP and RSS leaders convinced from the success of the earlier mobilization strategies that the Ram symbol was potential enough to secure political power.

III

The resignation of Chandra Shekhar's Government at the Centre and inevitability of holding the General Elections could not deter the VHP and its allies to abandon their plan of holding rally in the Boat Club. In the changed political situation the rally was turned into a demonstration of the pre-election preparedness of the BJP. In the course of his mass awakening programme in Bihar, Advani appealed the people in several meetings to "translate their Rambhakti into votes" for the BJP so that it would be able to build a Ram temple after forming the government.[57] The April 4 Rally was preceded by two-day Dharma Sansad (Parliament of Saints) which called upon the Hindus to elect such people who would promise them to construct Ram temple in Ayodhya, Sri Krishna temple at Mathura and Viswanath temple at Kashi[58] and exercise their franchise keeping clearly in their mind the ongoing polarisation between the Rambhaktas and Ramdrohis, and the sacrifice of the kar sevaks for the cause of Hindus. The April 4 rally was a shot in the arm for the BJP and also gave a clear indication of the BJP's determination to play the Ayodhya syndrome as its most potent winning strategy for the Tenth Lok-Sabha Elections. In the rally, the VHP and RSS, leaders declared their open support to the BJP in the elections since the latter had promised for the construction of the Ram temple at Ayodhya.[59]

57. *Times of India*, 27 March 1991.

58. *Times of India*, 3 April 1991. See also *Organiser*, 14 April 1991.

59. *The Hindu*, 5 April 1991.

The sustained communal mobilization after the Ninth Lok Sabha Elections is the important factor that influenced the voting behaviour of the electorate in the mid term Lok Sabha poll. Unlike the previous General Elections, the issues and trends in the Tenth General Elections were different in many respects. Firstly, the elections were most unpredictable as no political party was in a position to mobilize the deeply heterogeneous population on a broad spectrum of issues for which it stood for. Secondly, the issues in the elections assumed divisive and polarising nature. Thirdly, the tragic death of the Congress (I) leader and former Prime Minister, Rajiv Gandhi, in the midst of the election process gave a new twist to certain poll planks and left a deep impact on the voters' mind in the next two phases of polling in some parts of the country. Finally, the Muslims demonstrated an awareness by overcoming their caste, class, regional and linguistic barriers in the face of escalation of communal riots and rabid communal mobilization by the BJP and VHP. A six member Committee named as Qaumi Mushawarat Committee was formed and it acted as pressure group to extract maximum bargains from the non-BJP parties and demanded firm assurance and commitment from these parties to protect their interests and ensure security to their life and properly in return of their solid support and at the same time it tried to evolve a uniform pattern of support among Muslims in order to defeat the BJP candidates.[60]

For the first time three distinct political formations were dominating the election scene with divers poll planks. While the issues of corruption, poverty and price rise were forgotten in the elections the voters were offered a wide range of issues like political stability, social justice and threats to secularism to decide on. Unlike the Ninth General Elections wherein anti-Congressism became a dominant feature, in the Tenth General Elections a set of new political agendas appeared dominating India's electoral scene. Ever since the fall of V.P. Singh government, two political issues which subsequently

60. Prem Sankar Jha, "The Awakening Among Muslims". *The Hindu*, 12 June 1991.

became poll issues were the JD's plank of social justice and the BJP's campaign for the construction of Ram temple at the disputed place in Ayodhya. No election manifesto of a political party could have been completed without the reference to the Mandal Commission Report and Ramjanmabhoomi-Babri Masjid controversy, given the powerful impact of these issues on the political and social processes and the forces they unleashed.

Much before the announcement of the Tenth General Elections, the BJP got itself completely prepared to face the elections by adopting its two main poll planks, 'Ram' (Lord Ram) and 'Roti' (Bread) in its Jaipur plenary session. Few weeks later it again added another dimension of its slogan, 'insaaf' (justice) ostensibly to counter the Janata Dal and left front's secular agenda—the social justice to backward classes and under-privileged sections. In its National Executive Meeting the BJP adopted an important resolution which indicated its exclusive importance on the Ayodhya dispute as party's major campaign issue. The resolution read : just as Jalianwala was turning point in the freedom movement Ayodhya has become a turning point in the independent India. The march from Ramjanmabhoomi mandir to Ram Rajya will see the fulfilment of our dreams."[61] Even the party's National Executive promised to start the construction of the temple by October 1991, in case it is voted to power.

---

61. *The Week*, 17 February 1991, pp. 8 ff ; *Hindustan Times*, 17 March 1991. See also, Nilanjan Mukhopadhya, "The BJP : In Search of an Agenda", *Economic Times*, 18 February 1991. But interestingly, it was later on clarified by the BJP President, M.M. Joshi, about the party's position and he refrained from committing any particular time frame or modalities of constructing the temple. He clarified that, it is for the Ramjanmabhoomi Trust to construct the temple, while the BJP would remove all the hurdles in the construction of Ram temple (See *The Hindu*, 30 April 1991, *Hindustan Times*, 1 May 1991). But despite the party President's clarification Mr. Atal Behari Vajpayee went to the extent of fixing a tentative time period for building of a 'magnificant' temple in his Faizabad election meeting. (*Mainstream*, 8 June 1991, p. 8).

The credit for bringing Ramjanmabhoomi-Babri Masjid dispute to the centre-stage of Indian politics undeniably goes to the BJP and its leader L.K. Advani. Even since the opening of the gates of Babri Masjid the BJP/VHP/RSS/Bajrang Dal combine have been building mass support as well as expanding their support base through mobilisation for Ram temple on the site where the Babri Masjid stands today. In numerous public speeches, press conferences and interviews, the BJP leaders had made it clear that the Ayodhya dispute was going to be their main poll agenda in the elections. Given the BJP's sustained campaign and pre-election mobilization, it was not unusual that the BJP would give foremost importance to Ayodhya dispute in its campaign for the Tenth Lok Sabha polls.[62]

Behind the BJP's cynical and brazen use of the Ram symbol in the elections lie the party's success in various mobilization strategies such as Rathyatra from Somnath to Ayodhya, which had convinced the BJP leadership that mobilization for Ramjanmabhoomi issue not only helped it to penetrate into rural areas but would enable them to see through the Tenth General Elections. Further the BJP's right reactionary ideology and its social support base have their inherent limitations to draw mobilization for radical socio-economic issues of the country. Despite the tilt of the backward castes and lower castes to the BJP's fold the party's social base is still dominated by the upper castes, urban based middle classes and small entrepreneurs and businessmen.[63]

The party's election manifesto titled 'Towards Ram Rajya' explicitly spells out the BJP's stand on the Ramjanmabhoomi controversy which the party refrained to mention during the controversy in its 1989 election manifesto though the

62. Swapan Dasgupta, "Battle for Ram : Issue is the Denial of the Temple", *Times of India*, 15 April 1991.

63. Sumanta Banerjee, "Hindutva—Ideology and Social Psychology", *EPW*, 19 January 1991, p. 98. See also, Walter K. Anderson and Sridher D. Damle, "The Brotherhood of Saffron : R.S.S. and Hindu Revivalism" (New Delhi : 1987), p. 81.

Ayodhya dispute was exploited politically to the hilt by the BJP and Shiva Sena in the Ninth General Elections. The manifesto says, "BJP firmly believes that the construction of Sri Ram-janmabhoomi Mandir is a symbol of the vindication of our cultural heritage and national self-respect. For the BJP it is purely a national issue and it will not allow any vested interests to give it a sectarian and communal colour. Hence, the party is committed to build Sri Ram Mandir at Janmasthan by "relocating the superimposed Babri structure with due respect."[64] (emphasis added). One significant aspect of the manifesto is that while it falls in line with the party's stand on Ayodhya dispute adopted in Palampur in 1989, but it is silent about the means to solve the tangle. Rather the manifesto explicitly speaks the language of retributive justice and vehemence when it says that the party "seeks the restoration of Ram Janmabhoomi in Ayodhya only by way of a symbolic righting of historic wrongs...."[65]

Armed with the RSS's organisational acumen the BJP launched its high profile election campaign with its three main poll planks, 'Ram' (God), 'Roti' (Bread) and 'insaaf' (justice). By ostentious display of funds the party also launched its campaign through electronic media as well as print media and within a week after the announcement of the election dates the BJP seized the lead in the campaign. Throughout the country, one could notice two styles of campaign launched by the party. The party's top leaders apart from harping mainly on the Ayodhya dispute and identifying with issues of nationalism and pseudo-secularism also focussed on other issues like troubles in Jammu and Kashmir, issue of social justice and mismanagement of the economy. L.K. Advani who led the party in the election campaign said, "The main issues that would be in focus and especially his party would seek to mobilize public opinion on the issues of nationalism and secularism. All these issues are linked to Ayodhya dispute."[66] Further he wrote in the

64. See the BJP Manifesto for Tenth Lok Sabha Poll, "Towards Ram Rajya", p. 5.

65. *Ibid.*, p. 1.

66. *Times of India*, 16 March 1991.

Hindustan Times : "At one level the construction of the temple at the Janamsthan will satisfy the devotionalism of millions of Hindus who venerate Lord Rama as the Maryada Purushottam but equally crucial is the recognition of the fact that Lord Ram is the symbol of Indian nationhood whose importance is on par with the Indian attachment to mother India. Such a recognition overrides divergences of faith... Indeed the importance of Ramjanmabhoomi campaign cannot be overstated. The campaign has generated a mass nationalist upsurge motivated by an unprecedented determination to both remove a symbol of bondage as well as create a monument for New India."[67]

On the otherhand, the party's sister organisations like the VHP, the Bajrang Dal resorted to naked communal mobilization and scurrilous campaign at the grassroot levels. The cadres at the grassroot level projected the election as the fight between 'Rambhaktas' (BJP and its allies) and 'Ramvirodhis' (all other political parties) and portrayed Ayodhya controversy as a symbol of "minorityism" and "pseudo-secularism" demonstrated in public highly provocative and exaggerated video-cassettes on the police firings on the 'kar sevaks' in Ayodhya in October-November 1990 and pressed into service the rabble rousers of the VHP who in their vitriolic speeches whipped up the communal passions of Hindus by hanking back the audience to the events at Ayodhya in October-November 1990.[68] The BJP's latter kind of strategy met with success especially if we take into account most of the riot hit areas of Uttar Pradesh where voting trends clearly went on communal lines and the beneficiery of this polarisation was the BJP despite the sizeable presence of Muslims and OBCs.[69]

Apart from the campaigns by its leaders and sister organisations, the BJP used print media to carry its message in different

---

67. L.K. Advani, "Nationalism is the Kay", *Hindustan Times*, 16 May 1991.
68. See my article on Communal Mobilization in Faizabad in *Mainstream*, 8 June 1991, p. 8.
69. Ajay Singh, "Communalism played a major role in U.P.," *Times of India*, 23 June 1991.

languages on its pet issues like Ram Rajya, pseudo secularism and minority appeasement policy. Here we cite two such advertisements in the print-media which were written in a sophisticated style only to attract India's educated middle class mind.

"To Indians, Ram is an ideal, a symbol of integrity, justice and compassion" (*The Pioneer*, Lucknow, 12 May 1991).

One such interesting advertisement put up in the name of "Ramjanmabhoomi Nyas" (a non-political body and an affiliate of VHP) on the Ayodhya controversy which exhorted the majority community to assert themselves as their faith was in danger. This was done in view of the recent Bombay High Court judgement in unseating Siva Sena and BJP MLAs and guidelines and rules for election campaign stipulated by the Election Commission of India. The advertisement shows how the VHP has resorted to such disinformation campaign in order to justify its stand on the disputed mosque :

"You can run but you can't hide yourself from the facts.

* This is not a new 'political' struggle. It is the 77th attempt in the history to restore the Ramjanmabhoomi, our heritage. Thus far over 300,000 kar sewaks have laid down their lives in the 400 years.

* Pseudo-secularists want the mosque declared a national monument forgetting that Ram was an Indian and Babur an invader. It is a national dishonour if a symbol of invasion is so declared :

"Now Ask Yourself !"

Can even the most tolerant, most reason able and peaceloving Indian run away from his pride—the reason for his being ? The time has come to fight for our threatened faith.

"Hindus unite ! Act as one.

Not against anyone !

But in defence of our motherhood."

(Ramjanmabhoomi Nyas, *Tee Pioneer*, 11 May 1991).

The BJP put up 480 candidates as compared to 225 Lok Sabha candidates in 1989 elections. In selecting candidates the BJP fielded many sadhus, saints and even an actor and actress who acted as 'Ravana' and 'Sita', in the popular T.V. serial 'Ramayana'. The VHP and Bajrang Dal put up some of their leaders (who had led the so-called kar seva programme in October-November 1990) for Lok Sabha seats in U.P. with the support of BJP.[70] This was done apparently to demonstrate the BJP's sincerity of constructing Ram temple at Ayodhya and turning the elections as the referendum on Ramjanmabhoomi.

The BJP's single point campaign, *i.e.*, on 'Ram' and ignoring its two other poll planks 'Roti' (bread) and 'insaaf' (justice) was proved in my study of Faizabad Parliamentary constituency and Ayodhya assembly segment which falls under the former constituency.

To demonstrate the grip of 'Ram wave' over Faizabad and to avenge its humiliating defeat in Ayodhya in 1989 assembly elections, the BJP was determined to wrest the Faizabad Lok Sabha seat and Ayodhya Assembly seat from its main rivals, the JD-CPI combine and the Congress (I) in the Tenth Lok Sabha Elections and 1991 Assembly Elections which were held simultaneously. That for the BJP it was a battle for the heart and mind of Faizabad—the epicentre of Ram imbroglio, can be proved from its aggressive communal mobilisation and shrill campaign with the help of its RSS-VHP-Bajrang Dal and Durga Vahini combine. By fielding Mr. Vinay Katiyar, U.P. Bajrang Dal convenor, who played a leading role in the violent kar seva programme and storming of Babri Masjid in October-November 1990, the BJP had virtually made the Lok Sabha elections in Faizabad as a referendum on "Ramjanmabhoomi temple". By doing this, the BJP had been able to portray there Mr. Katiyar as the 'Rambhakta' (devotee of Ram) fighting with CPI, Congress (I) and SJP candidates, branded as "Ramdrohis".

70. For example U.P. Bajrang Dal convenor Mr. Vinay Katiyar, contested as BJP candidate for Faizabad Lok Sabha seat. Mr. S.C. Dixit the U.P. VHP leader contested from Varanasi Lok Sabha constituency.

The Bharatiya Janata Party's exclusive emphasis on Ramjanmabhoomi-Babri Masjid dispute in mobilisation of mass support around it was clearly discerned when the party's senior most leader, Atal Vihari Vajpayee addressed an election meeting of the party at Faizabad. At the outset of the meeting, the local leaders describing the Parliamentary and assembly elections as crucial for the Hindus since the election battle would be fought between the Rambhaktas on Rashtrawadis (the BJP and its allies) and Ram virodhis on Rashtra virodhis, (the JD, SJP, Congress (I) and the Left) exhorted the public assembled at the huge gatherings not to waste their vote by voting on caste lines. Mr. Vajpayee in his evocative and fiery speech concentrated mostly on his party's maid poll plank—'Ram' and appealed to the voters of Ram-ki-Nagri to give a massive mandate to his party so that within a couple of years it would be able to build a magnificent Ram temple. The Ayodhya dispute, he asserted, is not simple the question of constructing a temple or righting a historical wrong, rather it involves the larger question of reconstituting Indian nationalism Vajpayee declared amidst loud slogans of the party workers that rent the air : Jai Sri Ram...Jai Sri Ram !

Kar Seva ka balidan, Mang raha hai kamal nishan.

(The lotus symbol demands sacrifice from the kar sevaks).

Hindutva ne pukara hai, garam khoon hamara hai.

(Hindutva call out those who are hot blooded).

In the meeting it was very difficult to draw a dividing line between the core BJP workers from the large gatherings of their saffron brethren.

The BJP hopes that the Ram symbol would pave the way for attracting the OBCs, SCs to a transcendental cause that will make them to forget their underprivileged position, ignore their rights and in the process its main support base, the upper castes and urban based middle class would revive their weakening political hold. In numerous places around the Ayodhya township and rural areas BJP/VHP had put the following catchy slogans on the walls.

Jaat paat ko chhood diya, Sri Ram se nata jod diya.

(Having dissolved our differences of caste and sect, we all have established a bond with Sri Ram).

Jan jan ki yahi pukar, Ram bina jeevan bekaar.

(It is the opining of the every individual that without Ram, life is meaningless).

Jo Hindu hit ka kaaj karega

Wohi desh par raj karega (VHP, Bajrang Dal and Durga-vahini)

(He who works for the benefit of Hindus alone is fit to rule the country).

Since all the national political parties except the BJP had promised in their election manifestoes to maintain the *status quo ante* of all religious places of worship as on 15 August 1947 by enacting a suitable legislation, the VHP in order to counter such a move resorted to blatant falsehood in order to mislead the voters especially the Hindus about the real meaning of the '*status quo ante*' of all religious places of worship. Throughout Faizabad-Ayodhya twin cities one could see hundreds of posters put by the VHP which state : (translated from Hindi and English)

"Restoring the *status quo ante* of religious sites as on 15 August 1947 would mean what ?

*Shall the 'miraculously' appeared Ram be removed from the Ramjanmabhoomi temple ?

*Shall all the temples and Gurudwaras in Punjab and Haryana be reconverted into mosques ?

*Shall we have to think once again about Somnath ?

*Shall we have to remove from public places the statutes of Gandhi, Indira, Patel and Ambedkar and reconstruct the statues of Victoria and George V.

Nationalist, Patriotic citizens' Awake !

See through these conspiracies or else you will lose your all ! ! "

Soon after the tragic assassination of Rajiv Gandhi on 22 May 1991 on the eve of second and third phase of the polling for the Tenth Lok Sabha, the BJP changed in election strategy. It toned down its aggressive and shrill Hindutva campaign and shown it accommodative and moderate posture so as to acquire the broad support base for governance. In the changed political context, BJP virtually stole Congress (I)'s main poll plank "political stability" and given it equal importance with its Ramjanmabhoomi issue.[71]

The BJP's exclusive emphasis on Ramjanmabhoomi issue the and communal mobilization around it put its political rivals on the defensive. The party's senior leaders like advani, Vajpayee and M.M. Joshi in their election meetings continued to attack the Congress (I), the National Front and the Left parties for pursuing minority appeasement policy in the name of secularism. Even in an election meeting, Vajpayee called upon the Hindus to unite and support whole heartedly the BJP in the elections in order to end up the "vote bank politics" of the Janata Dal and Congress (I). Advani asserted in his meeting that, while Muslims are in favour of constructing a temple, only the pseudo secular parties are creating hurdles in the construction of temples.[72]

Having discovered suddenly the Bharatiya Janata Party to be a "communal party" when it withdrew its support from the National Front Government the Janata Dal learnt a great lesson and pined hands with the Left Front and fought election on secular agendas. The party had to pay more than it gained by aligning with the BJP in achieving its short term objective

---

71. Rajdeep Sandesai, "BJP is now Caught between two Rams", *Times of India*, 12 June 1991. At his Lucknow Conference L.K. Advani clarified that "Ayodhya is one issue which has affected the entire country. But our priority will be Kashmir, Punjab, Assam, formation of Union Budget and putting the economy back on its rail and then the Ram temple, if we are voted to power." (*Hindustan Times*, 9 June 1991). But in his Moradabad election Meeting, he maintained that Ayodhya is going to decide the 1991 polls (*Times of India*, 10 June 1991).

72. *The Telegraph*, 1 May 1991 and *Hindustan Times*, 9 June 1991.

of defeating the Congress (I) and ignoring its long term objective of emerging as a viable centrist secular alternative to the Congress (I). For the Janata Dal it was no longer the Congress (I) that was its main enemy in the Tenth General Elections rather, ironically it was the BJP with whom it had formed electoral alliance in the Ninth General Elections. The split within the party and other political compulsions forced the Janata Dal to align with the Left to fight elections for its two main agendas-social justice and implementation of Mandal Commission Report and threats to secular polity from the BJP. The party despite putting its premium on social justice had also put a great stake on the Ramjanmabhoomi-Babri Masjid controversy for its electorals success for the obvious reason of getting solid support from the Muslims who were made to believe by the party leaders that V.P. Singh "sacrificed" his chair at the alter for protecting the Babri Masjid.

There appears striking similarity in the manifestoes of National Front, CPI (M) and CPI with regard to the Ayodhya disput and these parties had stated out clearly their stand on the dispute. While maintaining their pre-election stand that *status quo* of all religious places of worship as on 15 August 1947 shall be respected, the NF-LF promised to solve the Ayodhya either through a negotiated settlement acceptable to both parties or by a court verdict which would be binding for all.[73] The National Front manifesto accuses the BJP and Congress (I) for fomenting communal virus and tension in the country for their political considerations. On the contrary, the people know that the NF and Left parties alone have stood rock like against these disruptive elements wihch are undermining the unity of India.[74]

V.P. Singh and the top JD leaders made the BJP and Congress (I) the main target of their attack. V.P. Singh in his election meetings defended the National Front government's stand on the Ramjanmabhoomi-Babri Masjid dispute and

73. See National Front Manifesto, p. 16, CPM Manifesto. p. 13. CPI Manifesto in *New Age,* 4 April 1991, p. 9.

74. National Front Manifesto, p. 3.

vociferously attacked the BJP for exploiting the religious sentiments of Hindus over the dispute.[75] In the 14 April rally for social justice at the Boat Club, which was organised by the National Front-Left Front to counter the VHP's rally held on April 4, V.P. Singh in his speech gave necessary thrust to the Janata Dal's campaign strategy on the Ayodhya controversy. He said : They wanted to fell the Masjid and build a temple in its place. We chose instead to let our government fall. It is not just a question of a mosque. If someone would want in future to demolish a temple, a Gurudwara on a Church, we shall not hesitate for a moment to sacrifice our government again rather than allow such anti-people acts to succeed. If our places of worship fall apart, the heart of India will break into pieces. The National Front Government would never allow that to happen."[76]

For the Janata Dal, Mandal Commission Report and the plank of social justice to the backward castes appeared a no hold barred electoral strategy for the Tenth Lok Sabha elections.[76a] The Janata Dal leadership firmly believed that their unequivocal support to the Mandal Commission Report's implementation would stem the tide of 'Hindutva' campaign particularly in North India and the backward castes, the scheduled castes and tribes in alliance with Muslims would secure the party's victory. To counter the BJP's vicious communal mobilization and Advani's Rathyatra programme, the Janata Dal in Bihar and U.P. organised pro-Mandal Commission rallies.

Former Prime Minister and the Janata Dal leader, V.P. Singh's secular image and claim for sacrificing the chair for the

75. *The Hindu*, 9 April 1991. In his election meeting at Faizabad on 10 May I heard him saying that he sacrificed his Chair of Prime Minister for the cause secularism and Hindu-Muslim unity.

76. Quoted in the JD's pamphlet, "Do not Divide the Nation in the Name of Rama".

76*a*. "Mandal is the Key Issue", V.P. Singh's interview with India Today, 31 May 1991, p. 16.

cause of secularism appeared spurious when he held parley with rank fundamentalist and communalist Shahi Imam of Jamma Masjid in Delhi in order to bag the Muslim votes. The Janata Dal leaders capitulation to Shahi Imam Sayed Abdullah Bukhari's dictates especially his insistence on having a say in the selection of Muslim candidates of the party had not gone well either with its ally, the Left Front of more articulate and progressive sections of Hindus and Muslims. Even though Muslims in North India particularly in Bihar,[77] had heavily tilted in favour of the Janata Dal, V.P. Singh's liasion with Shahi Imam darkened the secular image of the Dal, as it was nothing but a desperate scramble for garnering Muslim votes. The Janata Dal received a severe jolt when V.P. Singh's erstwhile 'Jan Morcha' colleagues deserted the party in protest against authoritarian style of V.P. Singh's functionings and his ponderings with Muslim fundamentalists to secure the minority votes. They accused that : "If the BJP was using Ram temple in the election to garner Hindu votes, V.P. Singh played the same game for garnering the Muslim votes."[78] While Janata Dal leaders strongly denied their acceptance of the 'conditions' laid down by Shahi Imam for supporting the JD, V.P. Singh justified his action of approaching the Imam : "We have our contacts with him. We used them. We are only asking for support on the strength of our manifesto. This is not a communal appeal. It is a political appeal. It is not a fatwa."[79]

The Shahi Imam on 3 May 1991 appealed the Muslims and oppressed classes to vote for the Janata Dal and Left Front candidates in the elections. He urged them to vote for the independent candidates in the constituencies where the JD and Left parties had not fielded their candidate.[80] However Shahi Imam's action had a far reaching consequence. The Imam not only out stepped from his position, but appealed to the Muslim

77. *Times of India,* 17 March 1991 ; *The Hindu,* 28 April 1991.

78. *The Hindu,* 19 April 1991.

79. *The Hindu.* 23 April 1991. See also, V.P. Singh's interview with *Illustrated Weekly of India,* 18-24 May 1991.

80. *The H'ndu,* 4 May 1991.

electorate to vote for a particular party at the time of communally charged campaign of the BJP, and this further communalised the political process. The Imam's appeal was projected by the BJP as fatwa and its leaders called upon the people to vote for the BJP on the issue of Ram Rajya vs. Imam Rajya."[81]

In contrast to the bluster campaign by the BJP, the JD published very few pamphlets and leaflets on various issues to counter the BJP and Congress (I)'s propaganda. One such leaflet titled "Do Not Divide the Nation in the Name of Ram" published by the Janata Dal which sharply attacks the BJP for playing 'Hind Card' over the Mandir-Masjid controversy.

USES AND ABUSES OF RAM

Uses : Hindus have always considered Ram as Universal God.

Abuses : BJP has reduced Ram to a sectarian hero in the service of the Party.

Uses : Gandhiji worked for Ram Rajya kingdom of God on earth.

Abuses : Ram Rajya for BJP is rule by right wing fanaticism in Parliamentary clothes.

Uses : The father of the nation served Ram until his last breath by serving his people.

Abuses : BJP used Ram for its own survival and growth.

Uses : For the true Hindu, Ram represents a Catholic tradition continued by Kabir, Nanak and Gandhi.

Abuses : In BJP's pseudo Hinduism Ram has been trivialized as a tool of intolerance and terror.

(Issued by Rajmohan Gandhi on behalf of the Janata Dal.)

The left parties however, did not denounce strongly the Janata Dal's run for Muslim votes. Instead, though both the

81. Based on my field study of Faizabad Lok Sabha constituency during the election campaign for Tenth Lok Sabha polls.

CPI and CPM did not appreciate V.P. Singh's move they and declined to hit their political ally over the issue.[82] In the Ninth General Elections the Left Front fought against the Congress (I) and the BJP on its principled stand against communalism and fundamentalism. But in the Tenth General Elections when its ally—the Janata Dal, hobnobbed with Shahi Imam, the Left parties could not denounce strongly the Janata Dal's opportunist tactics and chose to play safe by describing in as the Janata Dal's internal matter and expressing their concern over the Janata Dal's flirtation with the Muslim fundamentalist. The Left Front's lukewarm reaction to the Janata Dal's opportunism created an impression that the Left is not an equal partner to the Janata Dal—led National Front but a mere camp follower.[83] After the fall of the National Front Government on Ramjanma-bhoomi-Babri Masjid Controversy, the Left Front identified its defence of secularism to defence of V.P. Singh and utterly failed to restrain its favourite ally, V.P. Singh to rushing to Jamma Masjid. The most important issue before the Left which it studiously avoids is that it must gloss over whether by joining hands with the Janata Dal it has been able to check-mate BJP or force both the Congress (I) and the Janata Dal to abandon their opportunist and skin deep commitment to secularism. The anti-congressism of the Left and its vacillation with the Janata Dal has forestalled its effort to emerge as the catalyst for the anti-communal unity of all the Left-secular and democratic forces no matter whatsoever the deep concern and anxiety of the left parties over the growing communalisation of Indian politics.

The left parties in their election campaign continued to attack the Congress (I) for its compromises with fundamentalist and communal forces over the Shah Bano case and Ayodhya controversy which encouraged the right reactionary forces like the BJP to grow in strength. Unlike its political ally, the National Front, which gave top priority to the issues of social

82. *Sunday Observer*, 5-11 May 1991.

83. See the editorial "Left Tailism", *Times of India*, 2 November 1990.

justice and implementation of the Mandal Commission Report in its election campaign, the Left Front gave the foremost importance to threats to secularism from the Hindu communalists and perceived that "The BJP-VHP-RSS are using aggressive communal mobilization on the Ram temple issue by exploiting the religious sentiments of Hindus."[84] The Left see the "alarming" rise of the BJP as the greatest threat to the secular polity and as a shock to the secular forces in the country. The controversy around Ram temple, the Left Front believes not only threatens to polarise the people on religious lines but is also being used as a means to divert the peoples' attention from the real issues confronting them.[85]

The Congress (I)'s approach to Ramjanmabhoomi-Babri Masjid dispute, lacks consistency and coherence which can be attributed due to the party's electoral calculations that override the expediency of solving the communal time-bomb as was evident in the party's insincerity to seek a solution through expediting the judicial process and its cynical exploitation of the dispute in the Ninth General elections. The ruling Congress party then did not clarify its stand on Ramjanmabhoomi issue in the Ninth General Elections and allowed the VHP to conduct 'Shilanyas' in the disputed site. During the Chandra Shekhar Government's brief interlude, Rajiv Gandhi brought out a formula to solve the Ayodhya imbroglio. However, it failed to receive support from other political parties and contending parties to the dispute. But in the Tenth General Elections the party in its election manifesto took a similar position on the Ayodhya dispute like the National Front, and Left Front while pushing aside its 'Rajiv formula'. The Congress party is committed itself to find a solution either through a mutual negotiation or by the Court verdict if the former is not possible. The party is in favour of constructing the temple without

84. CPI (M) Manifesto, pp. 3-4.

85. M. Farooqi, "The Commitment of Left", *Hindustan Times*, 2 May 1991. H.K.S. Surjeet, "Forces of Destabilisation at Work", *The Hindu*, 20 May 1991.

destroying the mosque.[86] The Congress (I) had to modify its earlier stand on the maintenance of *status quo* of all places of worship as on 26 January 1950 as envisaged in the 'Rajiv formula' as a result of the electoral understanding reached with Indian Union of Muslim League. The Congress Party included in its manifesto the promise of a legislation "to maintain and restore the *status quo* of all places of worship as on 15 August 1947."[87] The Congress (I)'s electoral compulsion to win back the Muslims in North and South India was the real factor behind its quick patch up with the IUML, which had deserted the United Democratic Front in Kerala over the Congress (I)'s stand on the Ayodhya dispute and the Mandal Commission Report.

Rajiv Gandhi in his election campaigns attacked the BJP and National Front for exploiting the Ayodhya dispute for electoral purpose and dividing the country on the caste and communal lines.[88] While the local Congress leaders in Uttar Pradesh strongly advocated construction of the temple near the mosque but remained silent about the future and safety of the Babri Masjid. The local Congress leaders by adopting such strategy wanted to counter the BJP's propaganda against the Congress on the temple issue.[89]

The Congress Party's election campaign gave the issues of political stability and price rise as its top priority. The party's election campaign on the Mandir-Masjid dispute can be cited from our study of Faizabad Lok Sabha constituency. In the Ninth General Elections, the party's Lok Sabha candidate for Faizabad seat was confident of winning the Lok Sabha seat due to election eve manoeuvre by the Congress (I), like allowing the

86. See the Congress (I)'s Manifesto, p. 29.

87. *The Hindu*, 11 April 1991.

88. *Indian Express*, 19 March 1991 ; *The Hindu*, 1991.

89. Based on my interview with the Congress (I)'s Faizabad Lok Sabha seat and the Ayodhya assembly seat candidate and the local Congress leaders.

VHP to lay the foundation stone for Ram temple near the Babri Masjid and covert support extended by the local BJP-VHP units to the Congress (I) candidate. But the Congress (I) candidate lost to the Janata Dal backed CPI candidate. In the Tenth General Elections, the party's prospect of winning the Lok Sabha seat was gloom. Severely bruised by the Mandal and the Mandir issues, the Faizabad unit of the Congress party projected its old image of party which belongs to all sections of the people, which could be seen in the party's slogans and posters put in the city walls.[90] In contrast to his first election rally on the eve of the Ninth General Elections at Faizabad, this time, Rajiv Gandhi in his election meeting, appealed to the voters of Faizabad to overcome their caste and communal prejudices and vote for the Congress (I) which alone can provide political stability and defeat the communal and casteist forces. Despite adopting a broad platform of mobilization and feverish campaign the party's dubious stand on the Ayodhya dispute and the Mandal Report had darkened the party's prospect of winning the Lok Sabha seat and Assembly seats. The Congress party's old slogan of providing political stability had failed to cut much ice in an election fought on issues of a polarising nature.[91] After the assassination of its leader, Rajiv Gandhi, Congress (I)'s main poll planks remain unchanged and it more stridently propagated the need for political stability and threats to national security.

IV

The Lok Sabha election results were significent. Once again, the Congress Party failed to secure absolute majority

---

90. Two such slogans which were used widely were : Na Jaat Par Na Pat Par, Mohar Lagegi Haat Par (Neither for caste nor for creed, vote for Congress (I) ; *Hindu Muslim Sikh Isai, Sabke Liye Hai Congress (I)* (Hindu, Muslim, Sikh, Isayee ; for all is Congress (I).

91. This was also admitted by Arvind Singh, the Congress (I)'s Ayodhya Assembly seat candidate during my interview with him at Faizabad on 14 May 1991.

despite getting sympathy votes in some parts of the country in the second and third phase of the polling. The BJP, which had used all the resources, failed to create a pan-Indian Hindu identity by its efforts to capitalize the Hindu sentiments on Ram temple issue. Except in the Uttar Pradesh and Gujarat, where the party's Ram temple campaign paid much dividends, the BJP's performance in the Hindi belt is not satisfactory. Sustained communal mobilization by the BJP and its sister organisations and frequent rash of communal riots in these states, helped the party to polarise the electorate on communal lines to reap the electoral harvests.[92] While the Left maintained its *status quo*, the National Front's plank of social justice failed to convince the electorate especially the backward castes. The nation voted wisely and the voting analysis reflected the growing political and social diversity in the federal polity. Differences in the voting patterns among the states indicated significant interplay of forces both at the local, regional and national level.[93]

The CPI(M) accepts the BJP as the real winner in the elections thanks to the Ramjanmabhoomi-Babri Masjid controversy. The party perceives that without BJP's sustained campaign for Ram temple with the help of RSS/VHP it would not have extended its support base as well as increased its percentage of votes and seates in the parliamentary elections.[94] Interestingly enough, despite the limited success of the BJP's Hindutva platform even in the Hindi belt the BJP's ideologues describe the 1991 elections results as the mandate for constructing Ram temple at the supposed birth-place of Lord Ram and the BJP's success has been hailed as the emergence of "Hindu revolution."[95]

---

92. Vinod Sharma, "Campaigning in Ramlila Style", *Hindustan Times*, 19 May 1991.

93. Refer, *Bashiruddin Ahemad*, "The Reshaping of India's Policy", *Hindustan Times*, 25 June 1991. Also, Madhu Limaye, "Diverse Response to Party Planks", *The Hindu*, 25 June 1991.

94. *People's Democracy*, 30 June 1991.

95. *Organiser*, 7 July 1991.

Like the previous General Elections, the rise of BJP's strength in the Tenth General Elections, was the most interesting feature. While the party secured 11.8% and jumped from 2 seats to 88 seats in 1989 General Elections, in the Tenth General Elections it secured 119 seats and doubled double its popular votes, *i.e.*, 21.8% significantly in 130 Lok Sabha constituencies, while the BJP candidates came to second position in 1991 Lok Sabha polls.[96]

The BJP's spectacular success in U.P. and Gujarat can be attributed to the Ramjanmabhoomi campaign by the BJP. The gauche handling of the kar seva programme in October-November 1990, by the Uttar Pradesh Government, and the most important factor—the split in Janata Dal, helped the BJP to achieve a sweeping victory in the Lok Sabha elections and a marginal victory in the assembly elections. So much so, the Ayodhya factor that played such a decisive role in the BJP's victory in U.P. that, soon after the assumption of BJP in power, Chief Minister Kalyan Singh along with his party Legislators trooped to Ayodhya to offer prayer inside the disputed Babri Masjid complex before the idol, Ram Lala. Uttar Pradesh[97] Chief Minister Mulayam Singh Yadav's anti-communal rallies gave an edge to the BJP's counter mobilization on communal lines.

The BJP leadership even explicitly acknowledges Mulayam Singh Yadav's role in Ayodhya dispute, which contributed immensely to the party's success in the elections.[98]

Apart from communal issues, the BJP also very cautiously played up the caste factors which helped it to register its victory. For instance, in U.P., the BJP gave tickets to a large number of backward-caste party workers to make a dent on the growing consolidation of the backward-caste votes in favour of

96. *India Today*, 15 July 1990, p. 42 ; *Organiser*, 7 July 1991.

97. *The Week*, 7 July 1991, pp. 28-32.

98. K.R. Malkani, "BJP Facing a Wave and a Ravana", *Financial Express*, 23 June 1991,

the JD. At the same time, the party leaders by insisting on the economic criteria as the basis of job reservation, could hold forth its traditional support base.[99] In Uttar Pradesh, where the so-called "Ram wave" believed to have secured the BJP's victory, is however not supported by the analysis of votes. While the BJP's total popular votes came to 33%, the combined vote secured by the Janata Dal and SJP—who exclusively relied on OBCs and Muslim votes, far-outweigh the BJP's popular votes without adding popular votes secured by Congress (I) and Bahujan Samaj Party (BSP). But despite facts to the contrary, the RSS describe the BJP's victory in U.P. as unambiguous verdict for Ramjanmabhoomi temple. The RSS report says: "The single most outstanding signal that the election results have registered is the unprecedented popular support extended to the BJP in U.P., both for Lok Sabha, and Vidhan Sabha with regard to Sri Ramjanmabhoomi. It is an unambiguous verdict and a direction to the central and U.P. government to ensure that all hurdles are removed forthwith in the way for the construction of the temple."[100]

Communal politics over Ramjanmabhoomi-Babri Masjid conflict played a more determinant role in the Tenth General Elections compared to previous General Elections. The Ayodhya dispute has clearly taken a communal overtone, because the dispute is not an issue of communal challenge to secular state, rather, it is an issue which involves the larger question of redefining Hindu-Muslim relations. The 1991 Lok Sabha elections, proved that communal politics has come of age, as the main political parties resorted to covert and overt ways of manipulating the religious sentiments of the people. While the BJP is bent upon to effect a communal polarisation and assert majoritriarism through Ramjanmabhoomi issue, the Congress (I) and the Janata Dal-led National Front are manipulating the fear and anxieties of the minority communities. For the first time, Ramjanmabhoomi-Babri Masjid dispute at Ayodhya dominated the electoral scene as the

99. *Illustrated Weekly of India*, June 25-July 15, 1991.

100. *Organiser*, 21 July 1991.

the controversy has been turned into a politics of vote bank by the political parties. The Tenth General Elections gave a decisive twist to the Mandir-Masjid controversy as it is no longer a problem which involves the religious sentiments of Hindus and Muslims on ascertaining the historicity of a particular place.

The Hindu communalists had made three important issues, over the Ayodhya dispute, as their main battle cry on the eve of elections and during the election campaign. The Hindu communalists have been successful in linking up communalism with the religious sentiments and emotions of Hindus over the Ayodhya dispute and thus secure the legitimacy of their communal politics. The growing strength of Hindu communal forces proves this point clearly.

Secondly, the issue of Ramjanmabhoomi-Babri Masjid dispute is projected by the communalists as the example of pseudo-secularism practised by the political parties and intelligentia for their "disregard" of the sentiments of Hindus. Since the rabid communal propaganda and campaign may not pay electoral dividends and appeal cross sections of Hindus, the communal mobilization is given a nationalistic colour through recourse to universalistic doctrine nationalism, which will overshadow the communal nature of the campaign and draw the support of other sections of Hindu society. The BJP/VHP portrayed the Ayodhya dispute in their election campaign as a 'national issue' since Ram is a 'national Hero' and, further, the question of one's support on opposition to the movement for Ram temple was viewed from the context of his or her commitment to nationalism. L.K. Advani claimed that, "the campaign has generated an unprecedented determination to remove both a symbol of bondage as well as to create a movement for new India.[101] In all these three common themes, the communalists through sheer manipulation and distortion of facts, have been able to sway large sections of Hindus and

101. See Advani, n, 67.

injected into them a vehemently prejudiced attitude against the Muslims. The VHP and its allies, after the October-November firing incidents, at Ayodhya, launched a disinformation campaign about the death of hundreds of Rambhaktas in police firing which prompted the Uttar Pradesh Government to institute an inquiry to ascertain the exact number of deaths and to the utter dismay of the Bharatiya Janata Party and Vishwa Hindu Parishad, the government inquiry found that the list of dead kar sewaks submitted by the VHP is a take one as most of their 'martyrs' are still living.

Conclusion

As the raging controversy and its bloody fall-out of Ayodhya reveals no sign of abatement rather, poses ominous portents to the future of nation's body politics, here in the concluding chapter, we have tried to avoid reaching a hasty and tenuous conclusion on the politics of Ramjanmabhoomi-Babri masjid dispute of Ayodhya and its future. The volatile political process, the shifting perception of the parties towards the dispute and the rigid posture of the Vishwa Hindu Parishad (VHP) and the All India Babri Masjid Action Committee (AIBMAC) makes it difficult to arrive at concrete conclusions in our study. In our concluding assessment we have tried to sum up our study by linking the politics of Ayodhya dispute with one of its key aspects-secularism.[1]

The ostensible success of the Vishwa Hindu Parishad's sustained communal mobilization for Ram temple at the presumed birth place of Lord Ram has thrown a formidable challenge to the secularization proceess in India. The controversy over the disputed mosque in Ayodhya has raised a vital question of survival of the secular democracy in India. Because the Ramjanmabhoomi-Babri Masjid dispute primarily involves an issue of redefining the nature of Hindu-Muslim relationship in present day India and the role of the secular state to solve a contentions dispute which is intricately related with the faiths and beliefs of the two religious communities. Moreover, the role of state in the dispute is being perceived as crucial for the future viability of India as a secular democratic polity as neverbefore has the secular state came under such a grave threat to its very existence from the

1. Madhu Kishwar, "In Defence of Our Dharma", *The Telegraph*, 25 December 1990 and 26 December 1990.

onslaught of Hindu and Muslim communalists, as it is being seen over the Ayodhya dispute. The present controversy over secularism primarily arises from the mounting offensive of the communalists against the state.

I

The concept of secularism undeniably was the offshoot of eighteenth century European Renaissance and a longdrawn out battle for the political supremacy between the church and state which subsequently known as separation of ecclesiastic sphere from the temporal power manifested through the state. On the contrary the concept of 'secularism' adopted in the Indian constitution was basically the legacy of India's freedom movement and the composite cultural and social heritage. In the post independent India, the adoption of secularism is invariably symbolised as an important aspect of its cultural and political identity.

The word 'secularism' is the most used and abused term by the political and intellectual elites of India. The basic reason for the persistence of utter confusion on the concept is that, neither there exist a clear cut definition of Indian secularism in the constitution nor a common and broad understanding of the concept of secularism professed and practised by the political parties. In the context of the Ayodhya dispute, the issue of secularism in India has assumed a major political agenda in political process since the early eighties. Broadly speaking, there are two main divergent views among the political parties and intellectuals on the concept of secularism in India. Some argues that the concept must be understood from its strict dictionary meaning and the western notion of secularism which meant the separation of religion from the affairs of the public, is perfect, and must be practised and professed in India. Others strongly denounce the western concept of secularism as an alien or borrowed concept and strongly favour secularism that must be rooted in the indigenous cultural traditions and social ethos. It is in the political sphere that concept of secularism has been popular as the political parties provide interpretations of their own variant of secularism which suits to their political expediency.

The Indian variant is widely known as Nehruvian model of secularism, as it was Jawaharlal Nehru's vision that gave the warp and woof to the ideal of secular polity. The Nehruvian secularism envisaged India as a secular state friendly to all religions (Known as 'Sarva Dharma Samabhava at the elite level) but at the same time, the state is forbidden to practise, profess or promote any religion of its own. Secularism in its essence denotes "a national identity, which transcends the religious identity of a person but does not negate the identity."[2] The grand conception of Nehruvian secularism in its essence can be found in the words of Jawaharlal Nehru : "we call our state a secular one. The word 'secular' perhaps is not a very happy one. And yet, for want of a better, we have used its. What exactly does it mean ? It does not mean a state, where religion as such is discouraged. It means freedom of religion and conscience including freedom for those who may have no religion. The word 'secular' however, conveys something much more to me, although that might not be its dictionary meaning. It conveys the idea of social and political equality. Thus a caste ridden society is not properly secular."[3]

Inspired by the European experience, Nehru's vision of a secular India was contemplated on structural changes in the of socio-economic life of the people through modernization and industrialization. Planned economic development and application of science and technology for the development of human resources, it was believed, would in the long run wash off the age old social and primordial loyalities of the people and infuse them a sense of scientific temper and rational outlook and ultimately would rescue the people from the vulnerability of exploitation of their religious sentiments by the vested interests. The Nehruvian model of secularism went far beyond a mere legal notion of secularism and emphasised exclusively the development of higher values of human life and equal

2. G. Parthasarathy and S. Gopal, "Jawaharlal Nehru and India's Quest for a Secular Identity," *Occasional Papers an History and Society* (New Delhi : NMML, Teen Murti House, 1987) Vol. XLII, pp. 2-3.
3. Quoted in Parthasarathy and Gopal, n. 3, pp. 3-4.

opportunities for a fuller life to every citizen which Nehru termed as 'secular Democracy'. And for achieving the aim of "Secular Democracy", the socialistic path of development was accepted as the necessary concomitant for such transformation. In the aftermath of partition and Independence, Indian National Congress led by Jawaharlal Nehru accepted "secularism as the basis of a uniform and durable national identity in a multi-religious society" with the dominance of Hindus in all the spheres of national life.[4] It has been widely held that proclamation of India as a secular state after independence was a practical strategem rather than a mere ideology. In order to neutralise the Hindu political resurgence subsequent to partition and to remove the fear psychosis of minorities, especially the Muslims and bring them to the process of national consolidation, adoption of secular polity was a practical necessity for the nationalist elites. Hence, secularism in India provided equal protection to all religions and assured the minorities, that the dominance of Hindus would not threaten their cultural and religious identity in any way, and that they would be entitled to receive equal benefits in the economic and political sphere. Secularism, since its adoption, become the integral part of India's polity and the last forty four years of its operation has invariably established on integral link with the nature of nationalism and democracy.

The dominant aspects of Indian secularism is rooted in religion and religious practice and beliefs of the people and this has given rise to peculiarities in the practice of secularism.[5]

4. It is argued that Hinduism by its tolerance, plurality and absence of any fundamental dogma provided the 'religious basis' of Indian secularism. Nehru believed that the *success* of Indian secularism depends on Hindus who could be the mainstay of the secular democracy and can help the minorities to develop secular outlook and temper. See Parthasarathy and Gopal, pp. 17-19.

5. Prakash Chandra Upadhyaya, "The Politics of Indian Secularism its practitioners, Defenders and Critics", *Occasional Papers on Perspectives in Indian Development*. Number XI, (New Delhi : NMML, 1990), p. 1.

In the definition of the concept of secularism, the notion has neither separated politics from the sphere of religion in the governmental system, nor has it done so in the political process. The constitution declares India a 'secular state' but the constitution does not prescribes a negative code of conduct which can describe the activities of a party as anti-secular.[6] And this notion of secularism has given birth to a kind of party politics, where an aggressively communal party takes serious exception, if it is branded 'communal' and tends to justify itself as secular. A peculiar strand of Indian secularism is that the state has been viewed as a multi-religious entity with secular outlook and idiom.

It has been argued that since India has been the cradle of may religions and since the Indian people are deeply religious the state must not be neutral between religious and non-religious matter. Further, the state in India is neither anti religious nor irreligious rather it promptes all religions. But the second aspect of secularism that has been found in practice, is that, the state is neigther anti-religious nor non-religious and not even multi-religious but multi-communal.[7] The secular

---

6. Though the judiciary in few cases has been able to intervene and prevent the political misuse of religion but on the whole no such law ever has been enacted which can prevent the political parties and non-political organisations to exploit religious symbols and sentiments of the people for their political gains. In the Tenth General Elections, despite the Chief Election Commissioner's (CEC), frequent warning to political parties to desist from adopting corrupt practices in their election campaigns and in its public notifications, the Election Commission made clear that, "apeal on ground of religion caste, community or language or the use of religious or national symbols" is a corrupt practice which can be prosecuted under law. *The Hindu*, 28 April 1990. But it was witnessed of the most flagrant violation of the electoral laws by some political parties especially the BJP, the JD and the Congress (I) in their election campaign as these parties relied on sectarian and divisive issues for their election victory.

7. Rajiv Bhargav, "Strands of secularism", *Frontline*, 27 April 1991, pp. 50-51.

state gives preference and respect to the fanatical and obscurantist fringes in all religions.

In the ideological sphere, the Nehruvian secular platform received its approbation by the western educated liberal intelligentia who sought to invoke its secular spirit For the liberal intelligentia, communalism was looked upon as a regressive phenomenon, socially divisive and thus opposite to the values of secularism and rational outlook, and modernization was viewed as panacea for the evils of communalism.[8] These modernists rooted in west's liberal tradition are unable to comprehend the language of natives and their culture, and thus there exist a gap in the thinking of the secularists and the experience of the masses. The ongoing communal polarisation and growing strength of Hindu Communalists show the failure of the modernists and secular intelligentia to launch an ideological struggle against the communal forces of all kinds. While Hindu communal ideologues have emerged as the chief spokesmen of Indian culture and civilization, the liberal intelligentia, missing in remote, alienated and mired in the west's modernity.

Despite the ideological acceptance of Nehruvian secular model by the liberal intelligentia, enough secular advance has not been forthcoming. It can be safely argued that, since the beginning of the eighties, while the notion of communalism has received new meaning and dynamism, the liberal rhetoric of secularism is on the retreat, as the Indian society is striven by vibrant religiousity manifested through transregionalized of Hindu religious festivals with a glare of publicity, invention of new rituals and symbols, construction and innovation of sacred spaces, that dot the rural as well as urban landscapes and unending saga of communal riots that play havoc across the country. The ruling 'secular' party remains a mute spectator, when Hindu and Muslim communalists polarise the society on

---

8. Harbans Mukhia, 'The Liberal Evolutionary Model has not Worked, *Times of India*, 26 January 1989; Ashis Nandy, Secularists on the Run", *Manthan*, May-June. 1991, pp. 98-99,

religious lines and mobilize their co-religionist not only against each other but also against the state.

The communal politics arose during the pre-independence period and found its root in the divide and rule politics of the British. But how do we analyse the communal politics in the post-Independence period and especially in recent years when the communalisation of the political process has become the most distinctive idiom of Indian politics. We have in the begining made an indepth analysis of the shift in the political orientation of the Congress party in order to establish the fact that the emergence oι communal politics since the eighties should be understood in the context of overall shift in the strategies of mobilization by the Congress (I).

II

The communal mobilization on Ramjanmabhoomi-Babri Masjid controversy links communalism with the religious sentiments and emotions of the people through manipulation of powerful symbolic issues like 'retrieval of Ramjanmabhoomi' and 'restoration of the Babri Masjid' and seek to rally round the Hindus and Muslims, through appeals to their religious sentiments for a common cause. The present study reveals that, notwithstanding the involvement of various other issues like religious faith, identity and historicity of Ramjanmabhoomi, the controversy gained momentum only in 1980's and became a political issue by the intervention of the political parties in religious affairs. Moreover, other aspects of the controversy are related to the very origin of dispute but could not turn it into a communally sensitive and explosive one till the dispute entered into the political arena, and subsequently questions of the history, faith and identities of the two communities acquired political importance.

For the political parties, the Ayodhya dispute is an issue of Hindu-Muslim conflict which can be successfully capitalised for their political ends. When the political parties perceived the social situation in terms of communities and treat the contending parties as Hindus and Muslims, then a party either seeks to mobilize and appeal both sections by positing itself as the party which can maintain communal peace and harmony and represent divergent views and committed to solve the dispute by "respecting the religious sentiments of both Hindus and Muslims," or it can impart a sense of insecurity, suspicion and antagonism in the minds of either Muslims or Hindus and project itself as the real custodian of a community's interests. While the Congress (I) the Janata Dal and the left parties being to the first cetegory of parties in their involvement with the dispute, the BJP belongs to the latter category for its complication in the communal imbroglio in Ayodhya. The response of various political parties to the claims of Vishwa Hindus Parishad and the All India Babri Masjid Action committee and their involvement in the controversy is guided by electoral consideration than their concern to solve the dispute amicably and remove the communal tension. The present study of two General Elections and sustained communal mobilization prior to the elections proves, unambiguously, that the Ayodhya dispute is inter-alia a political issue. The political parties like the Congress (I), the BJP and the National Front have been enmeshed in the Mandir-Masjid tangle and unabashedly pander with communal forces and while trying to build and consolidate their vote banks by all means despite their commitment to build a secular state, on the contrary.

The fierce competition among the political parties to cash in on the dispute over the Babri Masjid has paid off politically to them. The BJP and the Janata Dal have increased their political strength by manipulating the religious sentiments of both Hindus and Muslims respectively. The Congress party tried to exploit the Hindu sentiments on the eve of Ninth General Elections and in the process appeased the Hindu communalists but failed to receive their supports but the Janata Dal and the BJP on the other hand, were the beneficiaries in the dispute. In the Tenth General Elections, these parties made the Ayodhya dispute a major plank in their election campaign. However, the BJP is the real gainer over the Babri Masjid—Ramjanmabhoomi controversy, compared to other parties due to its firm and consistent stand to demolish the Babri Masjid and construct a Ram temple in its place as well as its aggressive communal mobilization in support of the VHP's demand with the help of other members of the RSS 'Sangh Parivar' (family).

It would not be an exaggeration to argue here that the Ramjanmabhoomi-Babri Masjid controversy has helped the BJP to come to the centre stage of Indian politics at the cost of two centrist secular parties. Its unwavering Hindu image and communal politics has paid dividends in a situation of growing communal riots and polarisation. The party's strategy over the mobilization for Ram temple is not merely related to the construction of a temple. As indicated earlier, the BJP has successfully associated other issues like 'pseudo-secularism', 'minorityism', 'nationalism' and Hindutva and, thus has been able to gain support from the wide-spectrum of Hindus society. The catapultive rise of the BJP as an alternative to the centrist political parties and its ceaseless effort to keep alive the Ayodhya dispute is the most important reason for raising the concept of secularism as the major agenda in Indian politics. All the political parties view with grave concern that the growth of the BJP's political strength constitute the most serious threat to the secular polity in India. In its relentless crusade against the secular polity, secular political parties, and the secularists, the BJP and its communal allies, have given the political currency and found their paralance in the political vocabulary of the new concepts like "minorityism", "pseudo-secularism" and above all the "positive secularism".

III

The BJP attaches supreme importance to the Ayodhya dispute since the party has portrayed its involvement in the dispute as a "crusade against the pseudo-secular policy of other parties". 'Pseudo secular' implies, that those political parties and intellectuals who claim themselves secular but in practice are soft towards Muslim communalists and Muslims in general and antagonistic towards the Hindus in particular. In their campaign for Ram temple before and during the elections, the party leaders made secularism in India as the main target of their attack and frequently called upon for a national debate on issues of secularism and communalism. Apart from the Ayodhya controversy. Shah Bano case, Art. 370 which gives special status to Jammu and Kashmir and the Congress (I)'s failure to promulgate a uniform civil code are raised as supplements to their campaign against "minority appeasement." On 1st December 1990, BJP leader L.K. Advani challenged other political parties to fight elections solely on the issue of secularism and nationalism, so that it could be decided by the people what should be the real secularism in India.

Despite its serious attack on secularism, the party has not been able to explain clearly its concept of secularism.[9] In its Palampur Resolution in 1989, the party interpreted its own concept of secularism in a very precise and vague manner. Its resolution reads as, "........by the time the second court order of 1989 came, secularism had come to be equated with an allergy to Hinduism and a synonym for minority appeasement."[10] The party in its 1989 and 1991 General Elections manifestoes, again made a very brief and ambiguous interpretation of its concept of secularism. In the Ninth General Elections, the BJP mentioned in its manifesto, "BJP believes in positive secularism which according to our constitution makers meant 'Sarva Dharma Sambhava' and which does not connote an irreligious state. It certainly does not mean the rejections of our cultural heritage, the very foundation of this great nation." The BJP stands for 'Justice for All and Appeasement for None."[11] (emphasis added)

Despite the inadequacy of literature, it is clear that the BJP's ideology of secularism, is in direct opposition to the notion of secularism as depicted in the Indian constitution. The party advocates that the notion of secularism is not a new to India

9. The RSS and the BJP's mouthpiece *Organiser*, rarely enunciate the party's standpoint of secularism. Most of its issues carry a polemic against the Nehruvian concept of secularism and communalism, etc.

10. Bharatiya Janata Party, National Executive Committee Meeting, June 9-11, 1989, Palampur, p. 16.

11. See the BJP Manifesto for Ninth General Elections, p. 7.

since the traditions of secularism is innate to the Indian constitution. The concept of secularism put forth in the constitution is a western concept, while the indigenous brand of secularism rests on the affirmation of religion. The alien concept that has been imitated, negates the religion, because the secular polity was shaped by Nehru's flirtation with socialism and Marxian atheism. L.K. Advani says that,...... "secularism does not mean disowning our past heritage and culture. When I refer to heritage and culture, it certainly comphends the Vedas the Mahabharat and the Ramayana and all that ancient literature. Whenever one is talking about these......he is talking of what is essentially Hindu."[12]

The BJP denounce like the RSS and its family organisations, the prevalent concept of secularism as "Hindu baiting", "a premium of minorities", designed as to "keep down the Hindus", and directed against 'Hinduism', and the present policy of secularism, it is alleged, "not only against the interests of minorities but also against national unity, integrity of the country." The emergence of the BJP, the ideologues claim, as the protector of Hindu interests, proves that Hindu interests and sentiments were neglected in the name of protection of minorities under secularism.[13]

During Advani's Rathyatra trail, the Bharatiya Janata Party's notion of secularism with regard to the Ayodhya controversy was made clear when he gave an interview to India's best known English daily. The BJP leader justified his action of undertaking Rathyatra for what he called the inability and incapacity of other parties to understand and to respect the

12. See the Speech delivered by Shri L.K. Advani, M.P. and the President of Bharatiya Janata Party on August 7, 1989 in Rajya Sabha while participating the debate on Communalism, in "*Ramjanmabhoomi*" (New Delhi, BJP Publications, n.d., p. 2).

13. P.K. Nijawan, "The Party of India's Future", *Organiser*. Republic Day special, 1990 ; Ram Swarup, "Indian Secularism X-rayed", *Indian Express*, 2 January 1991 ; Nanaji Deshmukh, "Our Brand of Secularism needs a Second Look, *Manthan*, December 1980, Vol. XI, No. 12, pp. 9-13.

Hindu psyche. While commenting on the government's capitulation to the fundamentalists in the Shah Bano case and the temple issue at Ayodhya as the "characteristic example of pseudo-secularism", he justified the Rathyatra as a "crusade against pseudo-secularism and minorityism, which he also regarded as political issue."[14]

Ideological assault of the Hindu communalists on the secular state came to fore during L.K. Advani's bloody Rathyatra, when the BJP published a series of distorted and malicious propaganda lamenting over how secularism in India has been degenerated into pampering of minorities and disregarding the sentiments of the majority community and weakening their claims in their 'own' country.[15]

The BJP/VHP perceive the construction Ram temple at Ayodhya as "vindication of national honour" and outrightly reject the question of secularism when they demand for demolition of the Babri Masjid. The Hindu chauvinists view that, the issue of secularism is invoked by the "Baburwadis" and 'anti-mandir groups', in defence of the *status quo* of the Babri Masjid which is for them a symbol of 'national shame'. The Hindus, they claim, want that the old unhappy chapters of vandalism and forcible conversion of temples into mosques should be closed by the present generation of Muslims in a symbolic manner by forefeiting their claims over the Babri Masjid and handing it over to the Hindus and subsequently a similar gesture should be extended to Krishnajanamsthan (birth place of Lord Krishna) in Mathura and Kashi Viswanath in Varanasi.[16]

The BJP's advocacy of positive secularism and crusade against 'minorityism' must be understood in the historical

14 *Times of India*, 20 November 1990.

15. See the BJP's advertisements, "What does Secularism Mean", *Indian Express*, 28 October 1990; "When can the Court Decide", *Times of India*, 31 October 1990.

16. K.R. Malkani, "Concept of Secularism and Controversy around Ayodhya", *Mainstream*, 27 October 1990, pp. 37-38.

context. The BJP being the heir of Bharatiya Jana Singh and political organ of the RSS practise and profess a notion of secularism (which would differentiate it from other parties), whose ultimate aim is to redefine the existing secular framework of the polity and would marginalise politically the semitising religious minorities and establish the all pervading hegemony of majority community. Implicit in the meaning of this variant of secularism, Hinduism is presented as a tolerant and secular philosophy of life which includes diverse sects, cults and beliefs but consciously avoided in acknowledging the evolution of composite culture and society. The notion of secularism denounces the irreligious state. While it gives full freedom to all religions, it prohibits the state giving equal treatment to all religions. This concept advocates that the state can promote the 'religious world view'. Since the essential ingredient of Indian culture is Hinduism and Hindus are also the majority community, the secular state can not disown or ignore this reality. The state will be positively secular because it will be pro Hindu. This aspect of secularism not only favours the dominant community but also rejects the non-religious matter.[17] In this vision of secularism the 'faith' is placed above the rule of law of and constitution and at the same time it rejects the concept of theocracy as alien to Indian culture and strangely denounces all the modern notions of secularism that are prevalent in the present day world. The BJP and its saffron allies arrogate themselves as the spokesman of the Hindus and claim their right to construct a temple for Lord Ram to undo a historic wrong, and here, the state must not obstruct their move, because, "the whole world knows that the so called constitutional rights being claimed by the non-Hindus have been granted to them by the Hindus". When the move is opposed by certain sections within the Hindu-society, then, they are abused as 'traitors of Hindus, and pseudo-secular intellectuals' indulged in minorityism. But if the minorityism involves practising pro-Muslim and anti-Hindu policies, then

17. A.G. Noorani, "BJP's Talking Point: Its Concept of Secularism and Nationalism", *Frontline*, 25 May-7 June 1991, p 124.

we are assured that the majoritarianism would not involve any appeasement to any community, but it would be a fair and just system !

The Bharatiya Janata Party's ideology of positive secularism is not a new concept, but it is an integral ideological weapon of the Hindu communalists and their denunciation of secularism, explicitly indicate, the return to the old communal point of view widely enunciated by the RSS and Bharatiya Jana Singh. During the Golwalkar era naked and rabid anti Muslim stance had become the main source of the RSS ideology. Golwalkar's writings, of 30's and 40's still continue to be the only ideological guidelines for the RSS and BJP. M.S. Golwalkar, the RSS Supremo wrote in his book, we or our Nationhood Defined", and the similar kind of thinking very often found in the writings and speeches of the present day RSS/BJP/VHP leaders. He wrote "The non-Hindu people in Hindustan must either adopt the Hindu culture and language, must learn to respect and hold in reverence...may stay in the country wholly subordinated to the Hindu nation, claiming nothing, deserving no privileges...not even citizen's rights."[18]

If the critiques of secularism dubb the system as perverted and "contrived just to weaken Hindu Unity", its practitioners and defenders have also reduced the ideals of secularism to a sham when we specifically take into account the Congress (I)'s

18. M.S. Golwalkar, "We or our Nationhood Defined" (Nagpur : Bharat Prakashan, 1939. pp. 55-57.

For example, a recent booklet published by the Vishwa Hindu Parishad prescribes the conditionalities for the Muslim in India which reveals a crude psyche or the Vishwa Hindu Parishad and its other Hindu Communal outfits. The author of the booklet says, "Muslims should realise that if they have to have the right to stay on in Hindustan even after the formation of Pakistan they should give up their attempts to undermine the Hindu society. through conversions, stop cow slaughter, stop stoning Hindu religious processions and give up their hate spreading speeches," [Anand Pandya, ***Hypocrisy of Secularism*** (injustice to Hindu) Karnavati : [VHP Prakashan, n.d.], p. 18.

role in the Ayodhya dispute. It is now true that, the empty rhetoric and pompous claims of the Congress (I)'s leadership has become the most important hall-mark of the party's ideology. To cite, the party in its manifesto for the Ninth General Elections, viewed that : "one of the major issues in these elections is the future of secularism. The Congress has fought communalism everywhere ... The Congress reiterates its full commitment to secularism and its determination to continue the struggle in cooperation with like minded forces to eradicate all communalism from the body politic."[19]

Further, in a booklet published on the eve of Tenth Lok Sabha Elections, the Congress (I) claimed that, from Jawaharlal Nehru, Mrs. Indira Gandhi and down to Rajiv Gandhi, the Congress party has consistently maintained that India can not survive unless it is secular.[20] But now the vital question that must be raised in the mind of every political conscious citizen in the country is how far the Congress (I) has been able to resist and thwart the growing upsurge of minority and majority communalism in the political process.[21] The Congress party willy nilly succumbed to the pressure of Muslim fundamentalists and Hindu communalists in the Shah Bano case and the Ayodhya dispute. Reacting to the Congress party's role, the Times of India editorialized : "The alienation of Muslims will undoubtedly mark as the most grievous lapse on the part of Rajiv Gandhi Government...In retrospect the laying of the

---

19. See the text of Congress (I)'s manifesto in *National Herald,* 7 November 1989.

20. Pranab Mukherji "*Issues before the Nation*" (AICC-I) publication. New Delhi, n.d.

21. The curious irony of secularism in that, in its official form it appears as 'sui-generic'. The style of politics pursued by the ruling Congress party during Mrs. Indira Gandhi and Rajiv Gandhi's reign had in effect been anti-secular as we have earlier given an indepth analysis on this aspect. But still then, the 'anti-secular' policies appear secular because its practitioner were not only holding the mantle of secular state apparatus but also commanding enormous popularity and confidence of the large sections of people.

foundation stone of the Ram temple in Ayodhya on November 9 can be seen to be a dangerous turning point in the history of independent India. The seeds of disintegration of the secular vision of the country were sown on that day. History can not easily pardon the Congress for this direct and indirect contribution to the spectacular growth of Hindu chauvinist forces today and for the tightening hold of the fundamentalists on the Muslim community.[22] Because of the party's panderings with the forces of communalism and reaction it has demonstrated total incapacity to fight at the political and ideological level against these forces. The present generation of Congress leadership has betrayed the secular ideals which the earlier generation of the party's leadership had committed and dedicated their life for attaining.

IV

Behind the Ramjanmabhoomi-Babri Masjid dispute at Ayodhya lies the issue of power and politics which draws its sustenance from the questions of faith, identity, myth and history. For a disinterested observer, the Ayodhya controversy may appear as a conflict between the two religious communities over the legal ownership of a particular place considered to be hollowed one by them, but for an avid scholar of Indian politics, Babri Masjid is a crumbling shrine of communal discord in India. The Mandir-Masjid dispute has been politicised to such an extent that the possibility of an immediate solution appears remote because the dispute is not confined among the two contentious parties but the political parties are also deeply involved. The present study on the communal mobilization on Ayodhya dispute points that, the main threat to the secular polity does not come from the communal forces but from the opportunistic secular political parties like the Congress (I) and the Janata Dal for their compromising and conciliatory posture to the communal and reactionary forces. It is in this sense, the future of the Ayodhya dispute and its solution depend on the attitude of the political parties to the dispute.

---

22. *Times of India*, 28 November 1989.

Bibliography

Books

Advani, L.K., *Ramjanmabhoomi*, New Delhi : BJP Publications, n.d.

———, *Why BJP Withdrew Support from Shri V.P. Singh Government?* speech delivered by Shri L.K. Advani, M.P., in Parliament on 7.11.90, New Delhi : BJP Publications n.d.

Akbar, M.J., *Riot after Riot*, New Delhi : Penguin Books, 1988.

Anderson, Walter K. and Damle, Sridhar, K., *The Brotherhood in Saffron : The Rashtriya Swayam Sevak Sangh and the Hindu Revivalism*, New Delhi : Vistar, 1987.

Bakker, Hans, *Ayodhya*, Gorgington : 1986.

Banu, Zeenab, *Politics of Communalism : A Politico Historical Analysis of Communal Riots in Post-Independent India with Special Reference to the Gujrat and Rajasthan Riots*, Bombay : Popular, 1989.

Bardhan, A.B., *BJP : In Search of an Ideology*, New Delhi: Communist Party Publications, 1991.

———, *Appeal to all Countrymen*, New Delhi: CPI Publications, 1990.

Bhalla, G.S., *et al.*, *India : Nation State and Communalism*, New Delhi : Patriot Publishers, 1989.

Bhambri, C.P. *Political Process in India* (1947-1991). New Delhi : Vikas, 1991.

Bhat, S.R., *The Problem of Hindu-Muslim Conflicts*, Bangalore : Navakarnataka, 1990.

Bjorkman, James, Warner, ed., *Fundamentalism, Revivalists and Violence in South Asia*, New Delhi : Manohar, 1988.

Brass, Paul R., *Ethinicity and Nationalism*, New Delhi : Sage, 1991.

Bibliography

Books

Advani, L.K., *Ramjanmabhoomi,* New Delhi : BJP Publications, n.d.

———, *Why BJP Withdrew Support from Shri V.P. Singh Government?* speech delivered by Shri L.K. Advani, M.P., in Parliament on 7.11.90, New Delhi : BJP Publications n.d.

Akbar, M.J., *Riot after Riot,* New Delhi : Penguin Books, 1988.

Anderson, Walter K. and Damle, Sridhar, K., *The Brotherhood in Saffron : The Rashtriya Swayam Sevak Sangh and the Hindu Revivalism,* New Delhi : Vistar, 1987.

Bakker, Hans, *Ayodhya,* Gorgington : 1986.

Banu, Zeenab, *Politics of Communalism : A Politico Historical Analysis of Communal Riots in Post-Independent India with Special Reference to the Gujrat and Rajasthan Riots,* Bombay : Popular, 1989.

Bardhan, A.B., *BJP : In Search of an Ideology,* New Delhi: Communist Party Publications, 1991.

———, *Appeal to all Countrymen,* New Delhi: CPI Publications, 1990.

Bhalla, G.S., *et al., India : Nation State and Communalism,* New Delhi : Patriot Publishers, 1989.

Bhambri, C.P. *Political Process in India* (1947-1991). New Delhi : Vikas, 1991.

Bhat, S.R., *The Problem of Hindu-Muslim Conflicts,* Bangalore : Navakarnataka, 1990.

Bjorkman, James, Warner, ed., *Fundamentalism, Revivalists and Violence in South Asia,* New Delhi : Manohar, 1988.

Brass, Paul R., *Ethinicity and Nationalism,* New Delhi : Sage, 1991.

———, *The New Cambridge History of India—The Politics of India Since Independence*, Hyderabad: Cambridge University Press, 1990.

———, *Language, Religion and Politics in North India*, Delhi : Vikas, 1975.

Chakravorty, Bidyut, ed., *Secularism and Indian Polity*, New Delhi : Segment, 1990.

Chandra, Bipan, *Communalism in Modern India*, New Delhi : Vikas, 1988.

Das, Veena, ed., *Mirrors of Violence : Communities, Riots and Survivors*, New Delhi : Oxford University, 1990.

Dixit, Prabha, *Communalism : A Struggle for Power*, New Delhi : Orient Longman, 1974.

Dutt, R.C., *Challenges to Polity*, Delhi : Lancer, 1989.

Eliade, Mircea, *The Encyclopaedia of Religion*, Vol. 10, New York : Macmillan, 1987.

Elst, Koenraad, *Ramjanmabhoomi vs. Babri Masjid : A Case Study in Hindu-Muslim Conflict*, New Delhi : Voice of India, 1990.

———, *Ayodhya and After : Issues Before Hindu Society*, New Delhi : Voice of India, 1991.

Engineer, Asghar Ali, ed., *Babri-Masjid Ramjanmabhoomi Controversy*, Delhi : Ajanta, 1990.

Communalism and Communal Violence of India : An Analytical Approach to Hindu-Muslim Conflict in India, Delhi : Ajanta, 1989.

———, ed., *Communalism in India*, Delhi : Ajanta Publications, 1985.

———, ed., *Shah Bano Controversy*, Bombay : Orient Longman, 1987.

Golwalkar, M.S., *We Or Our Nationhood Defined*, Nagpur : Bharat Prakashan, 1939.

Gopal, S., *Anatomy of a Confrontation : The Babri Masjid-Ramjanmabhoomi Issue*, New Delhi : Viking, 1991.

Gould, Harold A., *Hindu Caste System*, Delhi: Chanakya, 1987.

Hasan, Mushirul, ed., *Communal and Pan-Islamic Trends in Colonial India*, New Delhi : Manohar, 1985.

Hasan, Zoya, *et. al.*, *State, Political Processes and Identity*, New Delhi : Sage, 1989.

Hobbesbawm, Erric and Ranger, Terence, ed., *Inventions of Traditions*, Cambridge : CUP, 1988.

Jayaprasad, K., *RSS and Hindu Nationalism*, New Delhi : Deep and Deep, 1991.

Joglekar, Sudhir, *Nation's Hope*, Bombay : BJP Publications, n. d.

Klyuev, Boris, *Religion in Indian Society*, New Delhi : Sterling, 1989.

Kumar, Santosh, *et. al.*, *Hindu Navosthan*, New Delhi : Suruchi, n. d.

Lal, Ramji ed., *Communal Problem in India : A Symposium*, Karnal : Dyal Singh College, 1988.

Maokenzie, D., *Indian Myth and Legend*, London : Gresham Publishing Co., 1972.

Mahmud, M., *Babri Masjid-Facts versus Fiction*, Faizabad, n. d.

Malhotra, Vijay Kumar, *Is it Sin to be Hindu in India*, New Delhi : VHP Publications, n. d.

Mishra, Chandra Vinay and Singh Parmanand, eds., *Ram-janmabhoomi-Babri Masjid*, Historical Documents, Legal Opinions & Judgements, New Delhi : Bar Council of India Trust, 1991.

Mukherjee, Pranab, *Issues Before the Nation*, New Delhi : AICC (I) Publications, n. d.

Namboodripad, E.M.S., *The BJP-RSS : In the Service of Right Reaction*, New Delhi : NBC, 1990.

Nandan, Deoki, *Sri Rama Janma Bhumi : Historical and Legal Perspective*, New Delhi : VHP Publications, n. d.

Nath, R., *Architecture and Site of the Babri Masjid of Ayodhya : A Historical Critique*, Jaipur : Historical Research Documentation Programme, 1991.

Nugent, Nicholas, *Rajiv Gandhi : Son of a Dynasty*, London : BBC Books, 1990.

Pandey, Gyanendra, *The Construction of Communalism in Colonial North India*, New Delhi : Oxford, 1990.

Pandya, Anand, *Hypocrisy of Secularism*, Karnataka : VHP Publications, 1990.

Pandya, Anandashankar, *Relevance of Hinduism in Modern Age*, New Delhi : VHP Publication, n. d.

Panikkar, K.N., *Communalism in Modern India : History, Politics and Culture*, New Delhi : Manohar, 1991.

Panikkar, K.N. *Appropriation of History and Historian's Role*, Presidential Address : Historiography, Calicut : South Indian History Congress, 1991.

Ramchandran, K.S., *Ramjanmabhoomi and The Marxist Historians*, Delhi : Historians Forum, n. d.

Rajgopal, P.R., *Communal Violence in India*, New Delhi : Uppal Publishing House, 1987.

Rao, C. Rajeswara, and Faizee, Shameem, *Babri Masjid-Ramjanmabhoomi Controversy*, New Delhi : Communist Party Publications, 1989.

Rudolph, L.I. and Rudolph, S.H., *In Pursuit of Lakshmi : The Political Economy of the Indian State*, Bombay : Orient Longman, 1987.

Sankalia, H.D., *Is Ramayan A Myth* ? New Delhi : PPP, 1973.

Sankhdher, K.K. and Wadhwa, K.K., eds., *National Unity and Religious Minorities*, New Delhi : Gitanjali, 1991.

Sen, Sukumar, *Origin and Development of the Rama Legend*, Delhi : Rupa & Co., 1977.

Seshadri, H.V., *et. al.*, *Why Hindu Rashtra*, Delhi : Suruchi, 1990.

Shah, M.C., ed., *Rajiv Gandhi in Parliament*, Delhi : Shipra, 1991.

Shakir, Moin, *Islam in Indian Politics*, Delhi : Ajanta, 1983.

———, ed., *Religion, State and Politics in India*, Delhi : Ajanta, 1989.

Sharma, R.S., *Communal History and Rama's Ayodhya*, New Delhi : PPH 1990.

Sharma, R.S., *et. al.*, *Ramjanmabhumi-Babri Masjid : A Historian's Report to the Nation*, New Delhi : PPH, 1991.

Shourie, Arun, *et. al.*, *Hindu Temples : What Happened to Them.* New Delhi : Voice of India, 1990.

Shukla, R.L. and Ahmed, Nilofar, *Babri Mosque or Ramjanam Temple*, New Delhi : Crescent, 1986.

Srivastava, Sushil, *The Disputed Mosque, A Historical Inquiry*, New Delhi : Vistar, 1991.

Suseelan, Babu, *India Under Siege*, New Delhi : VHP Publications, 1988.

Thapar, Romila, *et. al.*, *Communalism and the Writing of India*, New Delhi : PPH, 1987.

Thengadi, D.B., *Namboodripad's Anti-Communalism X-rayed*, New Delhi : VHP Publications, n. d.

———, *Exile and Kingdom : Some Thoughts on Ramayan*, Bangalore : Mythic Society, 1978.

Vanaik, Achin, *The Painful Transition : Bourgeois Democracy in India*, London : Verso, 1990.

Voice of India, *History versus Casuistry*, Evidence of the Ramjanmabhoomi Mandir presented by Vishva Hindu Parishad to the Government of India in December-January 1991, New Delhi : Voice of India, 1991.

Veer, Peter Vander, *Gods on Earth, The Management of Religious Experience and Identity in a North Indian Piligrimage Centre*, New Delhi : Oxford, 1989.

Weiner, Myron, *Indian Paradox : Essays in Indian Politics*, New Delhi : Sage, 1989.

Articles

Agrawal, Purushottam, "Sita and Shambuk—A Common Destiny", *Mainstream*, 18 May 1991.

A Group of Academics, "Advertising Discord", *Mainstream*, 26 January 1991.

Alam, Zaved, "Political Articulation of Mass Consciousness in Present Day India", in Zoya Hasan *et. al.*, *State, Processes and Identity*: *Reflections on Modern India*, New Delhi: Sage 1989.

Asad, Talal, "Anthropological Conception of Religion : Reflections on Geertz, *Man*, No. 18, January-March, 1983.

Asdhir, P.C., "Do not Push the Hindu Psyche too Hard", *Organiser*, 6 September 1987.

Bachelet, Patrizia Nonelli, "Ramjanmabhoomi Movement—The Real Issue", *Organiser*, 18 August 1991.

Bhatnagar, Aswini, "Opening of the Floodgates", *Illustrated Weekly of India*, 6 April 1986.

Bhambri, C.P., "Political Process in India", *Contemporary Affairs*, Vol. 2, Nos. 3-4, September-December 1988.

Bhambri, C.P., "India : 39 Years of Independence", *Indian & Foreign Review*, Vol. 23, No. 20, 15 August, 1986.

Bhargav Rajeev, "Right to Culture", *Social Scientist*, Vol. 18, No. 10, October 1990.

Brass, Paul, R., "1984 Parliamentary Elections in U.P.", *Asian Survey*, Vol. 26, June 1986, pp. 663-64.

Chopra, Pran, "Strategy of Survival", *Illustrated Weekly of India*, 24 May 1987.

Clad, James, "Hindu Revivalists Look Strong in State Polls : Awkward Allies", *Far Eastern Economic Review*, Vol. 147, No. 9, 1 March 1990.

Datta, Pradeep K., "VHP's Ram at Ayodhya : Reincarnation through Ideology and Organisation", *Economic and Political Weekly*, 2 November 1991.

Engineer, A.A., "Bloody Trail : Ramjanmabhhoomi and communal Violence in U.P.", *Economic and Political Weekly*, 26 January 1991.

———, "Lok Sabha Elections and Communalisation of Politics", *Economic and Political Weekly*, 6-13 July 1991.

———, "National Front Government and Communal Situation", *Economic and Political Weekly*, 26 May, 1990.

———, "Grim Tragedy of Bhagalpur Riots : Role of Police-Criminal Nexus", *Economic and Political Weekly*, 10 February 1990.

———, "Remaking Indian Muslim Identity", *Economic and Political Weekly*, 2 April 1991.

———, "Communal Riots In Muzaffarnagar, Khatauli and Aligarh", *Economic and Political Weekly*, 7 January 1989.

———, "Religion and Politics", *Mainstream*, Vol. 22, No. 14, 3 December 1984.

Farooqi, M., "National Unity and Secular Composite Culture", *Party Life*, Vol. 23, No. 3, March 1991.

———, "BJP Exposes itself as the Most Aggressive Communal Party", *Party Life*, Vol. 25, No. 10, October, 1989.

Freitag, Sandria B., "Sacred Symbol as Mobilising Ideology : The North Indian Search for a Hindu Community", *Comparative Studies in Society & History*, Vol. 22, No. 4, 1980.

Gandhi, Rajiv, "India Towards 21st Century", *Secular Democracy*, Vol. 19, Nos. 1-2, January-February, 1986.

Gandhi, Rajiv, "Communalisation of Politics, Education, Industry and Commerce: An Imperialist Strategy to Impede National Unity and Freedom Movement", *Muslim India*, October 1987.

Girdner, Eddie-J. and Siddiqui, Kalim, "The Political Economy of Communalism in India", *Asian Profile*, Vol. 18, No. 2, April 1990, pp. 147-62.

Goyal, D.R., "Ayodhya and After", *Mainstream*, 15 March 1986.

Grewal, O.P. and Tuleja, K.C., "Communalism and Fundamentalism", *Economic and Political Weekly*, 24 November 1990.

Gupta, Dipankar, "Communalism and Fundamentalism : Some Notes on the Nature of Ethinic Politics in India", *Economic and Political Weekly*, Annual Number, March 1991.

———, "Communalising of Punjab, 1980-1985, *Economic and Political Weekly*, 13 July 1985.

Gupta Indrajit, "Untenability of Rajiv Gandhi's Rule", *Mainstream*, Annual Number, 1989.

Gupta, S.P., "Ramjanmabhumi Controversy : What History and Archae ology Say", *Organiser*, Republic Day Issue, 1990.

Habib, Irfan, "Ayodhya Dispute-I and II, *People's Democracy*, 7, 14, April 1991.

Hardgrave, Robert L., "India on the Eve of Elections", *Pacific Affairs*, Vol. 57, No. 3 : Fall, 1984.

Hasan, Mushirul, "Indian Muslims Since Independence : In Search of Integration and Identity", *Third World Quarterly*, Vol. 10, No. 2, 1988.

Hasan, Zoya, "Changing Orientation of the State and Emergence of Majoritariarism in the 1980's", *Social Scientist*, Vol. 18, Nos. 8-9, August-September, 1990.

———, Zoya, "Minority Identity, Muslim Women Bill Campaign and the Political Process", *Economic and Political Weekly*, 7 January 1989.

Hussain, Monirul, "Muslim Question in India", *Journal of Contemporary Asia*, Vol. 19, No. 3, 1989.

Jadhav, Keshav Rao, "The Communal Problem", *Lokayan Bulletin*, November-December, 1989.

Jain, Girilal, "Hindu Revival", *Illustrated Weekly of India*, 7 December 1986.

Kamath, M.V., "The Philosophical Basis of BJP", *Organiser*, 24 February, 1991.

Kapoor, Coomi, "BJP : Coming into its Own", *Illustrated Weekly of India*, 26-27 January 1991.

Kapoor, Sanjaya, "Congress Shatters Hindutva Appeal", *Blitz*, 22 June 1991.

Karat, Prakash, "Separating Religion from Politics : The Rajiv's Style", *People's Democracy*, 15 March 1987.

Keshavan, Mukul, "Invoking a Majority : The Congress and the Muslims of the United Provinces, 1945-47", *Occasional Papers on History and Society*, No. 19, June, New Delhi : NMML, 1989.

———, "Communal Violence and Its Impact on the Politics of North India, 1937 to 1939", *Occasional Papers on History and Society*, No. 23, February, New Delhi : NMML, 1990.

———, "1937 as a Landmark in the Course of Communal Politics in U.P.", *Occasional Papers on History and Society*, No. 10, November, New Delhi : NMML, 1988.

Kohli, Atul, "Politics of Economic Liberalization", *World Development*, Vol. 17, No. 3, 1989.

Kotovsky, Griogri, G., "Certain Trends in Indians Socio-Economic and Socio-Political Development", *Asian Survey*, Vol. 24, No. 11, November, 1984.

Kothari, Miloon and others, "Defusing Ayodhya Crisis", *Mainstream*, 5 January 1991.

Kothari, Rajni, "Cultural, Contexts of Communalism in India", *Economic and Political Weekly*, 14 January 1989, pp. 81-85.

———, "End of the SecularCredo", Kothari, ed., *Politics and the People : In Search of a Human Agenda*, Vol. II, Delhi : Ajanta, 1989.

———, "Communalism : The New Face of Indian Democracy", in Kothari, *State Against Democracy*, New Delhi : Ajanta, 1989.

———, "Fundamentalism is Not the Essence of Hinduism", *Illustrated Weekly of India*, 7 December 1986.

Kumar, Pramod and Yadav, Bhupinder, "Communalism and National Integration". *Mainstream*, 9 February 1985.

Lal, B.B., "Archaeology of the Ramayan Sites Project : Its Genesis and Summary Results", *Manthan*, October, 1990.

Mallik, Yogendra K. and Vajpayi, Dhirendra, K., "The Rise of Hindu Militancy : India's Secular Democracy at Risk", *Asian Survey*, Vol. 29, No. 3, March 1989.

Manor, James, "Parties and the Party System" in Atul Kohli ed., *India's Democracy*, Princeton : Princeton University Press, 1988.

Madan, T.N., "Secularism in its Place", *Journal of Asian Studies*, Vol. 4 No. 4, November 1987.

Malkani, K.R., ed., *March On*, New Delhi : BJP Publications, 1991.

———, "Concept of Secularism and Controversy around Ayodhya", *Mainstream*, Annual Number, 27 October 1990.

———. "Nationalism and Colonialism in Historical Perspective", *Mainstream*, Annual Number, October-November 1989.

Miller, D., "Six These on the Question of Religion and Politics in India Today", *Economic and Political Weekly*, July 25, 1987.

Manthan, "Ayodhya Movement : A Search for the Roots of Nationalism and Secularism in India", *Manthan*, Vol. 12, Nos. 5-6, May June, 1991.

Mohan, Surendra, "Dissecting BJP-JD Relationship", *Mainstream*, 10 November 1990.

Moris Jones, W.H., "Forty Years of Indian Independence", *South Asia*, Vol. 10, No. 2, December 1987.

Mukherjee, Nirmal, and Banerjee, Ashis, "Neo-nationalism", *Seminar*, 313, September 1985.

Mukhia, Harbans, "Communalism and Indian Polity", *Mainstream*, 22 March 1986.

Muralidharan, M., "Fundamentalist Challenge to Secularism", *Janata*, 22 November 1987.

Nadeem, Abu, "A Mosque Where Ram Lives", *Mainstream*, 24 November 1990.

Nagar, Vishnu, "Mahatma Gandhi's Formula on Mandir-Masjid", *Mainstream*, 12 January 1991, pp. 9-10.

Nayak, Pradeep and Sikand, Yoginder, "Party-Politics and Communal Mobilization in Faizabad", *Mainstream*, 8 June 1991.

Nauriya, Anil, "Relationship Between State and Religion", *Economic and Political Weekly*, 25 February 1989.

Nijhawan, P.K., "Hinduism and Secularism", *Organiser*, 27 May 1990.

Nijhawan, P.K., "Left Movement in the Struggle for Secularism", *Marxist*, Vol. 8, No. 3, July-September 1990.

Noorani, A.G., "Indira Gandhi and Indian Muslims", *Economic and Political Weekly*, 3 November 1990.

———, "BJP's Concept of Nationalism and Secularism", *Front line*, 25 May-7 June, 1991.

———, "BJP : Child of RSS and Heir to Hindu Mahasabha", *Mainstream*, 27 July 1991.

———, "History of the BJP (1980-1990)", *Mainstream*, 30 March 1991.

———, "Moment of Truth for the Janata Dal", *EPW*, 29 January 1991.

———, "Sardar Patel on Babri Masjid, *Ma nstream*, 4 August 1990, pp. 11-28.

Omvedt, Gail, "Hinduism and Politics", *Economic and Political Weekly*, 7 April 1990.

Oommen, T.K., "Insiders and Outsiders in India : Primordial Collectionism and Cultural Pluralism in Nation Building", *International Sociology*, Vol. 1, No. 1, March 1986.

Pandey, Gyanendra, "Questions of Nationalism and Communalism", *Economic and Political Weekly*, 20 June 1987.

———, "Ayodhya and the State", *Seminar*, 364, December, 1983.

Panikkar, K.N., "Culture and Community Consciousness", *Social Scientist*, Vol. 18, No. 4, April 1990.

———, "Communalism in India : A Perspective for Intervention", *People's Democracy*, 17 March 1991.

Parthasarthy, G. and Gopal S., "Jawaharlal Nehru and India's Quest for Secular Identity", *Occasional Papers on History and Society*, No. XLII, New Delhi : NMML, 1987.

Puri, Balraj, "Can Caste, Region and Ideology Stem Hindu Wave", *Economic and Political Weekly*, 6 January 1990.

———, "Politics of Ethnic and Communal Identities", *Economic and Political Weekly*, 7 April 1990.

Rao, Rajeshwar C., "Ayodhya Issue Brooks No Delay", *Mainstream*, 4 June 1989.

Satyamurty, T.V., "State and Society in a Changing Political Perspective", *Economic and Political Weekly*, 9 February 1991.

Sagar, Vidya, "Secularism has Led to Aggressive Minorityism", *Organiser*, 23 April 1989.

Seshadri, H.V., "The Hindu has Discovered the Secular Fraud", *Organiser*, 27 July 1989.

———, "Wiping out the Blot of Foreign Slavery", *Organiser*, 5 January 1986.

———, "Menace of Communalism", *Mainstream*, Annual, 1989.

Seth, D.L., "Elitist Notion of Secularism", *Janata*, 3 August 1986.

Shahabuddin, Sayed, "Secularism & Neo Secularism in a multi-religious Society", *Muslim India*, 58, October 1987, pp. 435-36.

Shakir, Moin, "Political Economy of Rajiv Regime", *Link*, 25 January 1987.

Sharma, Narendra, "Election Results : Behind the BJP Debacle", *Mainstream*, 5 January 1985.

———, "Some Observations on 1989 Elections", *Mainstream*, 9 December 1989.

———, "BJP in Transition", *Mainstream*, 17 May 1986.

Shivanandan, S., "Hindu" Communalism and the Crisis of the State, *Mainstream*, 1 December 1990.

Shukla, Kali Shankar, "New Offensive of Hindu Communalism in U.P.", *Party Line*, Vol. 24, No. 12, December 1988.

Siddique, Majid, A., "Ramjanmabhoomi-Babri Masjid Dispute : The Question of History, *Economic and Political Weekly*, 13 January, 1978.

Singh, Randhir, "Theorising Communalism : a fragmentary note in the Marxist Mode", *Economic and Political Weekly*, 23 July, 1988.

Singh, V.P., "Religion Resides in Our Hearts, Not on Throne of Power", *Mainstream*, 17 November 1990.

Sinha, Abhay, "BJP Emerges Stronger Despite Left's Campaign", *Link*, August 1989.

Sinha, A.K , "The Origin of the Mosque", *Sunday*, 7-13 April 1991.

Sinha, Arun, "Elections, Parties and Political Void", *Economic and Political Weekly*, 28 October 1989.

Siwach, J.R., "Eighth Lok Sabha Elections", *Indian Journal of Political Studies*, Vol. 9, December 1985.

Surana, Pannalal, "In the Name of Religion", *Janata*, Independence Day Number, 1986.

Surjeet, H.K.S., "Bastion Against Communalism", *Illustrated Weekly of India*, 13 May 1990.

Thapar, Romesh, "Hindus: A Call to Arms", *Illustrated Weekly of India*, 7 December 1986.

Thapar, Romila, "Imagined Religious Communities? Ancient History and the Modern Search for Hindu Identity, *Modern Asian Studies*, Vol. 23, No. 2, 1989.

———, "The Politics of Religious Communities", *Seminar*, 365, January 1990.

———, "Syndicated Moksha?", *Seminar*, 313, September, 1985.

Upadhyaya, Prakash Chandra, "Politics of Indian Secularism : Its Practitioners, Defenders and Critics", *Occasional Papers on Perspectives of Indian Development*, No. 11, New Delhi : NMML, 1990.

Verma, Kewal, "Rajiv Gandhi and Secularism : Lessons from Muslim Women Bill Debate", *Mainstream*, 24 May 1986.

Veer, Peter Vander, "God Must be Liberated ! A Hindu Liberation Movement in Ayodhya", *Modern Asian Studies*, Vol. 21, No. 2, April 1987.

———, "Brahmans: Their Purity and Their Poverty", *Contributions of Indian Sociology*, Vol. 19, No. 2, 1985.

Verghese B.G., "The Essence of Ayodhya", *Mainstream*, 10 November 1990.

Warrier, K.V., "Rajiv Appeasing Communalism", *New Age*, 4 June 1989.

Selected Newspaper Articles

Abraham, A.S., "Case for Active Secularism : Leading Role for the State", *Times of India*, 15 October 1990.

Ahmad, Imitiaz, "Muslims and Boycott Call : Political Realities Ignored", *Times of India*, 14 January 1987.

Ahmed, Bashiruddin, "The Reshaping of India's Polity", *Hindustan Times*, 25 June 1991.

Bhalla, G.S., *et. al.*, "India, Nation State and Communalism", New Delhi : *Patriot*, 1989.

Bidwai, Prafulla, "VHP's campaign of Lies", *The Economic Times*, 14 December 1990.

———, "BJP in a cleft stick : Yatra's success a Liability", *Times of India*, 12 October 1990.

Chandra, Bipan, "RSS, BJP and Nationalism", *The Hindu*, 27 and 29 October 1991.

Chopra, V.D., "Fight Against Hindu Communalism", *Patriot*, 22 September 1987.

Das, Arvind N., "Pathology of Uncivil Society : Ritualism United Mandal-Mandir Move, *Times of India*, 5 October 1990.

———, "Hindu Fundamentalism : Danger to Social Fabric", *Times of India*, 25 April 1990.

Dasgupta, Swapan, "Battle for Ram : Issue is the Denial of the Temple", *Times of India*, 15 April 1991.

———, "Nationalist Disarray : Renewed Importance to Ayodhya", *Times of India*, 10 September 1990.

———, "Journey to Ayodhya : Hindu Nationalism Comes of Age", *Times of India*, 23 October 1989.

———, "Hinduism vs. Secularism : Change in the Little Traditions", *Times of India*, 7 May 1990.

Deshmukh, Nanaji, "Ayodhya : A Turning Point", *The Statesman*, 6 December 1990.

Document, "Congress Party and Secularism", *National Herald*, 20 May 1990.

Engineer, Asghar A., "Secularism and Pseudo-Secularism", *Indian Express*, 30 April 1991.

Ganguly, Amulya, "The VHP may Taken Over the BJP", *The Statesman*, 23 April 1991.

Gaur, Raj Bahadur, "Ayodhya : History of Religious Strife", *Partriot*, 18 December 1990.

Khare, Harish, "Sparing with Communalism : Why Sadhus are Setting National Agenda", *Times of India*, 20 October 1990.

Kishwar, Madhu, "In Defence of our Dharma", *The Telegraph*, 25, 26, 27 December, 1990.

Limaye, Madhu, "Verdict 91 : What it Means", *Hindustan Times*, 20 June 1991.

———, "Diverse Responses to party planks", *The Hindu*, 25 June 1991.

Madan, T.N., "Rambhakti on Powerplay : Politics of Hindu Fundamentalism", *Times of India*, 16 May 1991.

Mukhia, Harbans, "The Liberal Evolutionary Model has not Worked", *Times of India*, 26 January 1989.

Malkani, K.R., "Secularism is not a Mantra", *Hindustan Times*, 31 December 1990.

Namboodripad, E.M.S., "BJP Tie Up, Fatal for Opposition", *Times of India*, 12 October 1989.

———, "Secularism : A Fresh Look", *Indian Express*, 26 November 1990.

Sahay, Anand K., "Communal Politics and Elections", *The Hindu*, 30 March 1991.

Sandesai, Rajdeep, "BJP is now caught between two Rams", *Times of India*, 12 June 1991.

———, "Mandal, Mandir and Marxists", *Times of India*, 21 April 1991.

Satyanarayana, K., "How Janata Dal made room for BJP", *Indian Express*, 5 July 1991.

Sethi, J.D., "The Hindu Backlash", *Times of India*, 4 January 1985.

Sharma, Kalpana, "Judicial decrees on Religious Appeal", *The Hindu*, 25 May 1991.

Sharma, R.S., "Ayodhya May Be a Buddhist Site", *Times of India*, 6 December 1990.

Singh, Dinesh, "Congress Debacle in the North", *Indian Express*, 27 June 1991.

Singh, Jaswant, "The Tenth General Elections : Some Reflections", *Indian Express*, 5 July 1991.

Sinha, B.M., "Pseudo Secularism : Fashion of the Day", *Financial Express*, 20 January 1991.

SOZ, Saifuddin, "Ram is also Allah : BJP distorting a liberal concept", *The Statesman*, 19 June 1991.

Swarup, Ram, "Indian Secularism X-rayed", *Indian Express*, 2 January 1991.

Times of India, "Ninth General Elections, Babri Dispute not Major Issue", Pre-Election Survey, *Times of India*, 6 August 1989.

Tinmizi, S.A.I., "Was Babur really to Blame", *Times of India*, 24 February 1991.

Miscellaneous

BJP, *Presidential Address by Dr. Murli Manohar Joshi*, at Jaipur, New Delhi : BJP Publications, 1991.

———, *Documentation on National Executive Meeting Palampur*, 17 October, 1990, 9 & 10 November 1990, New Delhi : BJP Publications, 1990.

———, *Meenakshipuram Report*, New Delhi : BJP Publications, n. d.

Election Manifestoes, *Ninth & Tenth General Elections 1989 and 1991*, Published by Congress (I), The National Front, BJP, CPI, CPM.

Congress, *Congress Party and Secularism*, Document, National Herald, 20 May 1990.

CPI, *Three Eminent Personalities on the Ramjanmabhoomi-Babri Masjid Controversy*, New Delhi : CPI Publications, 1989.

CPI, *Communist Party of India and Fight Against Communalism*, New Delhi : PPH, 1986.

India Today, *Ayodhya : Exploiting the Issue*, India Today, 31st December 1990.

India Today, "BJP A new Confidence", *India Today*, 15 Februry 1990.

———, "Muslims : A Community in Turmoil", *India Today*, 31 January 1990.

———, "A Myth Exploded on Ayodhya", *India Today*, 15 January 1989.

———, "Hindus : Militant Revivalism", *India Today*, 31 May 1986.

JNU, "Political Abuse of History", *Centre for Historical Studies*, Jawaharlal Nehru University, New Delhi : 1989.

Lokayan Bulletin, "Series of articles on communalism", *Lokayan Bulletin*, 7-6, November-December 1989.

New Age, "Left Parties on Ayodhya Dispute", *New Age*, 6 January 1991.

Radiance Views Weekly, "The Babri Masjid, Series of Articles", *Radiance*, 25 November-1 December 1990.

Seminar, "Beyond the Vote—a Symposium on the 1991 Election and After", *Seminar*, 385, September, 19?1.

SVA, "On the Struggle Against Communalism", *Lokayan Bulletin*, November-December, 1989.

Teaching Politics, "Special Number on Ninth Lok Sabha Elections, Some Interpretations", *Teaching Politics*, Vol. 15, Nos. 3-4, 1989.

VHP, *Report on Sri Ram Janambhoomi presented by Shri Ashok Singhal, Secretary General, in Meeting of the Governing Council held on Ayodhya 26.1.90*, New Delhi : VHP, 1990.

VHP, *Evidence for the Ramjanmabhoomi Mandir* presented to the Government of India on December 23, 1990 by the Vishwa Hindu Parishad.

Following newspapers and periodicals from 1986-1991 have been consulted for the purpose of this dissertation :

Newspapers

1. Deccan Herald
2. The Hindu
3. Hindustan Times
4. Indian Express
5. National Herald
6. News Week

7. Patriot
8. The Statesman
9. The Telegraph
10. Times of India.

Periodicals

1. Economic and Political Weekly
2. Frontline
3. Illustrated Weekly of India
4. India Today
5. Link
6. Mainstream
7. New Age
8. Organiser
9. People's Democracy
10. Radiance
11. Sunday Observer
12. Sunday
13. The Week

Index

S